AF352270

e-Development toward the Knowledge Economy

e-Development toward the Knowledge Economy

Leveraging Technology, Innovation and Entrepreneurship for "Smart" Development

Elias G. Carayannis and Caroline M. Sipp

First published in 2006 by
PALGRAVE MACMILLAN
Houndmills, Basingstoke, Hampshire RG21 6XS and
175 Fifth Avenue, New York, N.Y. 10010
Companies and representatives throughout the world.

PALGRAVE MACMILLAN is the global academic imprint of the Palgrave Macmillan division of St. Martin's Press, LLC and of Palgrave Macmillan Ltd. Macmillan® is a registered trademark in the United States, United Kingdom and other countries. Palgrave is a registered trademark in the European Union and other countries.

ISBN-13: 978–1–4039–4244–9
ISBN-10: 1–4039–4244–7

This book is printed on paper suitable for recycling and made from fully managed and sustained forest sources.

A catalogue record for this book is available from the British Library.

Library of Congress Cataloging-in-Publication Data
Carayannis, Elias G.
        e-development toward the knowledge economy : leveraging technology, innovation and entrepreneurship for "smart" development / by Elias G. Carayannis and Caroline M. Sipp.
            p. cm.
        Includes bibliographical references and index.
        ISBN 1–4039–4244–7 (cloth)
        1. Information technology – Economic aspects. 2. Technological innovations – Economic aspects. 3. Knowledge management. 4. Economic development. I. Sipp, Caroline M., 1978– II. Title.
HC79.I55C35 2005
658.4′038–dc22   2005050962

10 9 8 7 6 5 4 3 2 1
15 14 13 12 11 10 09 08 07 06

Transferred to digital printing in 2006.

Contents

List of Illustrations

Tables

Figures

Boxes

Acknowledgements

The authors wish to acknowledge the many people working at the World Bank, the Inter-American Development Bank, USAID as well as numerous non-government organisations with whom they have had the opportunity to interact and collaborate with in relation to the contents to this book.

1
Introduction

> For countries in the vanguard of the world economy, the balance between knowledge and resources has shifted so far towards the former that knowledge has become perhaps the most important factor determining the standard of living – more than land, than tools, than labour. Today's most technologically advanced economies are truly knowledge-based.
>
> *World Bank* (1998)

Adam Smith defined *land, labor, and capital* as the key input factors of the economy in the eighteenth century. Joseph Schumpeter added *technology and entrepreneurship* as two more key input factors in the early twentieth century. He thus recognized the role and dynamic nature of technological change and innovation as well as path dependencies in shaping the health and future of the economy and moving away from the static approach of neoclassical economics.

In the late twentieth and the beginning of the twenty-first century, numerous scholars and practitioners such as Peter Drucker have identified *knowledge* as perhaps the sixth and most important key input and output factor of economic activity. We would like also to emphasize the role and significance of *technological and economic learning* as a driver of productivity gains and an accelerator of economic growth and prosperity (Carayannis, 1993; 1994a; 1994b; 1998; 1999; 2000; 2001a; 2002).

In other words, in classical economics, tangible resources (land), as well as human capital (labor) and financial capital are the key recognized factors of production while intellectual and social capital (i.e. knowledge stocks and flows) are all regarded as exogenous factors. In today's environment, *technology, innovation, and entrepreneurship* are not merely additional factors of production; they have become the key factors of production. Entrepreneurship in particular is the combination of talent, passion, and opportunity that serves to fully leverage technology and knowledge to foster innovations for sustainable socio-economic development accompanied by *knowledge, market, and network spillovers* in the form of both public and private knowledge goods (public domain knowledge versus intellectual property rights).

We thus feel that there is a clear role, opportunity, and challenge for entrepreneurs around the world to catalyze and accelerate socio-economic development and convergence and leverage the digital divide through bottom-up, entrepreneurial initiatives in the private sector in harmony and complementarity with top-down public sector policies that recognize and foster economic growth as driven by the accumulation of knowledge and new technological developments that create technical platforms for further innovations. These technical platforms, in turn, are drivers of economic growth. Technological innovation raises the return on investment, which is why developed countries can sustain growth and why developing economies cannot attain growth without it. Even with unlimited labor, natural resources, and ample capital, traditional economics predicts that there are diminishing returns on investment while experience shows that in the context of knowledge-based economies and societies, there may well be increasing returns to scale in an unlimited fashion: i.e. knowledge becomes increasingly valuable as it is shared. As J.B. Say (*circa* 1800) has stated, innovation is about changing the yield of resources, and, in this context, knowledge-based and knowledge-supported entrepreneurship via real and virtual, global and local (gloCal) knowledge infrastructures, such as the incubator networks we discuss later on, will be the preeminent driver of innovation in the twenty-first century. This perspective becomes particularly promising and enticing in the context of e-Development initiatives toward the Knowledge Economy (KE) that we profile in the case studies that follow.

There is ample and growing evidence that intangible resources such as knowledge, know-how, and social capital will prove to be the coal, oil, and diamonds of the twenty-first century for developed, developing, and emerging economies alike (World Economic Forum, 2002). Moreover, there are strong indications and emerging trends that there are qualitative and quantitative differences between the twentieth and the twenty-first century drivers of economic growth (Asian Development Bank, 2001):

> The world economy is in the midst of a profound transformation, spurred by globalization and supported by the rapid development of ICT [Information and Communication Technologies] that accelerates the transmission and use of information and knowledge. This powerful combination of forces is changing the way we live, and redefining the way companies do business in every economic sector.

We are currently going through a dynamic era for the economies of the world where a country can transition fast both upwards (see the case of Ireland) or downwards (see the case of Japan) and this trend has become increasingly more pronounced and in an accelerating fashion during the last decade. This new era is punctuated by (Dahlman and Aubert, 2001):

- Development of a service-based economy, with activities demanding intellectual content becoming more pervasive and decisive;
- Increased emphasis on higher education and life-long learning to make effective use of the rapidly expanding knowledge base;
- Massive investments in research and development, training, education, software, branding, marketing, logistics and similar services;
- Intensification of competition between enterprises and nations based on new product design, marketing methods and organizational forms;
- Continual restructuring of economies to cope with constant change.

The challenge and the opportunity in particular for advanced developing and transitioning economies is to evolve and possibly leapfrog from being lower to middle income, knowledge-, technology-, and know-how-importing and using countries to becoming high and sustainable income, knowledge-, technology-, and know-how-generating and exporting ones. For such a transition to be effective and sustainable key success factors are innovation and knowledge clusters and networks linking public and private, domestic, regional, and global sector research and technological development entities (OECD, 2001a):

> Innovation through the creation, diffusion and use of knowledge has become a key driver of economic growth and provides part of the response to many new social challenges. However, the determinants of innovation performance have changed in a globalizing knowledge-based economy, partly as a result of information and communication technologies. Innovation results from increasingly complex interactions at the local, national and world levels among individuals, firms, and other knowledge institutions. Governments exert a strong influence on the innovation process through the financing and steering of public organizations that are directly involved in knowledge generation and diffusion (universities, public labs), and through the provision of financial and regulatory incentives.

The Knowledge Economy, while relying on and leveraging heavily on technology and especially ICT, also needs a harmonious policy and institutional environment, a consistent regulatory framework, and a plausible business environment to promote innovation. Yet, this does not necessarily imply that the government is the sole actor responsible for developing toward the Knowledge Economy. Examples of viable strategies and interventions have shown how Knowledge Economy and e-Development allow for better integration and cooperation between the private and the public sector.

The significance and relevance of technology is two-fold. In one case, it widens the gap, leaving developing countries lagging. In the other, technology can optimize and maximize development efforts. Deeper cooperation among international donors and recipient countries is needed to allow the optimization role of technology to overcome the widening effect it imposes on the gap between North and South.

The convergence of transformations and discontinuities both in the means of production as well as the nature of the outcomes of economic activity (products and services) and the pronounced shift from *product-focused, tangibles-based* economies to *service-focused, intangibles-reliant* ones, necessitate rethinking and possibly reinventing ways and means to support the mission (as well as the business) of global, regional, and national policies and practices of economic development.

In this context, the validity of Joseph Schumpeter's and the Austrian School of Economics' principle of *creative destruction* is further corroborated. This principle underscores the importance as both a challenge and an opportunity of the continual replacement, renewal, and reinvention of socio-economic, technological, and political institutions, practices, and infrastructures. Hence, the role of private and financial sector development as an *enabler, catalyst,* and *accelerator* of bottom-up, entrepreneurial initiatives coupled with top-down creative and realistic innovation policies in developed, developing, and transitioning economies becomes increasingly central. At the core of our proposed domain of intellectual discourse, and especially using a systems approach, lie the processes of *higher order economic and technological learning* as developed in Dyker and Radosevich (2000), Matthew (1996), and cited in Carayannis (2000):

> The concept of economic learning captures the notion that some economies seem to be able to accommodate changes (e.g. products, technologies, markets) better than others. They do so partly through the flexibility of their firms themselves, but also through their capacities to promote inter-organizational linkages and collaboration and, above all, through the capacity of public institutions to imbibe and develop innovations, and then disseminate those innovations in various forms to firms, thus accelerating the process of adaptation . . . Matthew makes a useful distinction between first-, second-, and third-order economic learning. First-order learning takes place within firms (organizations). Second-order learning takes place between firms through arrangements like sub-contracting, licensing, consortia, equity partnerships or joint ventures. Third-order economic learning takes place both outside and within firms but in such a way that their operating conditions are changed. It is "meta-learning", or learning how to learn; it takes place at the level of the economic system as a whole.

In the developed countries, knowledge has become one of the key input and output factors of economic activity. In addition, new technologies are facilitating the process of globalization of economies and societies. In such a context, *technological learning* (Carayannis, 1993; 1994b; 2000; 2001) and *knowledge* have become crucial factors of economic, social, and *especially entrepreneurial development*, which empowers people and entrepreneurs across the world in taking advantage of opportunities and chances unknown and unexplored until recently.

The critical new role of knowledge in economic and social development therefore brings about the concept of the Knowledge Economy, which is simply another evolution of development phases following the agriculture economy and the industrial economy. This economy is based directly on the production, distribution, and use of knowledge and information. In more general terms, the Knowledge Economy is the theoretical framework and broad economic concept that outlines major forces in the economy driven and led by innovation and knowledge.

So far, it is primarily the developed market economies that have been able to take advantage of KE, gaining even more competitive advantage in the global economy and widening the gap between developed and developing countries. Yet, developing and transitioning countries still have the potential to catch up and leverage the concept of "Knowledge Economy" by utilizing one of its main driving forces – Information and Communication Technologies (ICT) – through the process known as *e-Development*.

Part I

ICT and e-Development Policies in the Knowledge Economy

2
Learning from Development Experience

> Ideas and knowledge have always been fundamental to the economic transformation of inputs into outputs. The fact that economists can now model that effectively does not represent an underlying change in the economy.
>
> Martin Richardson (2001)

The central motivation for this book is our belief that the "goodness of fit" between the stage an economy is in and the development strategy adopted (including the use of technology and the role of knowledge) determines the *quality, speed, and sustainability* of development (see Figure 2.1). In this context, our efforts focus on learning from development experiences, in particular those related to the formation and growth of small and medium-sized enterprises (SME), to develop a methodology for establishing *an optimal match typology* between development stage and development strategy.

Earning monopoly rents on discoveries is important for providing incentive for investment in technological innovation R&D. This is why protection of Intellectual Property Rights (IPR) is fundamental to growth, and traditional economics sees "perfect competition" as the ideal. Enhancing human capital also is critical for GDP growth. To make investments in technology, a country must have sufficient human capital. Economic growth is driven by the accumulation of knowledge and new technological developments create technical platforms for further innovations. These technical platforms, in turn, are drivers of economic growth. Technology raises the return on investment, which is why developed countries can sustain growth and why developing economies cannot attain growth without it. Even with unlimited labor, natural resources, and ample capital, traditional economics predicts that there are diminishing returns on investment.

We reviewed the economies of several nations within a spectrum of possible states of development as follows, and we related those to development pathways (see Figure 2.1):

(a) *Subsistence-focused*: where survival is the issue – e.g. Afghanistan today.
(b) *Commodity-based*: where commodities are the dominant means and goal of economic production and exchange and within that category a range from barter-based economies up to some transitioning economies.
(c) *Knowledge-based* (OECD, 1996): where knowledge is one of the key means and goals of economic production and exchange and one of the key economic resources with a high degree of utilization and sharing.
(d) *Knowledge-driven* (UK DTI, 1998): where knowledge is the major means and goal of economic production and exchange and the most valuable economic resource under continual renewal, sharing, and utilization. Technological innovation and economic learning are key modalities of economic development and growth.

This approach is partly inspired by the research findings of Robert Solow among others, as described by Easterly (2002):

> Nobel laureate Robert Solow published his theory of growth in a couple of articles in 1956 and 1957. His conclusion surprised many, and still surprises many today: investment in machinery can not be a source of growth in the long run. Solow argued that the only possible source of growth in the long run is technological change.
>
> Easterly (2002: 47)

Another conceptual pillar and source of motivation for our efforts is the work of Joseph Schumpeter on "creative destruction" and technological change, which was again listed as the preeminent driver of the process of sustainable economic growth "which incessantly revolutionizes the economic structure from within, incessantly destroying the old one, incessantly creating a new one. The process of Creative Destruction is the essential fact about capitalism" (Schumpeter, 1942: 82).

We consider entrepreneurial initiative as one of the main – if not *the* main – ways to drive technological change and catalyze and accelerate sustainable growth, hence our motivation to learn better from past entrepreneurial initiatives aimed at fostering economic development.

The convergence of transformations and discontinuities both in the means of production and the nature of the outcomes of economic activity (products and services) and the pronounced shift from product-focused, tangibles-based economies to service-focused, intangibles-reliant ones, necessitate rethinking and possibly reinventing ways and means to support *the mission* (as well as the business) of global, regional, and national policies and practices of economic development.

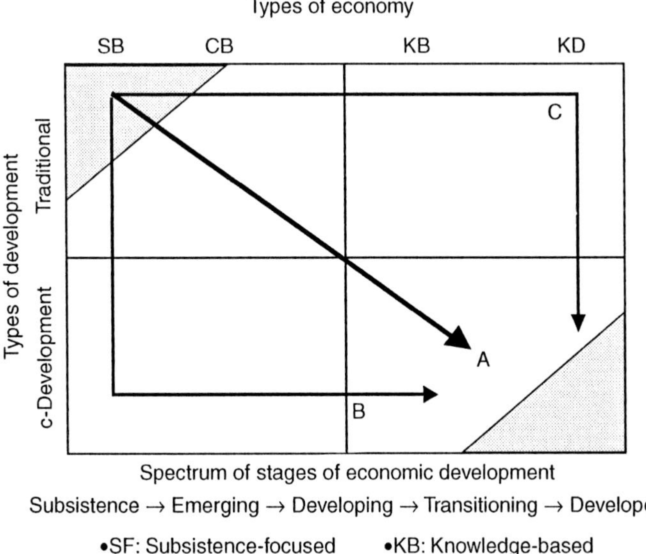

Attributes of pathways A, B, and C:
(A) Faster, easier and better way to move towards knowledge-based economy.
(B) Costly, slow but more common way in transitioning economies for moving towards the knowledge economy.
(C) Slowest, costly and more limited way.

Figure 2.1   e-Development pathways toward the Knowledge Economy destination

Source: adapted from Carayannis *et al.* (2005)

e-Development allows us to perceive the challenges and opportunities of development in a new light in terms of the *scope and speed as well as the quality of technological and economic change.* The role of ICT in the creation, diffusion, absorption, and use of Knowledge for Development (K4D), has been shown to be instrumental and with increasingly substantial and emerging potential (World Bank, 1998; World Bank Institute, 2001a, 2001b; Carayannis *et al.*, 2005; Carayannis and Popescu, 2005; Carayannis and von Zedwitz, 2005.

Definition of terms

In this section we attempt to define and operationalize the following concepts that we consider key to our research considerations:

- e-Development
- Knowledge Economy
- Innovation networks
- Knowledge clusters

- Technological learning
- Knowledge transfer
- Communities of Practice (CoP)
- Absorptive capacity
- Information and Communication Technologies for Development (ICT4Dev)

There are no well-articulated or established definitions for *e-Development* or the *Knowledge Economy* and that has been often a source of confusion as the following quotes indicate:

- We define *knowledge-based economies* as those which are directly based on the production, distribution and use of knowledge and information. (OECD, 1996, p. 7)
- *A knowledge-driven economy* is one in which the generation and exploitation of knowledge play the predominant part in the creation of wealth. (UK DTI, 1998, p. 2)
- For countries in the vanguard of the world economy, the balance between knowledge and resources has shifted so far towards the former that *knowledge has become perhaps the most important factor determining the standard of living* – more than land, than tools, than labor. Today's most technologically advanced economies are truly knowledge-based. (World Bank, 1999, p. 16)

Our working definition for the *Knowledge Economy (KE)* is as follows:

> The Knowledge Economy is a state of economic being and a process of economic becoming that intensively and extensively leverages knowledge assets and competences as well as economic learning to catalyze and accelerate sustainable and robust economic growth.

Our working definition of *e-Development* is as follows:

> e-Development is a set of tools, methodologies, and practices that leverage ICT to catalyze and accelerate social, political, and economic development or, in other words, *e-Development is ICT-enabled and KE-inspired development* that may enable the economies of developing and especially transitioning countries to become Knowledge Economies (see Figure 2.2). In addition:
>
> - e-Development is the means to reach the final end of Knowledge Economy.
> - e-Development is innovative since it provides for internal cross-sectorial strategies and capabilities, and externally it provides for a regional approach to better serve the needs of client countries.

In addition to the concepts of e-Development and the Knowledge Economy, we also introduce working definitions for two other important knowledge creation, diffusion, and use modalities that play a central role in our research on the role of technological learning for entrepreneurial development: namely, Innovation Networks and Knowledge Clusters. Our working definition of *Innovation Networks* is as follows:

> Innovation Networks[1] are real and virtual infrastructures and infra-technologies that serve to nurture creativity, trigger invention and catalyze innovation in a public and/or private domain context (for instance, Government-University-Industry Public-Private Research and Technology Development Co-opetitive Partnerships). (Carayannis *et al.*, 2005)

Our working definition of *Knowledge Clusters* is as follows:

> Knowledge Clusters (Carayannis and Campbell, 2005) are agglomerations of co-specialized, mutually complementary and reinforcing knowledge assets in the form of "knowledge stocks" and "knowledge flows" that exhibit self-organizing, learning-driven, dynamically adaptive competences and trends in the context of an open systems perspective. (Carayannis *et al.*, 2005)

Largely due to new technologies for efficient production, transmission, and processing of knowledge and information, other intangible resources such as know-how and social capital become the coal, oil, and diamonds of the twenty-first century (World Economic Forum, 2002). This trend is punctuated by several factors:

- Widespread adoption of innovative technologies to create new business models, reduce transaction costs, and enhance effectiveness and responsiveness of the public sector.
- Development of a services-based economy, with activities demanding intellectual content becoming more imperative.
- Increased emphasis on higher education and life-long learning to make effective use of the rapidly expanding knowledge base and build a competitive edge.
- Massive investments in research and development, training, education, software, branding, marketing, etc.
- Intensification of competition between enterprises and nations based on innovative product designs, marketing methods, and organizational forms.

We next define and discuss the concepts of technological learning, knowledge transfer and communities of practice:

Our working definition for *technological learning*, as developed by Carayannis (1992, 1993, 1994b, 1998, 1999, 2000, 2001a, 2002, 2004) and presented by Jelinek:

> Technological learning is defined as the process by which a technology-driven firm creates, renews, and upgrades its latent and enacted capabilities based on its stock of explicit and tacit resources. It combines purely technical with purely administrative learning processes. (Jelinek, 1979)

Teece *et al.* (1990) define learning as "a process by which repetition and experimentation enable tasks to be performed better and quicker and new production opportunities to be identified." Furthermore, they focus on the *nature* of learning as both an individual and an organizational process:

> Learning processes are intrinsically social and collective phenomena. Learning occurs not only through the imitation and emulation of individuals, as with teacher-student, or master-apprentice, but also *because of joint contributions to the understanding of complex problems*. Learning requires *common codes of communication* and coordinated search procedures. (Teece *et al.*, 1990)

Our working definition for *knowledge transfer* includes the following elements:

> Knowledge transfer is viewed from an *information theoretic* perspective (Shannon and Weaver, 1949), a *meta-cognitive* perspective (Simon, 1969; Halpern, 1989; Sternberg and Frensch, 1991), and a *linguistic* perspective (Chomsky, 1971; 1993) as a *knowledge transfer process*, where the human problem solver and technology manager is seen as both a technician and a craftsman (Schon, 1983), a "lumper" and a "splitter" (Mintzberg, 1989).
>
> The problem solver typically relies on *multi-layered technological learning and unlearning* (Carayannis, 1992; 1993; 1994a; 1994b; Carayannis *et al.*, 1994a; 1994b; Dodgson, 1991; 1993) to create, maintain, and enhance the capacity of individuals, groups, and organizations to transfer and absorb knowledge in the form of *embodied* and *disembodied* (von Hippel, 1988) technology in the form of *artifacts, beliefs*, and *evaluation routines* (Garud and Rappa, 1994) and *tacit* and *explicit* knowledge (Polanyi, 1958; 1966; Nonaka, 1988; 1994).
>
> Moreover, knowledge transfer occurs across scientific disciplines, professions, industries, economic sectors, geographic regions, and societies/countries (Reisman, 1989; Reisman and Zhao, 1991). This

motivates the linguistic view of technology sharing and absorption in the form of a firm's technological *absorptive capacity* (Cohen and Levinthal, 1990) as well as *transformative capacity* (Garud and Nayyar, 1994), since it requires effective communication among practitioners with often divergent *technical rationalities* (Schon, 1983).

The literature on knowledge transfer is organized into two mainstreams that deal with intra-organizational transfer and communities of practice, and inter-organizational transfer. However, Iansiti and Clark (1994) argue for a combination of external acquisition (capacity to access knowledge through relationships) and internal integration (ability to transfer knowledge within the organization) as one of the contributing sources to the performance of firms like NEC and Nissan.

The literature on intra-organizational knowledge transfer focuses on the factors influencing the efficiency of knowledge transfer. Hansen (1999) identifies the characteristics or capabilities of the sender and receiver, and the context. The literature on knowledge transfer within communities of practice focuses on the transfer and sharing of knowledge between people within a certain community of practice, where new knowledge is usually formed during the communication/interaction processes occurring within the group (Wenger, 1998). Extensive studies of distributed collaboration and knowledge sharing among business organizations show how communities of practice can enhance communications, improve organizational performance, and support collective goals. Wenger (1998) argues that production of knowledge is being shaped by organization context and relationships between professionals bonded together by a joint enterprise (CoP).

Our working definition for *communities of practice* is as follows:

Communities of practice (CoP) are defined as a persistent, sustained social network of individuals who share and develop an overlapping knowledge base, set of beliefs, values, history, and experiences focused on a common practice and/or mutual enterprise (Barab and Duffy, 2000). Wenger (2004) has identified three dimensions of communities of practice:

(1) Domain: the area of knowledge that brings the community together.
(2) Community: the group of people for whom the domain is relevant.
(3) Practice: the body of knowledge, methods, tools, stories, cases, and documents which members share and develop together.

Nonaka and Takeuchi (1995) state the importance of tacit company knowledge as the basis for communities of practice (CoP) and transforming it into explicit company assets. Wender and Snyder (2000) give examples of successful CoP both as internal company networking groups and with members from different companies.

The other stream within the knowledge transfer research, inter-organizational transfer literature argues that the outcome of knowledge transfer is highly dependent on the absorptive capacity of the recipient (Cohen and Levinthal, 1990).

Our working definition for *absorptive capacity* is as follows:

The notion of *absorptive capacity* refers to the capacity of the recipient to assimilate value and use the knowledge transferred. Similar notions of "learning" have been defined by Marshall (1965) as the acquisition and use of exiting knowledge and/or creation of new knowledge with the purpose of improving economic performance.

Braun (2002) introduces a conceptual model for knowledge flows that shows how a large company with high connectivity and an integrated infrastructure for information and knowledge exchange with communities of practice can lead to a higher level of trust and subsequent innovation and competitive advantage. He identifies the critical factors to consider in terms of knowledge exchange between organizations as follows:

- Adequate technology (infrastructure and data exchange);
- Trust and cooperative relationships;
- Common interest;
- Exchange of tacit and explicit company knowledge for the public good aspect of the company.

Our working definition for *ICT4Dev* focuses in the broad sense beyond the hardware and software aspects to encompass socio-economic and even cultural issues (ADB, 2001; FID, 1998):

ICT is at the convergence of a tripod made of three specialized domains, namely information technology, data and information, socio-economic issues to fuse the capabilities and functionality of each specialized domain into a holistic yet fluid domain that works to develop a customized information system for each user. Information technology (IT) or informatics was defined in 1990 as (i) the aggregation of information-related fields, such as computer hardware and software, telecommunications networks and equipment, and information-technology-based industries; and (ii) the application of these technologies in all economic sectors, publishing, broadcasting, libraries, databanks, and other information services industries. The major difference between IT and ICT is the emphasis given in the case of ICT to the communication aspects – the collaboration and connectivity that the technologies facilitate. A new vocabulary is emerging with reference to its electronic character using the prefix "e".

In this sense, ICT4Dev may allow commodity-based economies to evolve into knowledge-based and possibly knowledge-driven economies (see the cases of Ireland, South Korea, and Singapore among others; see also Figure 2.1).

e-Development allows us to perceive the challenges and opportunities of development in a new light in terms of the *scope and speed as well as the quality of technological and economic change.* The role of ICT in the creation, diffusion, absorption, and use of knowledge for development (K4D), has been shown to be instrumental and with increasingly substantial and emerging potential (World Bank, 1998; WBI, 2001a; WBI, 2001b) (see Table 2.1).

The set of tools, competencies, and applications of e-Development in the Knowledge Economy may be distributed among four main pillars of general development:

- Institution building
- Capacity building
- Policy making
- Investment making

The dimension of a more effective and efficient development resulting from e-Development interventions may be highlighted by the role of:

KE: The Knowledge Economy framework provides the foundation for the recognition of the potential of transitional and even developing

Table 2.1   Role of ICT in knowledge creation, diffusion, and use

e-Development brings about new ways of old interventions . . .

Privatization	e-Privatization
Deregulation	e-Legislation
Education and human capital	e-Learning
Government reform	e-Government and e-Procurement
Finance	e-Finance
Business climate	e-Government, e-Procurement, e-Taxation, e-Registration
R&D and innovation	Technology parks and incubators

. . . and creates room for innovative applications.

e-Society for increased participation of the civil society
Electronic flows of documents in the public administration to increase efficiency and transparency
Access to rural finance
Increase speed and flexibility
Improve general quality of services across industries and sectors of the economy
Opportunities for cross-country and cross-sectorial development

economies to catalyze and accelerate their development by leveraging ICT and e-Development practices.

e-Dev: e-Development may provide the ways and means to accelerate and catalyze the transition to the knowledge-driven economy including the potential for transitioning economies to leapfrog developed economies with less focus on e-Development in special and specific sectors or in niche markets.

ICT: ICT may allow commodity-based economies to evolve into knowledge-based and possibly knowledge-driven economies.

The knowledge-based economy creates *profit avalanches*. Entrance is easy for small, intelligent companies, but there is no space for organic growth; the market is instantly global and a newcomer can attain dominance very quickly. It also differentiates itself by the convergence of technologies, which removes market sector boundaries: wireless, satellite, cable, and telecoms no longer belong to discrete sectors (technological and sector convergence).

In a mobile information society, services also are different, impacted by the presence of the Internet, virtual organizations, or networked transactions. Information and Communication Technologies (ICT) are enablers of change; they release creative potential and knowledge and open up global markets and foster competition. Networked transaction economies resemble the most complex network: the human brain (Routti, 2003). The digital revolution can be a great equalizer, but national policies must be right to enable it. Proper training and education can make a networked transaction economy, or knowledge economy, more effective and efficient: *smarter*. This elevation requires methodical enhancement of the business development environment, for instance via business incubators. Advancement also requires enhancement of the network technology infrastructure, i.e. ICT. The state of the art is the virtual incubator, in which ICT extends and multiplies the effectiveness of business incubation at lower cost.

ICT opens up the possibility of a fundamental reengineering of business processes and wider economic structures to create the network economy and society. It permits every step in value generation to become smarter; value is being created less in the simple transformation of inputs into outputs but more in enlisting the new capacity and competencies created by ICT fundamentally to meet individualized and complex customer needs – whether business-to-business relationships or business-to-consumer.

Successful companies are becoming more networked, customer-focused and agile in which an ethic of demand-oriented service rather than producer-oriented production is conferring market share and value generation alike. Indeed more and more value generation lies in distribution, financing, marketing, and services rather than manufacturing the original product – important though that remains. Knowledge and the potential of ICT penetrate every link in the economic chain, not just the manufacturing core.

Another main contribution of ICT is as enabler of the democratic process of decision making in improving communications between citizens and their representatives, and increasing the visibility of governmental work. Many governments have already introduced online access, enabling citizens to make better use of their rights. Citizens participate electronically in the government, communicate with parliamentarians, or vote electronically.

In this context, information technologies could create a new type of citizen, one capable of monitoring the action of the elected representatives, of giving their opinion in real time on all subjects via the Internet. Moreover, an unlimited and non-restricted access to government information can increase market transparency, and can generate public value in other areas such as education and health with enormous potential savings. In summary, the new technologies foster the dissemination of information and knowledge by separating content from its physical location, and by making information, knowledge, and culture accessible, in theory, to anyone.

Hence, the need for e-Development interventions is stressed also by the development of the e-Economy and the increased competitiveness and openness that it brings about. The Knowledge Economy is fostering market transparency, integrating separate geographical markets and facilitating integration into innovative global markets. Moreover, the need for standardization, of both processes and policies, calls for the action of an over-arching organization that can provide appropriate guidance and advisory services to transitional economies willing and able to take advantage of the Knowledge Economy (see Figure 2.2).

Creative interaction between universities, scientists, and researchers on the one hand and industry and commerce on the other that drive technology transfer and innovation are necessarily rooted in the close physical location of universities and companies. There is already ample evidence around the world that high-tech clusters are built on this interaction, but *ideopoleis* – for example Helsinki, Munich, and Cambridge – go further. They have an array of other supporting factors – notably a sophisticated communications and transport infrastructure; financial institutions willing to provide the necessary risk capital to entrepreneurs and specialists in technology transfer; supportive public authorities that facilitate the network structures driving creative interaction; and are attractive environments for knowledge workers. Ideopoleis are emerging as the cities at the heart of dynamic, high-growth, knowledge-based regions.

The use of ICT might be used in developing countries that are the most disadvantaged by poor access to information to complement economic policies in order to boost efficiency and enhance market integration. In order to improve the efficiency, competitiveness, and responsiveness of their governments, and hence democratized governmental institutions, it is imperative to expand the number and variety of services, improve access to their services, and address crucial issues such as electronic procurement: "ICT can empower

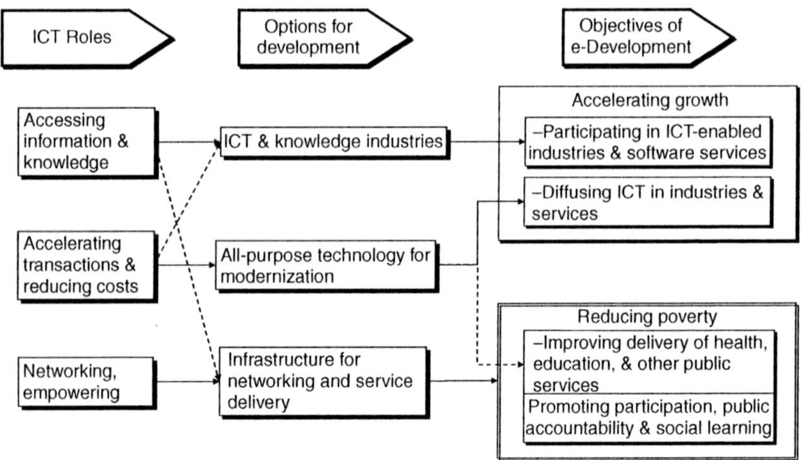

Figure 2.2   ICT roles, options, and objectives for development
Source: adapted from Hanna (2003)

the disenfranchised and their intermediaries . . . while promoting transparency of governmental actions and market outcomes."

Taking advantage of emerging information technologies requires policies similar to those needed for opening the market and free trade. For example, creating a modern public procurement is part of the process of an efficient, and a competitive market economy that is necessary for these countries' full integration into the global community. In this respect, ICT can help to achieve a competitive environment (open bidding), provides opportunities for the private sector (free access to public information), and thus government transparency, and elimination of a country elite's hold on the key sectors of the national economy.

Part II

e-Development Policies and Strategies toward the Knowledge Economy

3
e-Development Policies

A e-Development policies: challenges and opportunities

Transitioning and developing economies, such as those in the region of Europe and Central Asia (ECA), are exposed to significant risks of being left behind and becoming victims of the digital divide and even abyss rather than reaping digital dividends, without appropriate actions and interventions, balancing top-down public sector policies against bottom-up private sector initiatives focused on leveraging e-Development and Knowledge Economy interventions.

Moreover, the need for standardization, of both processes and policies, calls for action of an overarching organization that can provide appropriate guidance and advisory services to transitional economies willing and able to take advantage of the Knowledge Economy. The benefits for EU-accession candidate countries from engaging in the Knowledge Economy development framework are those generally predicted for the intra-industry integration and commerce, with general greater efficiency and cheaper and faster ways to conduct business (see Table 3.1).

The experience of advanced developing countries and newly developed ones has shown that ICT can be applied for a wide range of developmental goals (DOI, 2001):

(1) The first and the narrowest approach is developing ICT as a sector of the economy.

- The ICT along with the Science and Technology (S&T) sector is not limited to goods, such as hardware and software, but also includes value-added services.
- There are several reasons a country may be interested in developing ICT as a sector. ICT is a very profitable, high value-added business with good export potential. Plus, it serves as a locomotive industry that accelerates the development in other, "satellite" sectors of the economy. Several countries

Table 3.1   B2B estimated cost saving by sector through e-Commerce

Estimated savings	Sector
Less than 10%	Coal, food ingredients, health care
Above 10%, but less than 20%	Aerospace machining, chemicals, communications, computing, freight transport life science, media and advertising, oil and gas, paper, steel
Above 20%	Electronic components (above 30%), forest products, machining (metals)

Source: adapted from Brookes and Wahhaj (2000)

greatly benefited from utilization of the full potential of their S&T sector and have invested in creating a favorable environment for its development. The most notable success stories beyond the most developed countries are Ireland (software development industry), Costa Rica (hardware production), and Singapore and Malaysia (as ICT and communications hub for the region).

(2) ICT can be used to increase the efficiency of the government and business sector, thus accelerating economic growth in the country. Use of computer-assisted networks for intra-government operations greatly increases the efficiency of government.

- Other e-government solutions, such as information dissemination and interactive applications (i.e. e-taxation, e-registration, e-procurement, etc.) increase transparency and efficiency of both the public and private sectors. In the private sector, ICT can create new opportunities and drastically reduce trade and transactions costs by creating digital marketplaces to manage supply-chains, automating transactions, allowing local businesses access to global markets, and improving intra-firm communications. The cumulative effect of ICT adoption in private and public sector is a better competitive position of the country in the global economy.

(3) Finally, ICT can be used to achieve particular developmental goals: such as social justice, better health care, and better educational systems.

- Distance learning and training, e-health and e-society applications (increased participation of civil society in the political dialogue) are just a few examples of ICT applications for achieving narrow developmental goals. Many African e-Development projects supported by international aid agencies fall into this category. For example, thanks to Internet e-health applications, doctors in many remote areas can get consultant help from big medical centers both in and outside the country.

Box 3.1   Excerpts from "Creating a Development Dynamic: Final Report of the Digital Opportunity Initiative, July 2001"

Analysis of the approach to ICT policy taken by developing countries shows that ICT can play a significant role as part of an overall national strategy for development. In this respect, countries have pursued diverse strategies: some have focused on developing ICT as an economic sector—either to boost exports (Costa Rica and Taiwan) or to build domestic capacity (Brazil, India and Korea)—while others are pursuing strategies which seek to use ICT as an enabler of a wider socio-economic development process. Countries which use ICT as an enabler may be further subdivided into those which have focused primarily on repositioning the country's economy to secure competitive advantage in the global economy (Malaysia, Trinidad and Tobago) and those which explicitly focus on ICT in pursuit of development goals (Estonia and South Africa).

These varied experiences have revealed some important lessons about the role of ICT in development:

- An export focus can produce significant economic benefits, such as growth and foreign investment, but these gains do not automatically translate into progress on broader development goals.
- Building domestic ICT production capacity may address local needs and help strengthen domestic economic linkages, but it can significantly restrict countries' ability to adopt new technologies and to gain competitive advantage in the global economy.
- It is imperative to use ICT to improve the competitive position of a developing country in the global economy, but this may fail to meet some development goals if it diverts attention from fostering local markets and businesses.
- An explicit focus on using ICT in pursuit of development goals allows countries to achieve a wide diffusion of benefits from ICT and contributes to both broad-based economic growth and specific development goals.
- A number of interrelated factors should be addressed to maximize the benefits of ICT for development. These include building human capacity, creating incentives for enterprise, developing appropriate content and increasing competition, especially among telecommunications and Internet-related businesses.

Finally, the success of national ICT strategies is dependent upon the coordination and alignment of efforts undertaken by all actors involved, at global, local, and national levels.

The World Bank Comprehensive e-Development framework includes elements of all three approaches and combines them in a way unique to the conditions and development goals of a given country. Thus, understanding of the full potential of ICT is only the first step in e-Development.

In designing an e-Development strategy it is important to keep in mind that the advantages and opportunities offered by ICT remain extremely uneven. The digital divide phenomena are a reflection of deep social and economic inequalities both between and within countries, which can in the short to medium term be exacerbated by e-Development and ICT-related development interventions.

The convergence of globalization and technology forces and influences increasingly present new challenges as well as opportunities to transitioning and developing economies along with the more developed ones. The most developed countries with a strong ICT sector may be in a much better position than transitioning or developing economies, thanks to their residual endowments in technological infrastructures as well as human, intellectual, financial, and social capital stocks and flows, to exploit opportunities presented by globalization and free trade. In that sense, technology can effectively widen the development gap between "haves" and "have-nots."

Within a given country, ICT are rapidly adapted by most affluent and educated parts of the society, predominantly in urban areas. ICT most immediately benefit those who already are in a relatively advanced position, giving them even more leverage in economic, social, and governance matters. Benefiting society and economy at large, ICT have potential to widen the gap along geographical, educational, and income lines.

Hence, a well-balanced ICT and e-Development policy needs to shape strategies and pilots in a manner that will minimize the risks and maximize the benefits of economic development in the Knowledge Economy.

B   e-Development strategies components: the four pillars

In this section, we outline the key components of successful ICT and e-Development strategies derived from practical experience.

Analysis of the success stories shows that efficient e-Development should be based on the following four pillars:

(1) **Policy making** is the pillar concerned with the design and implementation of a clear strategy for e-Development in the country:

(a) Vision and commitment of the government are essential for a viable national action plan on ICT development;
(b) The action plan has to identify specific and realistic goals and targets to maintain consistency and sustainability, i.e. ICT manufacturing to boost export-oriented sectors (Ireland and Costa Rica); creation of ICT infrastructure to become a major communications hub in the region (Malaysia and Singapore);
(c) The action plan should also specify the timeframe and identify the - relevant actors involved in the implementation to ensure harmonization and synergies;

(d) All stakeholders, such as government, private sector, local authorities, and civil society should be engaged in the design and implementation of the action plan.

(2) **Institution building** concerns the creation of an appropriate institutional framework to oversee, design, and implement e-Development policy interventions:

(a) The creation of new institutions is crucial to increase efficiency and accountability in e-Development by linking actions to the most appropriate institution or body;
(b) An overarching organization may guarantee effective coordination among the various actors involved in e-Development, such as governmental agencies, private sector, civil society, etc.

(3) **Investment making** can include both domestic as well as foreign direct investments aimed at catalyzing and accelerating the development and use of ICT and e-Development-related technologies and initiatives.

(4) **Capacity building** includes investments in "hard" factors such as infrastructure (fixed and mobile telephone lines, computers, etc.) and human capital (skilled labor, literacy level of the population, etc.).

4
ICT and e-Development in the Knowledge Economy

A   Catalysts and accelerators of economic development

Innovative technologies are reshaping the global economic landscape, by improving speed and ease for communications and interaction among the various economic actors involved in the productive cycle. In addition, higher demand is rapidly decreasing costs and prices for ICT equipment and telecommunications services, and it is facilitating the liberalization of the trade and regulatory framework worldwide.

So far, it is mostly the developed market economies that have been ready to reap the benefit of such developments, leaving aside the opportunity for developing and transitional economies to participate in sharing this potential. Yet, the Internet and other technologies have the potential for allowing developing and especially transitioning countries to gain from the globalizing economy and to even catch up and leapfrog other, currently more developed economies. The SME sector is one particularly promising domain, where e-Development and Knowledge Economy concepts and practices could have a profound and sustainable impact.

Surveys of small- or medium-sized enterprises (SMEs) in developing countries, suggest that four types of information appear to be especially valuable (Goldstein and O'Connor, 2000):

(1) customers and markets;
(2) product design;
(3) process technology – operation, maintenance and repair of existing equipment, as well as new technology developments;
(4) financing sources and terms.

ICT may also benefit entrepreneurs by improving information available to their transaction partners, whether customers, financiers, or others. Besides reducing information search costs, the Internet or mobile telephony may actually improve the efficiency of the working of product and factor markets directly.

There are at least four different channels through which e-Commerce may impact on developing country entrepreneurs:

(1) making it easier for SMEs to access business-to-consumer (B2C) world markets;
(2) facilitating activity on the global market for agricultural and tropical products;
(3) allowing firms in poorer countries to tap into the business-to-business (B2B) supply-chains;
(4) allowing service-providing enterprises in developing countries to operate more efficiently and to provide certain services directly to customers anywhere in the world.

In developed economies, the Internet has proven to be more effective in the business-to-business (B2B) e-commerce applications, allowing big corporations to maximize and optimize their production and distribution chains. The Internet may empower small producers of intermediate products in developing countries to make contact with companies in the Western world and be part of their value chain by supplying products/raw material (provided that they can deliver on time, at a competitive price, and according to acceptable standard of quality).

Technology has made the global marketplace a smaller place, so suppliers in developing economies may be part of the international value chain that can include almost every supplier independently of location. Again, those companies that cannot (either financially or in terms of logistics) make a presence in the e-marketplace may be left behind, thus enhancing rather than alleviating the digital divide.

Box 4.1   B2C e-commerce for remote communities

The business-to-consumer dimension of e-commerce has been overestimated by industry analysts, even in the developed economies (given the bubble of the e-commerce in Western economies). Yet, the Internet has shown how it can have impact on economic transactions between companies and consumers, especially in specific sectors (i.e. travel, books, etc.). SMEs in transition economies can take advantage of this potential of the Internet, specifically by artisans in traditionally low-technology sectors. The OECD paper on e-commerce includes an interesting case study of a Guyanan weavers' cooperative formed by 300 women from the Wapishana and Macushi tribes producing hammocks and selling them through the web. The starting point of this experience is that most artisans live in remote villages and rural areas, and their very isolation may be one reason why their products have survived in the "global economy."

These products accrue value and interest exactly because of their unique character and rarity, attracting the attention of wealthy consumers in OECD

> countries. Moreover, emigrants from developing countries constitute another target market, if not another exclusive channel for marketing these unique products into OECD markets.
>
> From this experience we can assume that the Internet can be the channel for SMEs in developing economies to entice Western consumers by creating a niche market for their products and artifacts (as the Internet has created a niche e-marketplace for travel, books, and CDs in OECD markets).

Another extremely valuable application of e-commerce for SMEs in developing countries are value-added services such as tourism. The World Tourism Organization (1999) writes that "niche players are no longer constrained by the cost of breaking through geographic barriers. The niche player can now tackle global markets. For just a few hundred dollars of ISP charges and with some careful planning and design, world markets can be captured by organizations which, a few years ago, could not have contemplated looking beyond their own borders. Global distribution is available to the smallest players."

The very crucial point for e-commerce in transitional countries is the set of rules that the regulators put in place to ensure sustainability for electronic transactions. e-Commerce requires legal norms and standards, covering: contract enforcement; consumer protection; liability assignment; privacy protection; intellectual property rights; and process and technical standards, for instance regarding the way payments are accepted on the Internet and products are delivered to the final user; security; authentication; encryption; digital signatures; and connectivity protocols.

B   Prerequisites, catalysts, and accelerators

To identify the major challenges and opportunities in building a Knowledge Economy, an analysis of twenty-one countries has been carried out. The twenty-one countries include two groups: one group of newly developed and recently developed countries that have been able to dramatically improve their economic being by adopting a Knowledge Economy approach. The second group of countries includes the ten candidate countries for EU membership of central and eastern Europe plus Ukraine. In both cases, the analysis focuses on the main policy and interventions paving the way for a Knowledge Economy, to identify the measures critical to the promotion of ICT development. Three large categories have been identified: prerequisites; enabling environment/facilitators; and drivers/accelerators. Such a division allows for clearer identification of priorities and design of a logical sequence of actions for successful e-Development.

(1) *Prerequisites* are the very basic and essential requirements for e-Development in the country to become possible. However, their presence neither guarantees nor actively promotes adoption of ICT in the country. Prerequisites are a checklist of general political and

socio-economic conditions in the country. Thus, prerequisites are an absolute must but are passive in their nature.

(2) *Enabling environment/facilitators* is a set of measures that create favorable conditions for ICT adoption and development in the country.

(3) *Drivers/accelerators* are measures taken to accelerate ICT adoption and development in the country as well as in particular sectors. There is an important difference between facilitators and drivers: with facilitators the government provides necessary tools for e-Development to business and society, whereas using drivers the government actively promotes the use of these tools in a particular way.

The table below (Table 4.1) presents a classification of different e-Development activities and measures in infrastructure building, policy making, institution building, regulatory and legal framework, and human capital.

Table 4.1   Prerequisites, catalysts, and accelerators

Physical infrastructure		
Prerequisites	**Facilitators**	**Drivers**
	Most important: multiple and competing providers of services in telecom sector: in fixed networks, mobile services and ISP	
	Teledensity approaching 50%	
	Increasing international connectivity	
Basic infrastructure in place:	Digitization of the communication lines	Building of special high-speed networks for educational and R&D institutions
• Reliable network connections	Affordable hardware, Software and Internet rates	
• Teledensity (in fixed lines per 100) at least approaching 30%	Networking computers in schools, universities and government	Creation of "connectivity excellence pockets" with high speed connections for technology parks/ accelerators
• Computers are used in educational system, households, businesses and government	Building community access centers both free and paid	
	Increasing teledensity in rural areas	
	Building of reliable postal (delivery) services	
	Building a reliable online payment system for both businesses and private individuals	

Continued

Table 4.1 Continued

Policy making		
Prerequisites	**Facilitators**	**Drivers**
		Government actively involves the rest of the society in ICT use: adopts ICT for intra-government communications and provides variety of e-Government services online both for businesses and private individuals
	A political vision on e-Development in form of national ICT strategy with time-bound action plan. The strategy is focused on achieving well-defined targets and goals and is incorporated into a comprehensive national development strategy	Targeted policy interventions for the priority sectors, as identified in the strategy; examples:
Government oriented to building market economy	The action plan is supported by financial resources	• Active ICT awareness measures among general population
Favorable conditions for business development and FDI, especially in the area of SME	All stakeholders (government, private sector, local authorities, citizens groups, etc.) take part in the development and implementation of the strategy and the action plan	• Promotion of B2B and B2C e-Commerce • Promotion of high-tech SMEs • Promotion of ICT adoption by SMEs, targeting late adopters and laggards • Promotion of the dissemination of best practices within the business community • Promotion of cooperation between private sector and R&D institutions • Promotion of FDI in the ICT sector • Promotion of institutions providing access to capital for ICT sector
Institution building		
Basic institutional structure in place, meaning that there are institutions/ ministries responsible for regulation and	Creation of an overarching coordination council on ICT development and other institutions necessary for efficient coordination among different agencies involved in e-Development;	Institution building on micro-level to address specific policy priorities; examples: • Working group on e-commerce

Continued

Table 4.1 Continued

Prerequisites	Facilitators	Drivers
development of ICT sector, telecommunications in particular; clear division of responsibilities among different agencies is the key Viable banking and financial system, providing accessible capital, including venture capital, for SMEs	council should report directly to prime minister SME development agency Agency for export insurance Agency for FDI promotion Institution building at this stage heavily involves developing public–private partnerships	• Creation of government-supported venture funds and/or grant-making foundations to support R&D in ICT sector • Creation of public–private partnerships for ICT promotion among SMEs

Legal and regulatory framework

Prerequisites	Facilitators	Drivers
Basic regulatory framework for market economy is in place; special importance given to protecting shareholders' rights, regulations of privatization and fair competition, including anti-monopoly regulations Political stability and rule of law Control of corruption Favorable business environment, especially for SMEs: low barriers to entry, predictability of regulatory changes and implementation, business law enforcement, effective system	Privatizaion of the state-owned telecom provider Full liberalization of the telecom market; this is single most important element of ICT development Regulations of telecom sector promoting teledensity increase in rural areas; these regulations may be part of "package" for privatizing major telecom operator Introduction of regulations and requirement on use of ICT by the government, including government presence on the Internet Set of regulations on conducting business online including e-Document Act, e-Signature Act and Information Security Act	Major goal of government at this stage creation of regulatory system responsive to new market and technology developments Tax incentives for conducting B2B and B2C e-Commerce Creation of favorable conditions for FDI in ICT sector Creation of favorable conditions for R&D in ICT sector Regulation promoting cooperation between educational and R&D institutions and private sector Regulations promoting access to capital for high-tech SMEs Regulations fostering financial structures focusing on providing access to capital for ICT sector

Continued

Table 4.1 Continued

Prerequisites	Facilitators	Drivers
of solving business disputes, etc. Protection of intellectual property rights	Creation of favorable regulations for efficient commercialization of patents obtained by government-sponsored institutions	
Human capital		
Basic system of secondary and higher education is in place, resulting in generally well-educated population and low illiteracy level System of ICT-related higher education in place, producing high-quality graduates System of modern business education and training is in place	Introduction of ICT education in secondary and higher education Restructure educational system to realign with market economy Developing strong ties between private sector and educational system Developing system of life-long learning	Development of ICT vocational training Increasing number and quality of ICT graduates to level necessary for implementation of e-Development strategy Measures to prevent brain-drain in ICT sector and to attract skilled high-tech workers from abroad Development of distance education Special measures for development of business skills for players of ICT sector
Expected results		
Country is a "raw material," based on which process of building Knowledge Economy can begin	Country has created favorable environment for successful adoption of ICT	Government takes leadership role in building information society, actively promoting ICT sectors most relevant for country's development strategy

5
ICT and e-Development for the Knowledge Economy: Case Studies

In this chapter, we profile case studies where e-Development interventions geared towards the Knowledge Economy have had a significant impact.

We outline both examples of e-Development projects in select sectors and countries. We then profile selected countries in different stages of economic development (Chile, Mexico, Japan, China, Korea) to provide a more coherent and holistic conceptual framework, within which *top-down policies and bottom-up initiatives* would seem to have had a substantial set of *outputs, outcomes, and impacts* in catalyzing and even accelerating development. We also outline real case studies of the challenges and opportunities underlining development policy and practice.

ICT can be a powerful enabler of development goals because its unique characteristics dramatically improve communication and the exchange of information to strengthen and create new economic and social networks (DOI, 2001):

- ICT is *pervasive and cross-cutting*. ICT can be applied to the full range of human activity from personal use to business and government. It is multifunctional and flexible, allowing for tailored solutions—based in personalization and localization—to meet diverse needs.
- ICT is a key enabler in the *creation of networks* and thus allows those with access to benefit from exponentially increasing returns as usage increases (i.e. *network externalities*).
- ICT fosters the *dissemination of information and knowledge* by separating content from its physical location. This flow of information is largely impervious to geographic boundaries—allowing remote communities to become integrated into global networks and making information, knowledge, and culture accessible, in theory, to anyone.
- The "digital" and "virtual" nature of many ICT products and services allows for *zero or declining marginal costs*. Replication of content is virtually free regardless of its volume, and marginal costs for distribution and communication are near zero. As a result, ICT can radically reduce *transaction costs*.

- ICT's power to store, retrieve, sort, filter, distribute, and share information seamlessly can lead to substantial *efficiency gains* in production, distribution, and markets. ICT streamlines supply- and production-chains and makes many business processes and transactions leaner and more effective.
- The increase in efficiency and subsequent reduction of costs brought about by ICT is leading to the creation of new products, services, and distribution channels within traditional industries, as well as *innovative business models* and *whole new industries*. Intangible assets like intellectual capital are increasingly becoming the key source of value. With the required initial investment being just a fraction of what was required in the more physical-asset intensive industrial economy, barriers to entry are significantly lowered, and competition increased.
- ICT facilitates *disintermediation,* as it makes it possible for users to acquire products and services directly from the original provider, reducing the need for intermediaries. This not only can be a considerable source of efficiency, but also has been one of the factors leading to the creation of so-called "markets of one", leveraging ICT's potential to cater to the needs or preferences of users and consumers on an individual basis.
- ICT is *global.* Through the creation and expansion of networks, ICT can transcend cultural and linguistic barriers by providing individuals and groups with the ability to live and work anywhere, allowing local communities to become part of the global network economy without regard to nationality, and challenging current policy, legal, and regulatory structures within and between nations.

The unique characteristics inherent in ICT and the evidence from both micro-level initiatives and national ICT approaches suggest that a development-focused ICT strategy that leverages the powerful synergies of ICT as an enabler of social and economic development can lead to the creation of a development dynamic. The lessons learned point to five important interrelated areas for strategic intervention:

(1) Policy;
(2) Infrastructure;
(3) Enterprise;
(4) Human capacity;
(5) Content and applications (these will be referred to as components of the dynamic).

Taken together, these factors suggest that an approach which addresses several components of the dynamic is likely to be more effective than one which focuses in just one area. However, the development dynamic framework does not call for an "all or nothing" approach, nor does it suggest that such a dynamic can only be ignited if action is taken in all five areas at once. While acting on any of the components of the dynamic can produce valuable results, interventions taken across several component areas can generate returns to scale much greater than those achieved by a concentrated focus in any single area. As critical mass and threshold levels are achieved, *feedback, multiplier,* and *network effects* can ignite a virtuous cycle of sustainable development. Consider the following example, which takes a change in infrastructure access as its starting point:

Box 5.1   The e-Development dynamic

Investments in ICT infrastructure can lead to improved access by reducing costs and extending coverage to additional areas. This can have a catalytic impact on enterprises and provide additional incentives for increased adoption of ICT.

For example, it can help SMEs improve their competitiveness and expand market access. This in turn can create a feedback effect as demand for additional and faster access will entice additional investments in ICT infrastructure. The increase in both infrastructure and SMEs can lead, through spillover effects, to an increased demand for skilled labor and knowledge workers.

This increased demand for labor can then trigger additional investments in human capital. Such a combination of effects illustrates the connection between the different components that characterize the dynamic. To the extent that these interconnections are foreseen and addressed through complementary interventions, multiplier and feedback effects are realized, and the emergence of bottlenecks is avoided.

While the above example just looks at the generic case of a change in the conditions under which infrastructure is provided, the initiating effect could have started from any of the components of the dynamic—a change in IT policy, legislation favorable to enterprise creation, or a demand stimulus for increased deployment of ICT.

In South Africa the government requirement that all public procurement be done with electronic tenders led to a series of dynamic interactions between policy, enterprise, and human capability development. Similar results have been achieved through infrastructure roll-out policies centered on development goals. Estonia's Tiger Leap Program has demonstrated how ICT deployed to improve education can have positive impacts in other sectors. The complementarity between components of the "development dynamic" has substantial policy implications for national strategies focused on ICT as an enabler of development goals. Each of the five components has specific sub-components that allow policy makers and stakeholders to adopt and adapt them to reflect local priorities and conditions. This provides for a flexible policy tool that can be used in different contexts without tying countries to specific development paths.

A   Selected e-Development projects

e-Learning: ICT in vocational training, secondary and tertiary education

An examination of relevant statistical data is necessary to reveal the general status of development associated with e-Learning. Such data must include information regarding the number of Internet hosts, the number of PCs, the number of Internet users, and educational statistics including literacy rates and school enrollment.

As e-Learning is the application of information and communication technologies (ICTs) in support of distance learning, self-guided learning, and the traditional classroom (Development Gateway, 2003), it is vital to recognize that e-Learning encompasses aspects of both education and technology. School enrollment and literacy are essential information as is information concerning the general status of hardware in each country. Table 5.1 is representative of Latin American countries with complete statistics in conformance with the above criteria (Orbicom, 2003).

Vision 2016

In 1996, the government of Botswana set out to establish its long-term economic and social development goals in a national manifesto titled *Vision 2016*. The idea of the document, crafted by a nine-person presidential task-force was to create an outline of ideals for the development efforts in every sector in Botswana to follow, as well as propose tactics for achieving the goals. The overarching goal of *Vision 2016* calls for "an educated and informed nation," necessarily placing the improvement of educational quality and access at the forefront of the national mission. The mission details plans to enhance access to information through improved technological capacity and competence, as well as to "offer quality academic and professional programmes that ensure a commitment to, and a mastery of, lifelong learning skills as well as encouraging a spirit of critical enquiry" (Mutula, 2002).

The government of Botswana's 1996 mission has been followed with extensive efforts to ensure the implementation of these goals. Two well-known efforts supported by *Vision 2016* are discussed below, including the University of Botswana's Education, Democracy and Development Initiative (EDDI), and SMART Classroom, at the same institution.

Connect-ED

In 2002, USAID, in conjunction with the Ugandan national government, took a partnership approach to promoting access to and usage of, the Internet and computers for both teachers and students across the country. This project, which was also intended to standardize national public education, was entitled Connect-ED, short for Connectivity for Educator Development. Working under the umbrella project of USAID's LearnLink, operated by the Academy of Educational Development (AED), the Ugandan government implemented this online resource and training program for primary teachers in the country's public schools in 2002 (Connect-ED, 2003). This initiative by the government represented its acknowledgment that the most effective way to ensure the widespread understanding and

Table 5.1 Compilation of relevant e-Learning statistics

	Internet hosts/1000 people	Literacy rate (%)	Primary school enrollment gross (%)	Secondary school enrollment gross (%)	Tertiary school enrollment gross (%)	PCs/100 people	Internet users/100 people
Uruguay	21.1	97.6	109.4	98.1	36.1	11.0	11.9
Argentina	12.8	96.9	120.1	96.7	48.0	8.0	10.1
Chile	8.0	95.9	102.7	75.4	37.5	10.6	20.1
Brazil	9.6	87.3	162.3	108.5	16.5	6.3	4.7
Mexico	9.1	91.4	113.2	75.3	20.7	6.9	3.6
Trinidad and Tobago	5.3	98.4	100.4	80.8	6.5	6.9	9.2
Panama	2.7	92.1	111.6	69.2	34.9	3.8	4.1
Barbados	0.5	99.7	110.1	101.6	38.2	9.3	5.6
Costa Rica	2.1	95.7	106.8	60.2	16.0	17.0	9.3
Belize	1.4	93.4	128.1	74.0	0.9	13.4	7.3
Jamaica	0.6	87.3	99.6	83.3	16.4	5.0	3.8
Venezuela	0.9	92.8	101.9	59.3	28.5	5.3	4.7
Colombia	1.3	91.9	112.4	69.8	23.3	4.2	2.7
Paraguay	0.5	93.5	111.2	59.8	10.1	1.4	1.1
Guatemala	0.6	69.2	102.2	37.0	8.4	1.3	1.7
Peru	0.5	90.2	127.6	80.8	28.8	4.8	7.7
Ecuador	0.3	91.8	115.0	57.4	17.6	2.3	2.6
El Salvador	0.1	79.2	109.3	54.2	17.5	2.2	2.3
Bolivia	0.2	86.0	115.9	79.6	35.7	2.1	2.2
Nicaragua	0.4	66.8	103.5	54.0	11.8	2.5	1.4
Guyana	0	98.6	119.7	73.4	11.6	2.6	10.9
Honduras	0	75.6	106.0	32.0	14.7	1.2	1.4
Cuba	0.1	96.8	101.9	84.5	24.2	2.0	1.1
Average	3.4	89.8	112.6	72.4	21.9	5.7	5.6

Source: World Bank (2005)

usage of Uganda's young and growing Internet connectivity is through the public education system. The program primarily focuses on the confidence and capacity of teachers to integrate ICT into their classroom.

Much of Connect-ED's efforts in Uganda have been located in the actual teacher colleges and training centers, as well as through an online curriculum for training which actually posts the national curriculum guidelines along with other suggestions and training tools. By first training faculty and staff at the Institute of Teacher Education, Connect-ED was able to create a sustainable program through which the Ugandan staff members will be dispersed to various locations, to reach a wider audience of teachers, and spread the use of ICT (USAID, 2003). The three technical components of the Ugandan project include: the Digital Resource Library (DRL), which is a CD-Rom containing the national curriculum and other aids to help teachers craft and implement these lessons in the classroom; the Online Multimedia Curriculum, which includes engaging activities and other materials for learning and self-evaluation; and the Professional Development and Learning Environment (PDLE), a website designed to encourage Ugandan educators to continue using ICT to enhance their capabilities in the classroom (Connect-ED, 2003).

There is little analytical or critical literature available regarding this project to date. The homepage for Connect-ED has a "monthly reports" link, but this was last updated in 2001. However, the LearnLink project that was initiated by USAID and AED's efforts to expand ICT access in seventeen different countries between 1996 and 2003, through projects like Connect-ED, has published various sourcebooks and literature regarding its experiences in this field. LearnLink's most recent publication, a sourcebook called *Digital Opportunities for Development*, documents the project's findings in the chosen countries (four of which are in SSA) across all aspects of e-Learning and e-Health (LearnLink, 2003). By publishing such documents, this AED project hopes to contribute to the establishment of a general consensus regarding best practice for ICT and broader e-Learning projects.

South Africa: expanding ICT access in academic libraries

As a country that is leading the sub-Saharan Africa region on the path to enhanced ICT access, South Africa has reported excessive struggles with enhancing the connectivity and resources in its academic libraries over recent years. Though some officials in the country point toward the post-Apartheid societal divide between the developed world and third world conditions, many of South Africa's problems in this matter reflect upon issues facing all of sub-Saharan Africa. These include exorbitant hardware and literature access costs, high rates of technological illiteracy among the population, and the high number (eleven) of official South African languages (Darch, 1999).

Tanzania: a review of trends in government spending and support

For a United Nations conference in 2000 in Ethiopia, a research team of Tanzanian professors came together with the New York-based Partnership for Higher Education in Africa (the Partnership) to find and evaluate statistics revealing the government's financial backing and support of the deteriorating higher education system in the country. Though the research efforts focused on various aspects of the higher education institutions, a significant portion was focused on the policies, implementation, and future plans for ICT availability at the University of Dar es Salaam (UDSM) (Cooksey, 2001). Following the rocky transition decades of the 1980s, the government established the Institutional Transformation Programme (ITP), which has been the overarching guideline to Tanzanian education reform. Consequently, the Partnership's research team's critiques were fundamentally a review of the success and failure of Tanzania's ITP at UDSM.

The final product of the research was published by the Partnership at the UN Conference in Addis Ababa in 2000, and it documented the experience of various smaller efforts within the ITP at UDSM, including a partnership with African Virtual University in 1997, which lasted for two years. However, the researchers found that the project's success was hampered due to lack of equipment availability, or of adequate equipment when any was actually attained, and widespread support (Cooksey, 2001). Consequently, the available international courses provided by AVU were cut short, and the program has stalled at UDSM. Plans are currently in the works to establish an entirely independent, private AVU institution that will be hosted and monitored by UDSM.

Outside of AVU, the researchers looked into the accessibility of Internet and e-mail services at the university library, and found that the need to charge students to use these technologies were standing in the way of encouraging higher numbers of students to develop Internet literacy. Furthermore, it was noted that though the library had an extensive CD-Rom collection and subscribed to 550 different journals, students and faculty are inhibited from online resources that require fees (such as search engines and online journals) (Cooksey, 2001).

The fact that only eight computers were set up at the library in 2000 posed understandable obstacles, not only to the speed of research and information access, but also to the data-processing needs of all of the students. Any efforts to enhance the status of accessibility at the library of UDSM must begin with more equipment in the form of computers.

In 2000, at the time the Partnership presented their findings to the United Nations conference, plans were barely underway for putting the university administrative records and processes online. However, due to the small numbers of students with regular Internet and computer accessibility, this project looks to be a tall order for UDSM. This plan becomes particularly troublesome in light of the expected growth of university enrollment in Dar es Salaam from roughly 5,000 in 1997 to over 10,000 by the year 2003 (Cooksey, 2001).

The Partnership concluded its research findings with a shortlist of recommendations for the "steps that could be taken to promote the effective use of ICT at the University," listing the following:

- Computers need to be widely available for students, faculty and staff.
- Lecturers should require that their students carry out CD-Rom and Internet literature searches in preparation for research projects.
- Users need better CD-Rom and Internet training – not just on using the technologies but also in information retrieval skills. Researchers need to know how to phrase search queries and how to evaluate search results.
- An information retrieval skills cluster should be added to research methodology courses, to be team-taught by a librarian and a lecturer.
- Students need to learn how to type properly if they are to become active users of computers and ICT. A typing-tutor program should be installed on the campus network (Cooksey, 2001).

These recommendations echo the basic necessities shared by most African universities in regard to ICT expansion. This type of research performed by the Partnership is only preliminary to the process of actually enhancing accessibility at higher education institutions on the continent, and must be accompanied with a solid governmental support structure such as Tanzania's ITP, or Botswana's *Vision 2016* (see above).

UDSM is to be commended for the steps it has taken toward expanding ICT infrastructure within its walls over recent years; it proves a solid commitment to this ideal of economic and societal development. However, if the university community intends to more than double enrollment, accessibility takes on an entirely new, even more daunting task. This fact, too, is one that holds true for nearly all African universities in the opening of the twenty-first century.

Public-private partnerships for engineering education in Ghana and Uganda

In early March 2004, technology giants in the private sector paired with the historically black Prairie View A&M University in America to introduce two new efforts to enhance the quality of Engineering Education at two universities, in Ghana and Uganda, in the particular subject of product life-cycle management (PLM) training. The West Africa project, at Kwame Nkrumah University (KNU) of Science and Technology, developed out of a partnership between Prairie View A&M and a leading global outsourcing group, Electronic Data Systems (EDS).

EDS donated its Solid Edge software for 100 of the university's computer workstations in the form of an academic grant award, followed by a week-long training workshop on the topic of "The Application of Modern Design Modeling using Solid Edge" given by two Prairie View professors, and attended by KNU lecturers and teaching assistants. Significant emphasis was placed on the distinct nature of Prairie View A&M as a project partner, because of its role as a historically black college or university (HBCU) in the United States. The university's Engineering Dean Dr. Milton R. Bryant has emphasized that Prairie View particularly identifies with the struggle of students and administrators in Ghana to "achieve the road to success," and he strongly believes that the availability of this high-quality PLM software will "[offer] immediate benefits to [KNU's] diverse ethnic and socioeconomic student population" (USBE&IT News Services, 2004).

At the East Africa location, EDS joined with both Cisco Systems, the United States Agency for International Development (USAID), and the President of Uganda, Yoweri Museveni, to fund a grant that will bring high-quality network training and PLM software to Makerere University and the entire university system of Uganda. Though the collaboration is still in the formative stages, total funding could add up to over $14 million, divided roughly into $8 million from Cisco Systems, $2 million from USAID, and an undetermined amount from EDS. The backbone of the project will be ten Cisco Networking Academies that will be built and run at various locations throughout the Ugandan university system.

Further, EDS plans to build upon the Cisco Networking Academies with the provision of advanced computerized manufacturing training programs for university students, valued at approximately $4.2 million. The project is geared to enhancing Uganda's developing reputation as a growing "hub for manufacturing expertise and engineering in East Africa" (USBE&IT News Services, 2004). A notable characteristic of this ICT project is that it is an attempt to build upon the existing and already developing strengths particular to a region or country in Africa by investing in the human resource training at university level. This is a growing pattern among such projects in the SSA region, as it provides multiple levels of development through investing not only in a sector and human resource training, but also in the struggling university system.

University of Botswana: EDDI

Following his visit to Africa in 1999, US President Bill Clinton initiated the formation of the Education, Democracy, and Development Initiative (EDDI) model for African universities. The program was welcomed at the University of Botswana (UB), an institution that faced increasing pressure to "deliver well-trained and skilled workers to meet the increasingly sophisticated demands of the workplace," as well as find room within its overflowing classrooms to meet the demands of the excessive number of high school graduates in Botswana.

Though the program design consisted of four components, the essential focus was on instructional technology, referring primarily to "teaching and learning strategies through the use of modern technology and establishing a learner centered infrastructure" (Mutula, 2003). EDDI sought to use this instructional technology to provide distance learning options and opportunities for the numerous eligible students who could not get transportation to the university, could not get admission to the overflowing student body, or were full-time working professionals seeking another degree, studying in the evenings or at the weekends.

To oversee the integration of President Clinton's EDDI, UB established an e-Learning team (UBel) made up of the primary stakeholders at the institution. These members included the education technology unit, the university administration, the library, faculties, the students' representative council, the center for continuing education, and the IT department (Mutula, 2003). Among its essential functions is the administration of the hardware to the various departments, monitoring the continuous developments in e-Learning around the globe, relevant policy creation and implementation, and "promoting research and monitoring quality" (Mutula, 2002).

Lessons from EDDI have yet to be learned, evaluated, and documented since the project was just announced and in very initial stages in 2002. However, it does reflect the confidence that many countries in sub-Saharan Africa have placed in the extended learning opportunities model like that of the World Bank's African Virtual University, discussed above. The communication among the members of UBel is a key component to EDDI, and other countries and institutions are watching the University of Botswana to see how this approach is carried out.

EDS public-private partnerships in Ghana and Uganda for engineering education

The two projects led by Electronic Data Systems (EDS) with the partnerships of Prairie View A&M University, Cisco Systems, and USAID that were located in Ghana and Uganda are key examples of the growing trends in promoting ICT-related lifelong learning. The software donations of Solid Edge in both locations were aimed specifically at enhancing product life-cycle management (PLM) skills for engineering students at each university location, geared ultimately toward strengthening the manufacturing and engineering human capital for each country.

Namibia: the communication initiative

In 2002, the Swedish International Development Agency (SIDA) and the Danish organization Ibis worked together to create, fund, and implement this project for introducing and encouraging the "Internet as a tool for communication, information and participation among tertiary students in Namibia" (Belcastro, 2002). The project differed from those reviewed above, in that it was a field study researching the attitudes regarding the Internet that already existed in the project location, rather than a technical introduction of computers or other ICT capacity or training.

The researcher, Swedish student Helen Belcastro, found that "students have limited access to electronic media today, but a great interest in the use of e-mail and awareness of the potential of Internet communication. Many local ICT projects are weaving a growing web of Internet connectivity and paving the way for an increased and affordable access to the Internet" (Belcastro, 2002). She also praises the Namibian Government's dedication to education expenditure as essential to the continued expansion of ICT access and literacy.

University of Botswana: SMART classroom

One location of extended implementation and research in the "virtual university" field took place at the University of Botswana. In 2002 and 2003, the Education Technology Unit (EduTech) of the Centre for Academic Development at UB initiated an experimental form of teaching in a pilot project called the SMART classroom. The project was implemented in a first-year course required for the Masters in Education at UB, entitled "Trends in Early Childhood Development," and its broad focus was on shifting away from the traditional lecture-style of teaching and toward a more student-oriented and student-driven electronic sharing of information by enhancing their research and computer skills.

A distinguishing factor to this e-Learning initiative was the absence of international partners or development organizations and their funding. EduTech planned, staffed, and backed the entire program, paying only the $370 salary for the 40 hours worked by a project technical assistant. Among the benefits of the program were the "flexi-time" enabled by the nature of the course, allowing students with busy work schedules or families to learn the material in their own time, as well as the interactive approach that the program forces, requiring students to take the initiative to get online and find the information on the Internet or the media provided as opposed to the traditional lecture-style learning process.

Above all, the shift in the face of the curriculum increases IT-literacy, "which helps in personal employability and corporate competitiveness." The analysis of the project, by head implementer Kabita Bose, accentuates the difficulty in countries like Botswana, and many others in the SSA region, of encouraging an appreciation among students who have historically been incapable of developing an access to and a consequent need for ICT. When students are forced to utilize this technology for their courses, this wall can be broken down almost subconsciously (Bose, 2003).

In its 2001 publication, *E-Learning: The Partnership Challenge*, the Organization for Economic Cooperation and Development (OECD) more clearly articulated this challenge to IT-literacy efforts in SSA: "Individuals differ markedly in their appreciation for ability to learn from different types of communications, learning processes and materials. Interactive multimedia and the opportunity to combine various media resources, styles and methods is a key feature of ICT-enabled learning" (OECD, 2001b). Aside from technical computer or information system skills, it is extremely important for students and citizens to gain an appreciation of how information can be accessed and retrieved from ICT, particularly the Internet. The prospects for this tool to enhance an African's connection to the information available in the rest of the world are overwhelming, and a key benefit to the concentrated efforts of e-Learning.

Bose's review of the implementation documents an overall success in achieving the primary goals of EduTech's project. However, among the issues that arose throughout the duration are included a lack of access to ICT outside of the university setting for most of the students, as well as outside of the SMART classroom itself. As most of the students in the Master's program were primary teachers, the fact that no primary schools in Botswana have any computer access at all largely hampered the teachers' abilities not only to work on the class curriculum at their work, but also their opportunity to bring their new ICT skills to their own students. The Masters students also found that most of the computers available at UB in the computer labs were insufficient for the work required for their course (Bose, 2003). The slow pace of Internet connectivity was also a recurring issue. However, the successes were larger and more important than the obstacles. Bose remarks that the pilot project created a basis for standardization of further such e-Learning courses at UB, an imperative step in the process of expanding IT-literacy both at the university and in Botswana itself.

Digital Partnership

ICT-related education programs in African schools are fundamentally concerned with basic access and familiarity with document and Internet functions. These projects are targeted either at teacher confidence and training or at the students directly. However, the levels of teacher ICT competence are often equal to or below those of their students. Consequently, a common approach is the two-pronged one, training teachers and students in technology use at the same time. A prominent example of this method is the Digital Partnership (DP), which was borne of a formula common to e-Learning projects in SSA: a large, private firm supplies funding for a small-scale, experimental project in a particularly poor town. In this case, the firm was Western pharmaceutical giant Eli Lilly, donating 45 used computers to the infamously troubled Ivory Park Township that borders Johannesburg, South Africa (BBC, 2003). Preceding the creation of the Ivory Park School's computer lab courtesy of DP and Eli Lilly, the ICT presence at the school consisted of one telephone. The school has 1,400 students – the majority of whom had never had previous contact with computers or the Internet – as well as a teaching staff highly unfamiliar with the technology. Consequently,

DP focused its Ivory Park donation on training the teachers as well as the students, to ensure that the program would be sustainable. However, problems have arisen, as has been common with various recycled-technology programs like DP, with the maintenance costs of the second-hand computers and incompatible software (BBC, 2003).

This particular effort, however, is just one piece of a larger, coordinated effort to encourage such donations from various Western-based firms to classrooms in SSA. The Partnership itself was initiated by the International Business Leaders Forum, with support from the World Bank and other various international IT companies and their corporate users.

The DP's mandate was established at its 2001 inception as "an international partnership facilitating innovation and affordable access to technology, training and the Internet for learning, enterprise and development in developing and emerging market economies through a sustainable private/public partnership model" (Digital Partnership, 2003). The project anticipates the dissemination of 188,000 computers into classrooms in South Africa by 2005. The efforts of the DP over its first three years have been so successful that they have led to a formal partnership between DP's leaders and the Department of Communication in South Africa.

The Department has coordinated various community organizations and the school networking that is already in place, creating the domain of the South African Project Director to oversee this massive "rollout" of nearly 200,000 computers around the country through the Fall of 2004. The project includes the creation of six regional learning centers, funded by the South African Vodacom Foundation, where teachers can receive training and continued support.

The actual technical training is focused on teaching educators to "know how to apply technology to facilitate access to and use of information and communication for economic and social development" through various themed classes, including "Basic and Immediate ICT Skills Training", "Teach to the Future" courses that train teachers to incorporate technology in lessons, and the more specialized troubleshooting training program called "ICT Assistants Course." No conclusive statistics or evaluations of the South Africa Digital Partnership experience have been published yet, but they should have become available following the set closing date of September 2004 (Digital Partnership, 2003).

B   Selected country case studies

Argentina

The developing countries of Latin America utilize e-Government standards, particularly requirements for information disclosure, to combat corruption and to increase transparency of government. Now, it is possible for nations to release administrative and financial information about their government and its officials to their citizens through an efficient and low-cost medium. Argentina had concentrated a large portion of its e-Government efforts (prior to the leadership crisis of 2001) toward requirements for information disclosure, especially pertaining to financial information. In its attempt to increase transparency and fight corruption, Argentina realized the benefits of preventing conflict of interest within its government. In fact, Argentina's new system of online financial disclosure reduced the document acquisition time to less than forty-eight hours. Although Argentina maintains a law requiring documents to be supplemented in hard copy form, the Anticorruption Office at the Ministry of Justice managed to reduce its files of public official disclosures from 30,000 to a mere 1,800. This decentralization increased efficiency and lowered costs.

Chile

The strength of the Chilean economy is widely acknowledged. Take just one example: Chile is rated as the most competitive country in Latin America by the International Institute for Management Development (IMD) and the World Economic Forum as shown in Figure 5.1. Chile has the largest base of installed PCs in Latin America due to the population's purchasing power, the 0 percent import tariff for PCs, and the competitive costs among multinational and local assemblers.

The growth of Internet users has been explosive, especially in SMEs and homes. The availability of several types of connections and plans will maintain fast growth rates in the next few years. This will make Chile the biggest Internet-using country in Latin America when measured in Internet users for every 100 inhabitants. Among the available connections are commuted and

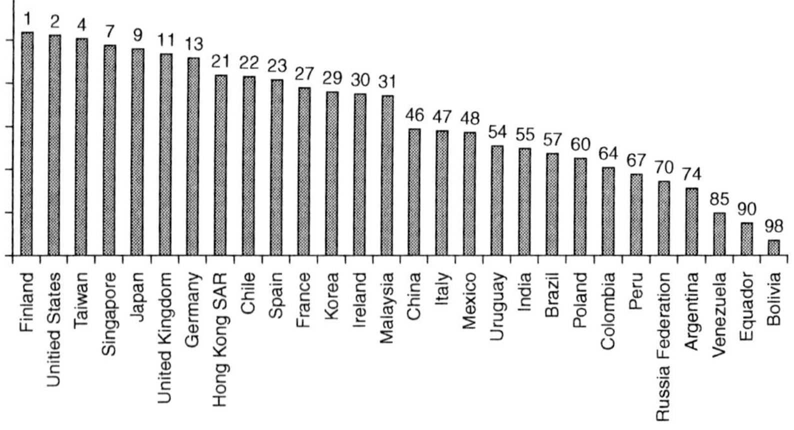

Figure 5.1   Competitiveness rankings 2004
Source: World Economic Forum (2005)

dedicated lines, ADSL (Digital Asymmetric Subscriber Line), Cable Modem, Integrated Service Digital Network (ISDN) and mobile directional short messaging (CORFO, 2003b).

The objectives of the government plan of Chile in ICT are:

- Internet for all; shortening the digital gap with politics of digital inclusion, increasing the use of ICT, and justness in availability of opportunities;
- Placing the state at the service of citizens, in an efficient and agile way; electronic government;
- Elevating the productivity and competitiveness of the companies;
- Educating the human resources of the country in ICT to be ready for the information society and the new economy.

Mexico

Several Latin American countries have initiated comprehensive e-Development efforts. Mexico, in particular, has recently launched an e-Development program that intends to revitalize ICT interests in the country. The Plan Nacional de Desarrollo, introduced in 2001 and still under development, proposed a 90 percent private sector control of new ICT deployment. The other 10 percent remains controlled by the federal government. Fiscal incentives are also being used to lure both foreign and domestic businesses into the market.

The e-Mexico plan aims eventually to strengthen democracy, solidify economic development, and overcome corruption with a strategy of educating as much as the population as possible through connecting more than 17,000 schools, libraries, and digital communities centers. This e-Learning component is viewed as central to any e-Development ambition. The program is attempting to reach nearly 85 percent of the 100 million inhabitants of Mexico. Once fully implemented, the e-Learning component of e-Mexico is expected to be the largest educational e-Learning network in North America, and one of the largest such networks in the world (ONETOUCH-SYSTEMS, 2003). The company heading the e-Mexico National Development Strategy is led by CEO and President Dennis Bertken of One Touch Systems™, which is also spearheading efforts in Brazil, after successful implementation of programs in the United States and Australia.

Mexico is still in the early stages of its e-Government efforts; in addition to its digital government strategy – which is the equivalent of the U.S. e-Government strategy – officials have developed an e-Mexico strategy. e-Mexico encompasses government, education, and health care, and seeks to deal with the issue of the vast Mexican digital divide. Less than 10 percent of citizens have Internet access. Officials want to have 80 percent to 90 percent online by 2006. Much of that will be done through satellite broadband access that is being developed right now for installation in community centers, libraries, schools, and other common locations nationwide. One of Mexico's biggest successes of the past year was its electronic tax filing initiative. In 2002, the country's entire population filed electronically, a mandatory measure made possible because citizens were able to access the system through terminals set up at local bank offices (Federal Computer Week, 2004).

Japan

In July 2000, as announced in the "Report" (Prime Minister of Japan, 2001), the IT Strategy Headquarters and the IT Strategy Council were established in order to promote and study ways for Japan to be an internationally competitive IT nation and they compiled the "Basic IT Strategy", which led to the enactment of the Basic Law on the Formation of an Advanced Information and Telecommunications Network Society (IT Basic Law) in January 2001. The Principles of Measures in IT Basic Law include promotion of electronic commerce and electronic government at national and local levels. This launch of the *"e-Japan Strategy"* had several goals, such as e-Government, which was set to be realized by 2003, and the market size of e-Commerce expected to grow to far exceed 700 billion dollars.

During March 2001, the "e-Japan Priority Policy Program" was adopted to materialize the e-Japan Strategy and clarify all measures the government should rapidly implement with priority in the five years from 2001. Roles of the private and public sectors were given in this program in which the private sector was to play the leading role in the area of IT.

The program also identified five areas in which measures should be intensively taken to realize their goals:

(1) Formation of the world's most advanced information and telecommunications networks;
(2) Promotion of education and learning as well as development of human resources;
(3) Facilitation of electronic commerce;
(4) Digitization of the administration and application of IT in other public areas;
(5) Ensuring security and reliability of advanced information and telecommunications networks.

To create a useful and user-friendly e-Commerce market, the following measures were set:

- Reforming regulatory frameworks which hinder e-Commerce;
- Making new rules;
- Introducing "Advanced Confirmation Procedures on Application of Laws and Ordinances by Administrative Bodies" (effective on June 1, 2001);
- Ensuring appropriate protection and use of intellectual property rights.

To finalize the efficient and consumer-friendly e-Government, every process of public services were to be digitized by FY2003. In addition to the above five areas, the government regards several cross-cutting issues as prerequisites for a successful e-Development strategy, namely:

- It is necessary to promote R&D on basic technology such as advanced networking or computing technologies through reinforced collaboration among industry, academia, and government.
- It is necessary to decrease the digital divide caused by differences in opportunities and abilities to use IT, due to geographic constraints, age, or technical infrastructure conditions.
- It is necessary to adequately and actively deal with newly emerging problems such as employment, IT training, cyber crime, and harmful information.
- It is necessary to attain international harmonization concerning various rules and standards.

These main points showed two e-Government plans. One was an attempt to bring forward the availability of completing administrative procedures online, such as making applications and providing notifications. The other was to decide techniques and policies on the use of the integrated circuit (IC) cards issued by administrative bodies, and promote their wide use in public services.

The "e-Japan Strategy II" (Prime Minister of Japan, 2003a) was decided by the IT Strategic Headquarters in July 2003. e-Japan Strategy II represents the second phase of the IT strategy of Japan: to became the world's most advanced IT nation and a "vibrant, safe, impressive and convenient" society through the active use of IT.

Given the successful development of IT infrastructures based on the e-Japan Strategy, the new strategy aims at taking leading measures in seven important areas that are closely related to the lives of the people. The areas are medical treatment, food, life, small- and medium-sized enterprises, knowledge, employment, and government service. Furthermore, the strategy focuses on advancing the development of new IT social infrastructures, which is essential for the sophistication of the active use of IT during this second phase.

Adjunct to the e-Japan Strategy II, the "e-Japan Priority Policy Program – 2003" (Prime Minister of Japan, 2003b) was adopted by the IT Strategic Headquarters in August 2003. This program features 366 concrete measures to be quickly implemented by the government; citizen-oriented one-stop service was to be realized in connection with e-Government. "The degree of user satisfaction" has been added to the index for evaluation.

The "e-Government Construction Plan" was adopted by the Ministries and Agencies Council in July 2003. The first comprehensive e-Government plan consists of general principles supported by a basic strategy and action plans that should be carried out by all ministries and agencies within two years (by the end of 2005 fiscal year).

The main goal is to realize:

(1) Citizen-oriented government service, to let people feel easy, safe, and comfortable in receiving 7 days-24 hours services and information via Internet on such as the e-Government portal;
(2) Simple and cost-effective-government, to promote Business Process Reengineering (BPR) and Enterprise Resource Planning (ERP) with outsourcing and up-to-date ICT for more flexible, efficient, and simple government.

China

China has been a "success story" in terms of many aspects of economic development driven by ICT, e-Development and Knowledge Economy initiatives (see the current Chinese mantra: "from factory to the world to laboratory for the world" as well as the huge trade surpluses and the other trappings of economic success – for instance China is home to the largest number of Rolls-Royce car owners in the world).

The challenge that remains is to assure a sustainable, long-term growth and for that purpose high-quality growth in terms of its breadth of scope and breadth of impact is required and targeted by a number of policies and related e-Development and Knowledge Economy practices:

(1) Strengthening markets for technology dissemination

New and improved technologies diffuse throughout an economy under the pressures of competition. It forces firms to adopt innovations, modify their products for better serving their clients, and change their processes to improve productivity. Least efficient enterprises are deemed to follow best performers rapidly or to disappear. Main diffusion agents are providers of these new technologies and related services – large as well as small firms. Customers, well informed on goods' prices and quality, play an essential role too.

The primary measures to be taken to strengthen markets should be:

- More open trade among Chinese provinces, allowing economies of scale and scope, and facilitating the diffusion of best products through price- and quality-based competition; eliminating tariff and non-tariff barriers between provinces – erected to protect local enterprises and related interests – is essential;
- Improve competition by establishing and enforcing appropriate laws, and eliminating privileges from personal and political connections;
- Support small firms providing services, consulting, technologies, and seeds to producers, farmers, and local communities; this requires adequate

incentives and removing regulatory and bureaucratic obstacles to their establishment and operation;

- Improve the system for technical norms and standards; China's exceptionally poor technical regulations and standards – such as product quality, work safety, and environmental protection – are a major obstacle to proper diffusion of modern technology and know-how in China.

(2) Redirecting technology-related policies

The mediocre diffusion of modern technology and related management methods owes much to the ways in which technology and industry policies are conceived and implemented:

- Over-concentration of attention, support, and incentives on designated industrial zones and high-tech parks, conceived to attract foreign firms and domestic firms for exports; this policy has been successful in many respects, but parks are a small part of the economy;
- Excessive fascination for high-tech production, without using high technology in the modernization of agriculture, manufacturing, and services;
- Neglect of the policy instruments increasing the receptiveness to, and adoption of, new technologies in the industrial and rural tissues;
- Too much technology push in R&D projects – supported by government funds, designed by government institutes, with little involvement of users;
- Disproportionate focus on large firms, even though smaller ones are a major source of technological dynamism and renewal.

A new mindset is needed in the design and implementation of the government promotion of technology. Priority should go to:

- Technology fertilization of the "average industry" over "high-tech" productions;
- Technological culture over advanced research;
- Bottom-up initiatives over top-down ones;
- Support to smaller firms over larger ones.

Three sets of measures are at the core of what needs to be done:

- Redeploying government programs for technology diffusion;
- Stimulating innovation in enterprises;
- Promoting innovation sites and clusters;
- Redeploying government programs for technology diffusion.

Some of China's policy measures for technology diffusion have had reasonable success, but most leave considerable room for improvement.

Massive efforts are needed for retooling and expanding overall government support to disseminate knowledge and technology. The government should not directly support or push the adoption of technology by enterprises and other economic agents. Instead, it should create an environment to facilitate development, commercialization, and use of improved technologies, including establishing appropriate organizations. The government should expand technology diffusion programs by:

- Restoring and expanding the networks of centers that support manufacturing technology;
- Revamping the design and infrastructure for agricultural and rural development;
- Setting up Engineering Research Centers and Productivity Centers.

Korea

The Government of Korea should complement its extensive liberalization of foreign business activity with measures that can strengthen the incentives of foreign firms to transfer technologies and skills. This agenda includes the implementation of corporate governance reform, the strengthening of national innovation systems and intellectual property rights protection, and the upgrading of human capital and measures to enhance its mobility, including the dismantling of barriers to mobility between foreign and domestic firms. Improving the level of English-language knowledge and skills would enable Koreans to work in FDI firms and gain higher positions in foreign-owned entities, and would enhance the learning effects to be gained from serving in such positions. In addition, the following measures should be considered:

- Improved information to potential or actual foreign investors about the risks and opportunities associated with ventures in Korea ("invest-in-Korea-services"), and particularly with respect to opportunities in knowledge-intensive areas;
- Measures to catalyze a more effective domestic market for business services;
- Strengthened cooperation between domestic and foreign firms in research and development through the expansion of foreign participation in government-supported R&D projects;
- Examination of how other economies, including Ireland, Singapore, and Chinese Taipei, have spurred foreign firms to develop backward linkages in order to strengthen the technological capability and competitiveness of domestic suppliers.

This should be complemented by according special attention to the following matters:

(1) Promotion of high value-added services

Services represent a rapidly growing share of knowledge-based activities, although this development has taken place at a slower rate in Korea than in most other OECD countries.

The knowledge-based economy is highly dependent on a competitive services sector. The more interlinked the provision of goods and services, the more sophisticated the products and the greater the capacity to satisfy increasing consumer demand. Furthermore, as incomes rise, the demand for services tends to increase faster than the demand for goods. The production of services is less standardized and less capital-intensive (but typically not less knowledge-intensive) than the production of goods. Meanwhile, technical progress, in particular in ICT, partly by facilitating storage and trade, is exerting a major impact on the functioning and organization of many services. "Knowledge-based services" now account for a larger and more rapidly growing share of the economy than "knowledge-based manufacturing" in practically all OECD countries.

Another set of factors influencing the role of services relates to industrial organization. In many OECD countries, there has been a pronounced shift in the way that businesses organize service-related functions. To a growing extent, manufacturing firms tend to outsource what they perceive as their non-core functions – thereby fueling an apparent growth in the services sector. The trend toward greater outsourcing is typically driven by:

- *Competence.* The increasing sophistication of information, financial, computer, research, and training needs by business, and the rapid evolution of new techniques and products in these fields has made it difficult for firms to maintain competitive competence in these areas. To do so would require the accumulation and maintenance of a knowledge base in diverse disciplines that, in most instances, firms would be hard pressed to justify.
- *Cost and efficiency.* Firms specializing in support functions are often able to provide their services at lower cost, while offering a wider choice of innovative products, reflecting the positive effects of competition (in-house services were likely to be shielded from such competition, a condition which lowered the need to maximize efficiency and to innovate).
- *Specialization.* The trend in industry in recent years has been towards consolidation and concentration on core competencies, providing increased opportunities for independent suppliers of goods and services.

Outsourcing by large and small firms alike is set to grow in Korea in tandem with the emergence of innovative, knowledge-based service providers. However, in Korea and, to a lesser extent, Japan, this trend has so far been weaker than in most other OECD countries; companies have preferred to retain control of many service-related functions in-house. The obstacles to outsourcing in Korea include the emphasis on vertical hierarchical structures, and barriers to the mobility of workers. In addition, a number of regulations continue to constrain the service sector's ability to innovate, adjust, and grow.

There is no panacea for stimulating greater competitiveness and higher growth in business services. However, several areas require reform:

- Continued removal of regulatory barriers to market entry and exit;
- Initiating creation and expansion of new service markets by promoting outsourcing of services in the public sector;
- Reforming financial support to innovation and government-supported research programs to make them more applicable to the services sector; current incentives are primarily geared to the needs and opportunities of manufacturing operations;
- Reviewing education and training policies to support the development of the human resource skills needed to support knowledge-based industries, most of which are service-oriented;
- Exploring ways to adapt intellectual property rights to more effectively meet the needs of services industries;
- Improving data on services industries; this will benefit services providers, users and investors alike, while providing the basic information required by governments to formulate policy;
- Continuing work in the WTO–GATS framework to identify effective strategies for liberalizing trade in services on a multilateral basis;
- Fostering a better functioning market for knowledge-based consultancy services, without resorting to public consultancy services as these can impede the development of private consultancy services;
- Improving conditions for investment in intangible assets (see below).

(2) Promoting investment in intangible assets

Traditionally, the private sector and the government have focused their attention on investment in physical assets, such as machinery and equipment. In the knowledge economy, however, the source of value has shifted from physical content to knowledge content. The development of knowledge-based activities is critically dependent on conditions conducive to investment in so-called intangible assets (e.g. innovations, worker skills, patents, brand names). The weak state of services in Korea, for instance, is related to a bias in favor of investment in plant and equipment relative to investment in intangible assets.

Venture capital is important for enabling investment in intangible assets, especially in new, explorative firms and industries. Risk-taking is a key element in venture capital, and excessive government guarantees regarding the financing of intangibles can counteract the innovativeness that it aims to encourage. The problems with measuring and disclosing intangible assets are particularly severe in a debt-oriented economic system such as Korea, since intangibles cannot generally be taken as collateral for bank loans. This is especially troublesome for new firms without a track record, and in services where tangible assets tend to be limited. The prevailing situation in Korea in this regard may appear paradoxical, since some new enterprises within these categories recently have found themselves drowning in equity funding. However, where systematic information on intangible assets is difficult to come by, it is particularly difficult for the market to evaluate which new firms are viable and which are not. Although a similar situation is observable in other OECD countries, there are special complications in Korea.

These are partly rooted in "cultural factors," such as the lack of preparedness to adopt new ideas. They are also a result of the weak Korean tradition in providing information about business operations, which has brought about a habit of reliance on inadequate information in investment decisions, providing little shelter from overly high expectations in new growth areas. Whereas any excesses in that respect should be expected to correct themselves sooner or later – although inevitably resulting in painful lessons and unwanted distribution effects – the current situation should lead to a strengthening of the demand for better transparency in business operations.

The valuation of intangible assets is influenced by attitudes. The government can exert a certain influence in this respect as well. The following are a few concrete initiatives that may be considered for building a more hospitable policy set-up for investment in intangibles in Korea:

- Publicizing and broadly disseminating cases of successful development of intangible assets by Korean citizens and companies, such as the patenting in the semiconductor area; the successful development of Korean software, such as the Hangol word-processing and Korean game software; and cultural and literary achievements;
- Broadening the support for innovative efforts away from traditional R&D support;
- Examining options for introducing tax incentives to stimulate training (e.g. exempting profit tax on profits used for paying for personnel training);
- Reviewing and correcting government policy bias in favor of physical investment;
- Promoting research and evaluation to document successful cases (best practice) of foreign–Korean cooperation, and developing the means to diffuse such information effectively;
- Improving enforcement of intellectual property rights protection.

(3) Improving conditions for small and medium-sized enterprises

In the OECD as a whole, SMEs make up over 95 percent of all enterprises (99 percent for Korea) and account for 60 percent to 70 percent of jobs (74 percent for Korea in 1997). The share of SMEs in employment tends to be somewhat lower in manufacturing, ranging from 40 percent to 80 percent (69 percent for Korea). Korean SMEs fared particularly badly during the financial crisis. Average value added fell and some 20,000 small firms went bankrupt when the *chaebol* delayed payments to their SME suppliers.

The problems confronting big parts of the SME-sector in Korea, however, are of a more long-term nature, go beyond the role of the *chaebol* and are related to the knowledge-based economy. While productivity differentials between large firms and SMEs have narrowed in some low-tech traditional industries – e.g. textiles, clothing and footwear, and food processing – they have increased in industries where technological competitiveness matters most – e.g. machinery, electronics, and transportation equipment. On average, value added per employee in SMEs relative to large firms fell from 55 percent in 1980 to 39 percent in 1997. Several factors interact to hamper the development of SMEs, including:

- product market competition, including subcontractor systems;
- public procurement practices;
- formal and informal business practices, and
- access to skilled labor and technology.

Improved SME performance matters not only in its own right, but also because small firms are less likely to suffer "lock-in" with respect to existing plants, technologies, and organizational structures, making them important for innovation and commercial experimentation with new technologies. At the same time, SME operations are typically characterized by high turbulence and churning, and the social benefits of their commercial experimentation tend to exceed the private ones. In the knowledge-based economy, policy intervention must crucially be conducive to entrepreneurship and risk-taking, but should not shelter SMEs from change. Today, information and communication technologies open up new opportunities for combining the advantages of small scale with those from networking among SMEs (and/or between SMEs and larger firms, or between firms and other actors such as research institutes). Networks can also serve as an instrument to enable government policy to reach out more effectively. It is essential that networks are driven by the identification of market opportunities, however, and policies should be conducive to such "demand-led" approaches. The available experience suggests that successful network development requires a combination of measures facilitating the provision of venture capital, public procurement, technology diffusion, programs, and incentives conducive to training, regulatory reform, etc. (Schmitz and Nadvi, 1999).

In short, there is a case for consolidating present programs and increasing consistency among different policies, phasing out those that aim directly at protecting SMEs; enhancing markets and programs to strengthen the diffusion of technology and skills; and improving the broader entrepreneurial climate through the creation of a social and economic environment – including government institutions – which is more friendly to small business development.

Part III

e-Development Case Studies

In this part of the book, we present a number of cases illustrating the various forms of e-Development and a broad set of country profiles to present the various degrees of e-Development achieved by *developed, transitioning*, as well as *developing* countries.

e-Development evolves around five main categories: *e-Business, e-Government, e-Society, e-Health, and e-Learning*. In Chapter 6 we have chosen to illustrate some of these aspects before entering into a more in-depth analysis of specific countries to profile their e-Development status and their moving from e-Development toward the Knowledge Economy.

Because this topic is by nature evolving rapidly, we gathered as much current data as possible. However, there are instances where this was not possible. Statistical data are mostly available upto 2003. For some projects, either completed or still ongoing, progress toward the achievement of results was not always reported on.

6
Best Practices by e-Development Component

We first identified a number of best practices among e-Development interventions that illustrate the various forms which e-Development can take. Table 6.1 overleaf provides an overview of these projects, by e-Development component.

A   Improving business environment/ promoting entrepreneurship

Mauritius: Contributions Network Project

A joint public and private sector initiative, the Contributions Network Project (CNP) (www1.worldbank.org/publicsector/egov/mauritiusCNPcs.htm), is spearheading the government initiative to foster electronic interaction with businesses and citizens. The CNP revolutionizes the way employers interact with the government for the submission of PAYE and VAT returns. There will be no need to file separate returns for VAT and PAYE. Employers can send a single return for VAT and PAYE electronically, as well as effect electronic payment of both taxes in one single account. The option for separate returns and payments has, however, been maintained.

The Contributions Network Project connects all large employers, and the majority of small ones, to the relevant government tax departments via a single point of contact. The system enables employers to submit their returns directly through a two-way, fully electronic system. In return, employers receive confirmations from the respective departments. Payments are also made electronically through a direct debit arrangement. The payments covered under the project include PAYE (Pay As You Earn), Corporate Income Tax, VAT (Value Added Tax), NPS (National Pensions Scheme), NSF (National Savings Fund), the IVTB levy, and company registration.

The CNP is a phased approach in which the first phase consisted of e-Filing and e-Payment of Value Added Tax (VAT). The second phase included e-Payment of National Pension Fund and National Saving Fund contributions. The third phase incorporated e-Filing of corporate

Table 6.1 Best Practices by e-Development component

e-Development component	Improving business environment/promoting entrepreneurship
Projects	Mauritius: Contributions Network Project
	European Union: European Business Angel Network (EBAN)
	United Nations: virtual microfinance market
	Japan: portal on e-Venture capital
	France: center of formalities of the companies
	Singapore: start-up e-Adviser
	Japan: small and medium-sized enterprise agency
	Japan: Osaka City support center for SMEs
	Japan: online services for start-up companies J-Net 21
	Canada: business gateway
	Singapore: Registry of Companies and Businesses
	Hong Kong: Electronic Service Delivery (ESD) Scheme
	China: one-stop shop "Digital Beijing"
	Vietnam: one-stop business services for investors
	Iceland: customs declaration on the Web
	Jamaica: automated customs services
	Philippines: ICT-based system for import procedures
	Chile: government e-Procurement system
	Brazil: Comprasnet e-Procurement system
	Hong Kong: Electronic Tendering System (ETS)
	Australia: Commonwealth electronic tender system
	European Union: public procurement
	Philippines: pilot e-Procurement system
	Mexico: Compranet procurement system
	Spain: integrated management of wealth & income tax
	Portugal: tax electronic services
	Canada: NETFILE online tax filing
	France: online subscription and payment of VAT
	Chile: online tax system
	Bulgaria: improving transparency & state emphasis on SMEs
R&D promotion	
	Singapore: intellectual property marketplace
	Sweden: Gothia Science Park
	Sweden: creative center business incubator
	Netherlands: BTC Twente Incubator
	Portugal: Novas Empresas e Tecnologias (NET)
	Finland – TEKES: supporting innovative enterprises
	Denmark: Patent and Trademark Office
	Netherlands: promotion of innovation through Dreamstart Program
	Portugal: Centro Promotor de Inovação e Negócios
	Brazil – ReACCT: networking for science and technology projects

Continued

Table 6.1   Continued

e-Development component	Improving business environment/ promoting entrepreneurship
	SME Capacity Building
	WBI: Europe and Central Asia Virtual University Malaysia: teaching company scheme Ireland: Enterprise Ireland Portal
	Supporting rural enterprise
	e-Choupal, India: e-Commerce solution for fragmented rural farmers Russia: rural information and knowledge system Drishtee, India: e-Development services for rural populations

information and e-Payment of fees to register companies. The final phase includes e-Payment of corporate tax. As of June 2001, at least 9.5 percent of PAYE and 11.6 percent of VAT were handled electronically by the CNP.

European Union: European Business Angel Network (EBAN)

The European Business Angel Network EBAN (http://www.eban.org) is a non-profit association that provides means of introduction between investors (business angels) and SMEs. Membership in EBAN ensures entrepreneurs access to the largest European network of contacts in the Business Angels field through various matching operations, such as computer matching, investment newsletters/magazines, investor forum and fairs. The website provides online secure matching information.

Internet BAN in France, http://www.business-angels.com/site/, provides online secure matching information system for entrepreneurs and investors. Funding requests are posted on the site after selection by Professional Networks or one of its partners (technological parks, specialized organizations, etc.). The investor who wants to get in touch with an entrepreneur clicks on a dedicated icon, which transmits the investor's profile to the corresponding entrepreneur. The entrepreneur decides whether or not to follow up on the contact.

United Nations: Virtual Microfinance Market

United Nations Conference on Trade and Development created the Virtual Microfinance Market (http://www.vmm.dpn.ch), an information exchange designed to facilitate interactions between MFIs, private investors, governments, and other participants in the microfinance market. The virtual finance market is aimed at creating sustainable market links between commercial investors and microenterprises in developing countries and is expected to permit the investment of millions of dollars at the grassroots level and the creation of thousands of jobs.

Japan: portal on e-venture capital

Chamberweb, the portal site of the Japan Chamber of Commerce, enables entrepreneurs to present their complete set of business plans to two venture capital firms to get the possible funding. The venture capitalists provide the evaluation and comments through e-mail, and for those who present feasible business plans that have potential, venture capitalists provide necessary funding (see http://www.chamberweb.jp/ – Japanese only).

France – Center of Formalities of the Companies

The Centre de Formalités des Entreprises (CFE) acts as a single contact point to the various administrations, such as the local trade register, the taxation office, the administrations in charge of social security and pensions, the statistical office, etc. Once the enterprise has given the required information to the CFE, the CFE transmits this information to the other relevant administrations such as the Statistical Office (INSEE). INSEE also plays an important role as it is in charge of the national enterprise directory and gives a national identification number to the new enterprises (see http://www.cfe.ccip.fr/ – French).

Singapore: start-up e-Adviser

The start-up e-Advisor Web portal is launched jointly by the Ministry of Trade and Industry (MTI) and the Ministry of Finance in Singapore to help new businesses get registrations, licenses, and permits online. It functions as a one-stop licensing center, and provides information on the available government-assistance schemes to guide new businesses (see http://www. ecitizen.gov.sg/business/startupeadvisor/).

Japan: small- and medium-sized enterprise agency

The SME agency http://www.chusho.meti.go.jp/chu_top.html (limited English translation) provides comprehensive SME-related legal information through its website. Users have access to search for all kinds of legal and regulatory information through the regulatory database.

Japan: Osaka City support center for SMEs

Osaka City support center for SMEs (http://www.akinai-aid.ne.jp – Japanese only) offers a 24-hour online advice service by experts. Clients can choose an adviser from among the sixty business consultants and other advisers registered with the center. Clients will get a reply from the selected expert within 48 hours and are encouraged to give evaluations for the advisory services, which they get for further improvement. The center offers other programs, including "b-mart," which provides a forum for generating business opportunities, "e-liaison," which links enterprises and universities, and "IT@BRIDGE," which provides IT support for SMEs. These services are run largely by staff from the private sector rather than Osaka city officials. The center also collaborates with local industry and public entities.

Japan: online services for start-up companies, J-Net 21

The Japan Small and Medium Enterprise Corporation (JASMEC), a public agency that plays a significant role to implement Japan's SME policy, ventured a portal service called portal site J-Net 21 (http://j-net21.jasmec.go.jp/index.html – Japanese only). It functions as a one-stop shop for SMEs, connected electronically to various administrative bodies as well as private entities, where all the necessary procedures to create a business can be completed for start-ups and also valuable information for expanding business opportunities can be obtained for SMEs at their early stage. The integrated system provides variety of information and guidance, such as initial examination of business concepts, information on permits and licenses required for establishing a business, investors and necessary contacts, referral to additional information sources, and more. It also provides training sessions on know-how, such as preparing business plans, money management, foreign investment, ISO certification, tax planning, and more.

Canada: Business Gateway

Business Gateway (http://businessgateway.ca/en/hi/) provides a single access point to all government services and information needed to start, run, and grow a business, including forms and detailed information regarding the following topics: business start-up, entrepreneurship, registration, planning, financing, private sector assistance, micro-credit, government assistance, taxation on goods and services tax, payroll deductions, corporate income tax, human resources, employment, recruitment, training, hiring subsidies, legal requirements, management skills, regulations, selected federal regulations for business, exporting, importing, preparing to export, marketing abroad, financing, import duties, permits, business statistics and analysis, business indicators, sector profiles, Canadian statistics, innovation, R&D, technology, intellectual property, research, product development, mergers and acquisition, and bankruptcy.

Singapore: registry of companies and businesses

The Registry of Companies and Businesses (RCB: http://www.rcb.gov.sg) is a Singapore government agency that administers the business registration and regulates the formation of business firms. It provides information about registered particulars of business entities through its website. The RCB simplifies the business registration processes through the Internet, enabling the applicants (1) to obtain a business name by downloading and sending the application form within 24 hours; (2) to get issuance of a Certificate of Registration which is valid for three years. Payments for these services are also done online. Singapore's administrative start-up formalities are far more simplified than those of some EU member states, which took a maximum of 120 days (Commission of the European Communities, 1997). A foreigner intending to be a business owner is merely required to produce an Approval-in-Principle Employment Pass from the Employment Pass Department without registration. The application forms can be downloaded at the RCB website.

Hong Kong: Electronic Service Delivery (ESD) Scheme

The Hong Kong ESD Scheme (http://www.esd.gov.hk/) is an innovative project providing online public services to the community. Its website is one of the world's first bilingual (English and Chinese) one-stop portal providing integrated electronic public and commercial services. The Scheme covers a wide range of over seventy types of electronic public services provided by over twenty government departments and public agencies. Examples of public services include filing of tax return, renewal of driving and vehicle licenses, application for business registration, payment of government bills, registration as a voter, job search, application to become a volunteer, tourist and investor information, etc., all accessible through just a few clicks. The private sector operator developing and maintaining the system will also provide value-added commercial services (e.g. sale of event tickets, registration for educational courses, etc.) and advertisements via the same portal website. Users can search for services through three mega-channels: "People," "Business," and "City"; through nine service types: "Transport," "Citizenship," "Education," "Employment," "Finance," "Household," "Leisure," "Business," and "Tourist"; through the list of departments and agencies providing the services or through interactive search. Services are available 24 hours a day and seven days a week. Services can be accessed via personal computers with Internet connection; public computer facilities installed in district offices, community halls, post offices and public libraries; or smartly designed public kiosks installed throughout the city in train and subway stations, shopping centers, supermarkets, cultural and exhibition centers, and government offices.

China: one-stop shop, "Digital Beijing"

Beijing, the capital city of China, began its "Digital Beijing" initiative in the year 2000. Zhongguancun e-Park (http://www.zhongguancun.com.cn) is a pilot project that applies the latest computer and Internet technologies to improve the efficiency and responsiveness of government. Since the e-Park system went online in 2000, more than 6,000 businesses in the Beijing hi-tech park of Zhongguancun have been able to apply for a license, file monthly financial reports, submit tax statements, and conduct thirty-two other "G2B" and "G2C" functions online. The system has greatly increased government transparency and efficiency, and reduced the opportunities for corruption. The mayor of Beijing announced that in five years most government administrative functions in the city would be performed online as they are in e-Park.

Zhongguancun Science Park is the first and biggest national science park in China, established in 1988. Located in northwest Beijing, it covers about 100 square kilometers. Inside the Science Park, more than 6,000 hi-tech enterprises in the fields of information technology, biology, medicine, and others have their offices. Large multinational information technology (IT) corporations such as IBM, Motorola, Microsoft, Lucent, HP, and Epson have R&D institutes here. Thirty-nine prominent universities and colleges, such as Tsinghua University and Beijing University, are also located within the Park. More and more companies are moving into the Park, attracted by its hi-tech business development environment and preferential tax treatment. Companies in the Park generated a total of $12 billion in revenue in the year 2000 and $200 million in foreign investment, so they clearly contribute significantly to China's economic welfare.

The e-Park has applied the latest computer and Internet technology to build a common administrative platform that connects all government departments. The central database and website allow data sharing and workflow integration among all the departments. Now the government works as an integrated body and shows only one face to the public. The system includes five functions, all of which are accessed from the same homepage:

(1) *e-Application*: The first step a company must take to set up operations in the ZSP is to apply for approval from ZSP to get a "hi-tech company certificate." "e-Application" is a web-based program that provides applicants with all forms and documents to be prepared as well as related laws, regulations, requirements, and procedures – everything they need to know about setting up a company in the Park.

(2) *e-Registration*: After a company is initially approved, it must provide additional information to register with other ZSP departments, like the statistics bureau, the finance bureau, the quality control bureau, etc. Companies can do this via the Internet as well.

(3) *e-Reporting*: Each hi-tech company must report about 100 pieces of operational data, such as revenue, tax, costs, cash flow, and so on, to the appropriate government offices each month. This is now done entirely online.

(4) *e-Administration*: There are several documents that companies must file on a regular basis, and these are now all filed online.

(5) *e-Consulting*: Government officials can provide interactive online consulting services about any of these procedures, and can provide answers to FAQs by e-mail or fax.

Vietnam: one-stop business services for investors

Hanoi and Ho Chi Minh City started business services agencies in 2000, launching websites called Hanoi Ministry of Planning and Investment and Ho Chi Minh Department of Planning and Investment, respectively (World Bank, 2000). The service agencies provided investor, including foreign participants, with business-related information ranging from general business climate to investment license applications. Each investment application can be submitted online and processed in less than one day. Technical assistance was provided by a business advisory body funded by a Japanese government grant, and implemented by MIGA. Total cost for the project amounted to US$200,000, which was funded fully by the Japanese government grant. The one-stop business services enabled investment applicants to reduce time and cost for application process. Thanks to the websites, investors were able to save several thousand dollars that had been paid to professional agencies for investment applications.

Iceland: customs declaration on the Web

The project (http://www.tollur.is) is an interactive online service by the Icelandic Directorate of Customs. The website allows users to receive and send answers to customs declarations and use digital signature as a safety measure.

The benefits include: facilitation import/export procedures for businesses and particularly SMEs by making customs declarations possible over the Internet; fully automated customs procedures by getting up to 100 percent of the declarations electronically transmitted.

In addition, through this system, the declaration time and clearance is now measured in minutes. Digital signature is used as a safety measure which is new in transactions with the government and may lead to wider usage by businesses as confidence grows.

Jamaica: automated customs services

The importation of goods and collection of duties had been primary processed manually, based on a paper-based system. The inefficient custom system had resulted in time-consuming importation entries and often miscalculated duty collections. For improving the custom administration, the Jamaica Customs Department decided to introduce automated custom services using customized software developed by Fiscal Services Limited (FSL), a government-owned information technology company. The automation project initially confronted various difficulties, including resistance from customs brokers and customs officers for technical and monetary reason, and underdeveloped telecom infrastructure (e.g. shortage of phone lines). However, 98 percent of customs procedure has been shifted from manual to electronic entry, and the project has delivered the following successful outcomes: (1) customs processing time shortened from 2–3 days to 2–3 hours; (2) the importation revenue increased from J$12 billion in 1998 to J$24 billion in 2002 despite little or no economic growth; (3) inconsistency and errors in duty collections reduced; and (4) changes of tariff rates were quickly and accurately accommodated.

Philippines: ICT-based system for import procedures

Both business and government in the Philippines were concerned about the delays and corruption associated with customs and importation. An ICT-based system was introduced to address these concerns. Importers create a single electronic declaration, which is processed to calculate payments due and to undertake risk analysis, which identifies shipments that may require physical inspection. The online system has allowed a move to cashless procedures in which verification of duty/tax payment is sent electronically from authorized banks to customs. The verification is automatically reconciled against processed declarations and a release order is then issued. The release order is sent electronically to the Customs warehouses that hold shipments. The result is a much faster service for business. "Cargo is released between four hours to two days, as opposed to eight days in the earlier system." Reconciliation of payments – which used to have a four-month backlog – is now done within the day, and there are fewer errors. Finally, because the customs staff no longer handles cash or physical documentation, the pressures and opportunities for importers to make corrupt payments have been largely removed.

Chile: government e-Procurement system

Recognizing the potential benefits of IT, the Chilean Government established a Communications and Information Technology Unit (UTIC) in 1998. The UTIC was given the mandate of coordinating, promoting, and advising the Chilean Government on the development of IT in the areas of employment, information, and communications. One area of reform in which the UTIC was particularly successful was in pushing forward a comprehensive reform of its procurement system.

Under the government procurement e-system (http://www.compraschile. cl/), companies that wish to do business with the public sector do not need to search through newspapers or the Web for information about bidding opportunities. Instead, they need only to register a single time in the areas in which they do business (e.g. office furniture, construction services, IT consulting, etc.). Whenever a public agency needs to purchase goods or contract a service, it will fill out a request in the electronic system, specifying the kind of operation and including all the documentation and information associated with the request. Automatically, the system sends an e-mail to all the private companies registered in that selected area, minimizing response time and providing an equal opportunity for all firms. The system also provides, online, all the information related to procurement operations, including the public organization's name, address, phone, e-mail, fax, and position of the public officer in charge of the operation. Finally, at the conclusion of the bidding process, the e-System provides the results: who participated; the proposals; the economic and technical scores; and, lastly, who won the bid or obtained the contract. Historical information about the public organization's purchases and contracts is also made available. Currently, there are 4,200 firms registered in the new procurement system.

Brazil: Comprasnet e-Procurement system

Comprasnet (http://www.comprasnet.gov.br) is an e-Procurement application addressing the interaction between the federal government and its suppliers. The Comprasnet service frees the potential suppliers from having to present legal and administrative documentation for every tender, and reduces the cost of supplying to the federal government. Another advantage is that the integration of the procurement system with the financial/payment system enables automatic settlement of the government's payment obligations, assuring timely payment of the contracts. The application enables control over prices of specific goods and services, reduces paperwork and human resource inputs, and increases transparency. The demonstration will highlight key achievements such as significant savings on the process itself, on the initial lowest prices on each tender (over 20 percent), and time spent on the process (over 70 percent on time reduction).

Hong Kong: Electronic Tendering System (ETS)

The ETS (http://www.ets.com.hk) is an Internet-based electronic tendering system for the Hong Kong SAR Government. It was developed and operated by Global e-Business Services Limited (GO-Business), a subsidiary of Computer and Technologies Holdings Limited. ETS is mainly designed for displaying, disseminating, and submitting tender information for the Government Logistics Department (GLD). It includes the display of tender notices, contract award notices and General Terms and Conditions, despatch of tender documents, receipt of offers, etc. By subscribing to the service of ETS, subscribers can logon to the system and enjoy additional functions such as online registration as GSD-registered suppliers, updating of company information, downloading tender documents and clarifications, submitting queries on tenders, and submitting tender offers whenever they wish, and wherever they are. Today, ETS is being operated and managed by GO-Business as a powerful and robust online electronic tendering platform. It links the supplier community worldwide directly with GSD, which is the central purchasing, storage, and supplies organization for the government of the Hong Kong Special Administrative Region serving over eighty government departments, subvented organizations, and certain non-government public bodies. As of 1999, GSD procured around US$873 million worth of goods and services.

A total of 429 tenders (which accounted for 73 percent of the total number of tenders, with value below HK$10 million per tender, issued by the GSD) have been issued through the ETS since its launch in April 2000. By March 2001, the system had attracted 1,260 subscribers. A total of more than 1,000 tenders had been issued through the system which contributed to a total value of HK$1 billion, accounting for 72 percent of the total number of tenders issued within that value range and representing 74 percent of tender values. Through the Internet-based ETS, GSD could rapidly expand its potential supplier pool and thus create a much more competitive environment. As a result, GSD would be able to receive more competitive offers and with more choices. ETS could effectively assist GSD in the reduction of paper usage in printing large number of paper-based tender documents to be collected by suppliers. Furthermore, ETS has brought in many new suppliers (both local and overseas) who had not participated in GSD tenders when only paper-based methods were available. For suppliers, ETS could dramatically shorten the time and save the cost for preparing and submitting bid offers for GSD. In terms of the research, it takes 3 days and 31 minutes respectively through courier and fax sending a 42-page document from Ottawa to Hong Kong and it costs around US$30 and US$4. While the document is sent via Internet, only 2 minutes and US$0.11 is required. It means 2,160 times faster and over 270 times cheaper when submitting documents through ETS compared with the courier option.

Australia: Commonwealth electronic tender system

In conjunction with its Government Online Strategy, the government has released a Commonwealth Electronic Procurement Implementation Strategy, which sets out specific initiatives in this area. Specifically, the government commits to build, in conjunction with agencies, the foundations for online transactions in common government business operations such as procurement and payments, grants and tender processes (http://www.tenders.gov.au). The government will adopt electronic purchasing and payments to the extent that proven technologies allow, with targeted stimulation of supplier involvement to promote government procurement objectives.

This strategy sets the following major goals in the area of Commonwealth electronic purchasing and payments:

- To pay all suppliers to government electronically by the end of 2000, with this facilitated by the issue of electronic remittance advice to all suppliers;
- To deal electronically with all those simple procurement suppliers who wish to by the end of 2001;
- To conduct 90 percent of purchase-related transactions with suppliers to government through electronic means by the end of 2001. However, this depends on supplier readiness. The government will continue to support and facilitate suppliers toward this goal. It will also provide a single

supplier registration process to facilitate secure electronic business transactions with the Commonwealth, and facilitate electronic invoice presentation by suppliers to government.

The initial focus of the electronic purchasing component of this strategy is on simple procurement. The strategy proposes to supplement current purchasing approaches for simple procurement through the use of electronic marketplaces. Electronic marketplaces are essentially electronic catalogues of goods or services hosted on electronic trading networks that link buyers and sellers. Electronic marketplaces are expected to offer agencies more support, greater accountability, and improved statistical information gathering, for simple purchases. It will also provide more flexibility and efficiency for complex purchases. The government will investigate the preferred option of stimulating existing electronic marketplaces where appropriate, combined with the use of emerging electronic marketplaces.

European Union: public procurement

The SIMAP (Système d'Information pour les Marchés Publics) website (http://simap.eu.int) is the official procurement site of the European Union. This site provides specific tools like the electronic online notification service and background information on rules and procedures, both at European and national levels. For suppliers, the site provides information on the procurement market. It makes it possible to search opportunities in all linked (or hosted) databases and sites (purchaser profiles), including smaller contracts and third countries acquisition; a special search and retrieval mechanism allows the selection of specific opportunities, even below the thresholds or outside the European Union. The purchaser profiles will make it possible to directly access the tender documents relating to the call for tenders that the browser is interested in or to consult the annual acquisition plan of a certain contracting authority.

Philippines: pilot e-Procurement system

In November 2000, the Procurement Service of the Department of Budget and Management (PSDBM), with the assistance of the Policy, Training, and Technical Assistance Facility (PTTAF) of the Canadian International Development Agency, launched the Internet-based Electronic Procurement System (EPS) pilot (http://www.procurementservice.net). The EPS is composed of: Public Tender Board to provide access to information and distribute bid packages; Electronic Catalog to support purchases of goods and services by public sector agencies; and Supplier Registry for the registration of suppliers wishing to do business with government agencies.

Initially, the EPS will serve as the official system to advertise and distribute specifications for public bidding opportunities by the government of the Philippines, Procurement Service, and other government agencies. The EPS also contains information related to doing business with the government such as rules and regulations, press releases, a directory of government agencies and contacts, planned and historical agency procurement, bid matching for suppliers, potential competitors, winning bidders, and an FAQ section. In the future the system will be extended to support other aspects of the procurement process including direct purchases, bid submissions, central accreditation, and payments.

Mexico: Compranet procurement system

Mexico's federal government established Compranet (http://compranet.gov.mx/) for government procurement as part of its efforts to curb corruption by automating procurement procedures. By facilitating a process of bidding and reverse bidding online, it seeks to make government purchasing more efficient and transparent. The system allows the public to see what services and products the government is spending its resources on and which companies are providing them with these services. There are more than 6,000 public sector tenders logged daily, and more than 20,000 service-providing firms are regular users. Other countries in the region are looking to imitate Mexico's successful Compranet.

Spain: integrated management of wealth and income tax

The many services provided via the Internet (http://www.aeat.es) are organized according to the type of taxpayer (large companies, SMEs, tax practitioners, professionals, and other taxpayers). These services cover all the process of tax management (information, electronic tax return filing and payment, certifications, etc.). The objectives of the project are helping the taxpayer meet his/her tax responsibilities, simplifying the procedures, and facilitating – where possible – an earlier tax refund. The project has already won several national and international awards, among those the 2000 WITSA (World Information Technology and Services Alliance) Global IT Excellence Award. The comprehensive management of taxes and procedures by Internet, in a top level of security and confidentiality framework, is an important objective for the Spanish Tax Administration.

Portugal: tax electronic services

The service, operational since 1997, covers all forms of tax (www.dgci.mailcom.pt). The tax services provided include online filing of tax forms, downloading of offline solutions, file import from business account packages, specific solutions for account services, interactive tax filing for users with a lesser understanding of tax procedures. In addition payments and enquiries can be made through the use of ATM networks. Internet delivery of tax forms prevents errors and allows earlier access to critical information that can be used to control fraud and tax evasion.

Canada: NETFILE online tax filing

The NETFILE website (http://www.netfile.gc.ca/), launched on November 1, 1999, introduced the newest electronic filing option to Canadians. For the 1999 taxation year, CCRA invited 3.8 million Canadians to submit their tax returns using NETFILE. The project proved to be more successful than expected: attracting 443,654 returns – rather than the expected 380,000. The transmissions were acknowledged within two to five seconds, well below the two-minute confirmation response time that had been estimated. Based on the results of a survey for the 2000 tax year, CCRA offered the service to approximately 22 million Canadians. More than 1.4 million taxpayers had filed their returns through NETFILE by the April 30 deadline. Electronic filings through NETFILE, TELEFILE, and E-FILE now total 7.9 million returns, more than 34 percent of the tax filing population.

France: online subscription and payment of VAT

TéléVA (http://tva.dgi.minefi.gouv.fr) is a package of services for declaring and paying VAT to the General Tax Directorate by means of a single transaction on which the VAT return and payment order are sent in the same message. TéléVA provides businesses with a convenient and secure way for declaring and paying VAT. Benefits include the availability of the service, 24 hours a day, seven days a week, until the last minute of the last day of the due date, a personalized service because the software automatically chooses the relevant forms for a given taxpayer, and other services offered such as online documentation on VAT, last-minute information, FAQ, and a technical hotline. TéléVA provides the taxpayer with sophisticated automatic controls, online acknowledgement of receipt and the possibility of viewing past VAT declarations and payments over a three-year period. Currently the paper-processing of VAT in France represents 30 million forms and payment orders a year which are dealt with by approximately 2000 tax officers. TéléVA is expected to provide the tax administration with huge productivity gains and to speed up the process of collecting VAT.

Chile: online tax system

In 1998, the Servicio de Impuestos Internos, SSI (Chilean Internal Taxation Service) developed an Oracle Internet-based online taxation system (http://www.ssi.cl) with the following three objectives: (1) reducing the cost and increasing the accuracy of tax collection; (2) equipping Chile's tax authority with the resources it needed for the foreseeable future; and (3) offering taxpayers throughout the country a higher standard of service along with swift, easy access to vital tax information.

The system was developed in two main phases. During the first phase, the system only provided information about the Chilean tax system, which benefited not only the Chilean citizens, but also foreign investors, making the tax system more transparent and information more easily accessible. In the second phase, the focus was on making the site more interactive, including online tax filing and data entry by the taxpayers, reducing input errors, printing costs, and processing time.

Within three years the system attained remarkable results: over 400,000 taxpayers had checked their assessments online; 183,548 returns were sworn, and 89,355 income tax returns had been received. The Chilean exchequer had collected $1.943 billion through the electronic system. Managers at SII prepared the online system for a potential 1.8 million tax returns per annum, in addition to 950,000 VAT returns each month.

Bulgaria: improving transparency and state emphasis on SMEs

In 2000, a United Mortgage Electronic Registry was created with a unique number for every real estate in Bulgaria. Now, when an entrepreneur goes to the bank for credit, he declares whether he will use a mortgage, and gives the precise address of his property. The bank resorts to the specialized service to check whether the real estate has other burdens and then reserves a place for the mortgage. Thus, during a two-week period the bank checks and considers a request for credit, the property stays reserved, and no other bank can put a mortgage on it. And one can check from anywhere in the country whether a mortgage has been put on a property. This has enhanced accountability, improved transparency, and helped both financial institutions and entrepreneurs in the access to finance. Through the central registry both debtors and creditors will be able to make security interests public, secure priority of security interests, and safeguard against relying on property already encumbered by third-party security interests.

B   R&D promotion

Singapore: intellectual property marketplace

The Intellectual Property Office of Singapore (IPOS) introduced a new marketplace platform (http://www.surfip.gov.sg) enabling intellectual property (IP) owners, potential buyers and sellers, and licensees virtually to come together and commercialize IP assets. It provides a platform listing what types of IP are available for licensing, and what types of IP customers are looking for. SurfIP benefits SMEs that may lack the capital to take a product to market, may be looking for licensees, and also may be willing to take out a license to commercialize patented technologies. It provides an opportunity for licensees and licensors to meet and establish contacts for commercialization of patented technologies. The SurfIP website also provides a comprehensive IP information service connected to a number of patent databases around the world to obtain an integrated IP information.

Sweden: Gothia Science Park

Gothia Science Park (http://www.swedepark.se) offers a creative and dynamic environment with activities, services, and premises well suited to facilitate start and growth of high-tech start-ups. Emphasis is on development of companies, start-ups from the University of Skövde and spin-off ventures from already existing companies. It is also open to knowledge-based companies wanting to establish close to the University of Skövde. Its focus is on: science park including incubator facilities; technology, business and management support; spin-off program – education on entrepreneurship for development of products and business ideas. Close cooperation with the university of Skövde gives access to the technical competence within the fields of IT, industrial economy, virtual engineering, and health care.

Sweden: Creative Center Business Incubator

Business Incubator at the University of Jönköping (http://www.creativecenter.cc), is in the south of Sweden. So far, students and Ph.D. students have started up over 130 new ventures through the supporting concentrations of Creative Center. Creative Center is a non-profit organization. The funding for a project-based work comes from both the private and public sector appreciating the creation of new businesses. Processes and activities are around three areas:

(1) Inspiration and start-up: students and Ph.D. students are offered professional advice and practical services in order to establish their new ventures.
(2) Business incubator: the new ventures are offered business incubator facilities. This means a flexible infrastructure for the entrepreneurs and self-employed when they are establishing their businesses. The facilities are favorable since the resources are shared and partly sponsored but also since it creates an entrepreneurial environment and culture. Services offered: mentorship program, networking activities, seminars, support in developing business ideas, incubator managers.
(3) Network and growth: creative center stimulates cooperation between the knowledge-intensive new firms and is actively involved trying to build new clusters. The ventures are also given guidance and advice in the financial process where sometimes seed- and venture capital is raised.

In five years (1996–2000) over 150 new ventures have been established (80–90 of those are still in business. Sixteen of these companies are located in the Creative Center Business Incubator and approximately 240 full- and part-time jobs have been created, investment attracted from both internal and external sources adds up to a total of SEK 127 million. They mostly work within the area of service, IT, and consulting.

Netherlands: BTC-Twente incubator

BTC-Twente (http://www.btc-twente.nl) is located at the Business and Science Park in Enschede, in the eastern part of the Netherlands, near the border with Germany. Its objective is to promote and support the start-up and growth of innovative enterprises in the Business and Science Park, Enschede. The Park is situated at the doorstep of the University of Twente, which has 1,200 scientists and some 6,000 students. BTC-Twente has been operating since January 1983. It has net office space of 3,000 sq m and production space of 1,500 sq m. It offers excellent facilities for incremental growth to all its tenants. BTC-Twente does this by bridging the gap between industry and education. An important partnership has been forged between the BTC and the local university and polytechnic school, whereby the education establishments provide vital technological know-how and developments and the BTC the incubation space and professional business services.

In terms of facilities, BTC-Twente provides inexpensive and flexible space: from a single 12 sq m office to a 180 sq m unit for light manufacturing. Furthermore, the centre offers a wide array of essential business support services that include reception, telephone answering, secretarial services, management consulting, technology marketing, and many other "big business" resources to match small business budgets. Price and quality of services are therefore entirely in accordance with the needs of pioneer companies.

Portugal: Novas Empresas e Tecnologías (NET)

Founded in 1987, Novas Empresas e Tecnologias (NET) of Oporto (http://www.net-sa.pt) has the mission of helping the creation of innovative business and technological enterprises, with a great potential growth and low failure ratio, promoting the launch of small enterprises, and supporting the modernization of existing SMEs.

Its area of influence is north of Portugal and its development activities are in two distinctive areas: (1) the creation and incubation, which includes a set of services provided to the enterprises, such as the use of rooms and management supporting services; and (2) support to existing SMEs trying to develop a modernization project.

NET has pioneered in Portugal the "Idea Contest," with a monetary prize, aimed at stimulating entrepreneurship and promoting innovation with prospects of success, contributing to the renewal of business in the northern region of Portugal, through the creation of new enterprises. NET is also involved with other BICs in several international innovative projects.

Finland: TEKES, supporting innovative enterprises

The government-run TEKES Foundation (http://www.tekes.fi/) gives grants and loans to small- and medium-sized businesses seeking to develop specific ICT applications. Its funding is targeted at projects which produce new know-how or bear high technological and commercial risks. The projects to be funded promote sustainable competitiveness, commercialization of research results, and emergence of new business activities.

Besides providing financial support for R&D projects of particular enterprises, Takes also has so-called "technology programs." They are used to promote development in specific sectors of technology or industry, and to commercialize the results of the research work. The technology programs are planned in coordination with TEKES, enterprises, and research institutes. TEKES usually finances about half of the costs of programs. Below are some interesting examples of the technology programs:

- Digital Media Content Program 1996–1999. The primary aim of the program was to support the creation of profitable business in the new media industry. It supported new multimedia businesses, particularly SMEs, not by financing the development of individual products, but by helping them to access, develop, and acquire fast and efficient content production processes, enhanced business skills, and improved distribution networks.
- The Information Networking in the Construction Process Program – VERA 1997–2002. The VERA program is a great example of building synergy between ICT and traditional sectors. The VERA program aims to develop information networking solutions to compile and record information flows in a building during its entire life-cycle. The projects undertaken in the program deal simultaneously with construction process and information technology solutions. Participants have included construction companies, property owners, architects and designers, and software houses. Data can be transferred between different software suites as the building is designed, built, and subsequently used.

Denmark: Patent and Trademark Office

In order to encourage the Danish SMEs to make use of the IP system, the Danish Government has initiated a two-year project, and the Patent and Trademark Office KDPTO has developed IPscore (http://www.dkpto.dk/int/patents/ipscore.htm) as a practical management tool. The IPscore manages and evaluate patents and trademarks to give a picture of the strategic value for companies of a patent or a trademark. The DKPTO has established a call center with the objective of handing IP-related inquiries of SMEs. The center provides through guidance on IP matters and on commercial services of DKPTO, i.e. patent application. The center handles approximately 150 telephone inquiries per day.

Netherlands: promotion of innovation through Dreamstart Program

Dreamstart (http://www.dreamstart.nl) is an initiative of the Dutch Ministry of Economic Affairs in line with the Ministry's policy to generate more new technology-based firms, i.e. technostarters. Its mission is to create awareness amongst universities and research institutes that technology research can be translated into commercially successful business. Furthermore Dreamstart intends to generate technology driven companies active in a wide range of technology areas. Its objectives are two-fold:

- To become a center of competence for technostarters offering them coaching, advice and entrance to a potential European market.
- To become a coordination platform in the Netherlands for the different regional incubators, stimulating synergy and cooperation, enhancing the quality of the services offered and avoiding fragmentation of initiatives.

In order to reach its objectives Dreamstart organizes and participates in various events aimed at creating awareness amongst researches and students. In these events Dreamstart cooperates with a wide range of directly related organizations such as venture capital organizations, universities, banks, etc.

Dreamstart maintains a website providing information on a wide range of matters which may be crucial in setting up a new company. Links with various other organizations are provided. The website also contains an inspiration part, which offers the possibility for technostarters to get into contact with other starters and discuss their problems and challenges.

Portugal: Centro Promotor de Inovação e Negócios

The Centro Promotor de Inovação e Negócios (CPIN) is an immaterial BIC, whose mission is to become a benchmark as an Integrated Solutions Provider to technology-based entrepreneurship. CPIN works in close partnership with Taguspark (http://www.taguspark.pt), the biggest and most successful science park in Portugal. The physical incubation facilities are provided to entrepreneurs by Taguspark (5,000 sq m, more than 110 tenant technology-based firms), whilst CPIN concentrates its action in the "soft" part of the incubation process, acting in the entrepreneurs and projects evaluation, support to business planning, coaching, specific consultancy, IP assistance, S&T commercialization, growth and internationalization processes, technology management, etc.

A self-owned methodology for evaluation of entrepreneurial skills has been developed and tested and is now in regular use. A new development is now under course for linking entrepreneurial capacities, intangible assets and success potential in the early stages of knowledge-based firms.

Brazil: ReAACT, networking for science and technology projects

The Rede para Administração de Apoio à Ciência e Tecnologia (ReAACT) is a web-based system designed to manage the entire cycle of science and technology projects, from project proposals to final reporting. Through ReAACT, the Support Program for Scientific and Technological Development

(PADCT) program succeeded to automate expensive and time-consuming procedures to manage scientific and technological projects. The participants of ReAACT include a proposal team, agencies technical staff, program coordinators, consultants, and advisory committees. Project proposals can be submitted via the Internet, and evaluated and monitored by coordinators and consultants for deciding whether they will be approved or not. There were 1,580 contracted proposals, involving 1,453 institutions and 5,173 applications, up to July 2005. In addition, automations of administrative procedure resulted in enormous cost reduction: R$38,195 for paper, R$1,144,598 for mail, R$1,000,000 for air tickets and daily expenses. Also processing time decreased from nine months to five months.

C   SME capacity building

WBI: Europe and Central Asia Virtual University

Europe and Central Asia Virtual University ECAVU (http://www.iis.ru/ecavu – Russian only) is an association of universities in ECA region that coordinates and facilitates distance learning activities by universities and helps them build capacity in distance learning. The activities of the association will be based on the common language – Russian.

ECAVU helps bridge the growing gap between the best international education practices based on the most recent achievements in information technologies and the pace of education system development in CIS states. Thanks to the ECAVU, participants in CIS universities have access to economic and business-oriented courses designed by the world leaders in the area, such as the London School of Economics. Such courses help address the training and continuing education needs of entrepreneurs in the region.

Malaysia: Teaching Company Scheme

Malaysian SMEs experience difficulties in their research and training activities due to a lack of skilled labor in the country. To address the problem, a concept first introduced in the UK called the Teaching Company Scheme (TCS) was employed. The program creates partnerships in which academics and students join with companies to contribute to the implementation of their strategies on the technical or management side. The TCS not only supplements the SMEs' financial and human capital, but also improves the links between public and private sector in the country.

Ireland: Enterprise Ireland Portal

Benchmarking is a systematic process for profiling and evaluating a company's effectiveness in terms of productivity, quality, innovation, and other business practices, by comparison with the "Best In Class." Enterprise Ireland offers access to a benchmarking tool for quantifying performance and assessing SMEs' competitive strengths and weaknesses based on Just-in-Time (JIT), Total Quality Management (TQM), and employee involvement techniques. Using a European database of 2,500 companies, SMEs receive an objective rating against best international practice. The Irish Benchmarking Forum, a cluster or network of companies and academia, delivers a vehicle for this new approach. By sharing their experience, SMEs are able to improve the development process and more quickly than if they work by themselves. By using benchmarking as an integral part of their development initiatives, numerous dramatic results, i.e. machine efficiency up 15 percent and business increased 25 percent, were achieved by Irish SMEs. Instant benchmarking tool is not accessible via the Internet, but the website promotes the awareness of benchmarking (see http://www.enterprise-ireland.com).

D   Supporting rural enterprise

e-Choupal, India: e-Commerce solution for fragmented rural farmers

e-Choupal was established by ITC's International Business Division, which is the largest exporter of agricultural commodities in India. The objective of e-Choupal is to make a sustainable efficient supply-chain of Indian agriculture through vertical integration of fragmented rural farms. Through its website, e-Choupal provides varied information regarding weather, knowledge of scientific farm practices, and market prices of agricultural commodities in local language. In addition, in order to raise productivity and enlarge capacity of farmer risk management, e-Choupal aggregates the demand for inputs for production, storage, and marketing of their products, eliminating involvement of numerous intermediates. ITC makes profits by procuring products at lower costs, skipping costly intermediaries; at the same time, they can offer better prices to farmers. Rural farmers can access e-Choupal at local kiosks. Since established in June 2000, e-Choupal has created 1,300 kiosks in 8,000 villages across four states, becoming the largest initiative among all Internet-based interventions in rural India. ITC plans to expand its kiosk network up to other eleven states in the country over the next a few years.

Russia: rural information and knowledge system

The Agricultural Reform Implementation Support (ARIS) Project was funded and implemented by the World Bank and the Russian Federation between 1994 and 2000. The objective of this project was reform of the agro-industrial sector that accounted for around 25 percent of the Russian economy. The main objectives of this project included introduction of agricultural support services through the establishment of a market information system, and farmer information and advisory services. Agricultural Market Information System (MIS) covers roughly one third of Russia, providing weekly and bi-weekly producer, wholesale, and retail process on a wide range of agricultural products through the Internet, ARIS websites, mass media, and other communication methods. Such price information services have resulted in great reduction of the variation of prices of the ten products covered by MIS within participating regions, and a 20 percent reduction in price variation across the participating regions. Farmer Information and Advisory Services (FIAS) provides newly emerging and restructured farmers with information, knowledge, technology, and training necessary for agricultural production and management of agribusinesses. Between 1999 and 2000, agricultural enterprises receiving FIAS consultations had grown on average by 23 percent, while those not receiving such consultations had seen deterioration by 9 percent.

Drishtee, India: e-Development services for rural populations

Drishtee is a comprehensive platform for rural networking and marketing services enabling Indian villagers to access both government and private services though ICT. The localized Intranet between villages and a district center provides access to various services, including online land record, registration and applications of income and domicile certificates, market-related information on cereal crops, government, health, and education benefits. Villagers can reach Dristee at local kiosks, and each kiosk is owned by a villager, called a *Soochak*, with government financial assistance. A *Soochak* procures the hardware by himself, and earns commission from transactions. This business model spread to Indian rural areas; the number of kiosks increased to over 300 kiosks as of July 2005. A single kiosk covers two to ten villages with population of 5,000 to 10,000. At villages that set up a kiosk around 15 percent of the village population uses the service (see http://www.drishtee.com).

7

e-Development toward Knowledge Economy: Country Profiles

e-Development's role and validity in developing countries is two-fold: on the one hand it sustains development efforts and on the other it helps to bridge the gap, decreasing the digital divide.

e-Development (intended as a dynamic and flexible mix of technology and development policies and interventions) is a new phenomenon: technology and development can, and should, co-exist to increase efficiency and maximize intervention impact. It leverages, catalyzes, and combines *people*, *culture*, and *technology* for optimal *availability, awareness, accessibility,* and *affordability* of knowledge-based goods (digital and tangible) and can serve as a powerful *communication, cooptation,* and *coordination* device for development.

The innovative nature of e-Development and the need to adjust development intervention and policies to the specific needs of any given recipient country does not allow for the standardization of e-Development interventions. Yet, the benchmark of a set of countries (a mix of developing, transitioning, and developed countries for as total of 23 countries)[2] has allowed for the identification of a number of e-Development best practices on a global scale via the analysis of technology- and innovation-focused policies and interventions in newly developed and advanced developing countries.

We first introduce the framework on which we based our individual country assessments, then we present a summary of our findings, that is for each country we list e-Development-related strengths and weaknesses, as well as findings from the country's experience, before presenting the in-depth assessments for e-Development toward knowledge economy.

A Framework for e-Development profiles

The country profiles for e-Development toward knowledge economy that we present in Chapters 8, 9, and 10 have been developed based on the following framework:

- *e-Development and Knowledge Economy overview*: based on country-specific factors, such as its political structure, economic performance, and major e-Development indicators and ratings.
- *Policy and regulatory framework for e-Development*: includes a historic background and an overview of the government's awareness on e-Development and the Knowledge Economy, a review of the institutional framework, the public–private partnership on e-Development, policies and strategies on e-Development, major legislation supporting e-Development, and e-Government applications.
- *e-Development Knowledge Economy ICT infrastructure issues*: such as the telecommunications sector, ICT penetration, and ICT products and services (hardware/software).
- *e-Development and Knowledge Economy human capital issues*: covers education, training, awareness, availability of quality workforce, and public–private partnerships in human capital development.
- *e-Development and Knowledge Economy PSD issues*: including business environment issues, privatization, e-Business/e-Commerce development, business development issues, foreign direct investment, research and development, SME development, and enabling environment for e-Business (Business-to-Business: B2B; Business-to-Consumer: B2C; and Business-to-Government: B2G).
- *e-Development and Knowledge Economy FSD issues*: covers the role of ICT in the financial sector, capital market development, e-Finance, retail banking, and bank supervision.
- *Bilateral and multilateral e-Development and Knowledge Economy activities*: includes projects from the World Bank Group, the European Union, the United Nations, and other multilateral or bilateral organizations, if applicable.

B   Summary of e-Development profiles

We introduce below a summary of our findings from the analysis of each specific country which presents e-Development-related strengths and weaknesses, and knowledge gained (Tables 7.1, 7.2 and 7.3). We grouped the countries according to their relative stage of development (as defined in the note 1 to Chapter 7).

Table 7.1 Country profiles: summary of findings for developed economies

Country	Strengths	Weaknesses	Knowledge gained
Australia	<ul><li>Facilitation of access to finance for SMEs</li><li>R&D incentives</li><li>Investments in human capital</li><li>Institutional and regulatory framework</li><li>Public–private partnership</li></ul>	<ul><li>Location: Australia is remotely located from major economic centers</li><li>Geography: territorial extension of the island and its scarcely populated hinterland</li><li>Internal digital divide</li></ul>	<ul><li>Size does matter: reaching dispersed population in rural areas has been a challenge for Australia</li><li>Fiscal incentives are pivotal to facilitate R&D and foster innovation</li></ul>
Finland	<ul><li>Early deregulation of the telecom market and privatization of telecom operator</li><li>Low telecommunications access charges</li><li>Wide adoption of mobile technology; provision of universal service not tied to fixed networks only. A telecom company may provide these services also through its mobile networks</li><li>Promoting high level of competition in the ICT industry</li><li>Public–private investments and partnership in R&D</li><li>Support of R&D for SMEs</li><li>Access to finance for R&D</li></ul>	<ul><li>ICT sector too much related to only one company – Nokia</li><li>e-Government is somewhat underdeveloped</li><li>No favorable conditions for FDI</li><li>Public sector plays too big a role in national economy</li><li>Data security problems are the biggest hindrance to the utilization of the Internet in business</li><li>Heavy taxation of labor</li><li>Small population and limited domestic market</li><li>Low level of entrepreneurship</li></ul>	<ul><li>Building of information society in Finland has some idiosyncratic features, e.g. Fins are known as creative, persistent and hard working; very interested in all kinds of new technology, adopt it rather enthusiastically. These human and cultural factors can potentially contribute to a very large share of Finnish e-Development success. Finnish case study stresses the importance of "soft factors" for e-Development</li></ul>

Continued

Table 7.1 Continued

Country	Strengths	Weaknesses	Knowledge gained
	• Promoting networking both within ICT cluster and between the cluster and "traditional economy" • Human capital and education • Connecting schools to the Internet • Introduction of electronic ID cards		
Ireland	• Favorable macro-economic conditions • Export-oriented economy • Favorable taxation regime; Ireland has the lowest rate of corporation tax in Europe • Very highly educated workforce • One of the highest levels of PC ownership in the world • Proactive role of government • Maximum liberalization of telecom market • Rapid progress since in developing broadband capacity, especially in international connectivity • Creation of favorable ICT-related regulatory environment • ICT skills training with heavy emphasis on introduction of	• Limited domestic market • Relatively underdeveloped banking sector with low use of electronic payments • Relatively high cost of Internet access and slow connection speeds available for residential Internet users • Conditions for producing ICT for export better than conditions for "consumption" within the country	• Ireland government very good at creating and satisfying demand for IT professionals in the country: booming ICT production sector creates demand for skilled labor, government's heavy investment in higher education allows for "production" of many IT graduates, which, in turn helps to create favorable conditions for investment in country's ICT sector. Two trends re-enforce each other • Ireland's e-Development experience particularly relevant to Romania and Ukraine, e.g. creation of export-oriented ICT industry may benefit these countries greatly, including solving major problems such as brain-drain • Ireland's focus on building modern infrastructure as a prerequisite for

	• ICT-related courses in higher education system • Government-supported promotional campaigns • Maximum adoption of ICT by government • Adoption of public–private approach to e-Development		• successful building of information society pays off; maximum liberalization of telecom market helps country to quickly advance to leadership positions in e-Development
New Zealand	• Small size of country allows for quick response to changes of global environment • Open and transparent regulatory environment • Multicultural, well-educated population • Recognition of opportunities and challenges in ICT sector • Adoption of international standards in all economic and social fields	• Short supply of technical graduates from tertiary institutions • Brain-drain of IT workers attracted by greater opportunities overseas • Lack of an innovation culture • Varying ICT-literacy in the community • Uneven distribution of infrastructure capability at reasonable cost, particularly in rural communities • Shortage of management, leadership, and entrepreneurial e-Commerce skills	• To overcome digital divide between rural and urban areas, New Zealand government intervened actively in privatization and deregulation process of telecom market • Despite small and remote domestic market, government of New Zealand still able to develop innovations in ICT sector and to attract FDI • Instead of creating national ICT standards, New Zealand complied with preexisting international ICT standards • Government of New Zealand fostered an open and fully deregulated ICT market
Singapore	• Very proactive role of government • Far-sighted approach of government: first ICT-related	• Small domestic market • High interference of the government in the economy, deemed sometimes as	• e-Development is not only about infrastructure: human capital and awareness are crucial to ensure success

Table 7.1 Continued

Country	Strengths	Weaknesses	Knowledge gained
	actions in mid-1990s • Heavy investment in telecom infrastructure (almost 90% of household, academia, public and private sector connected) • Institution building has been essential • Creation of appropriate legal framework • Gradual opening of telecom sector	ove-regulation	• e-Development is not only about Internet and telecom: Singapore is now becoming an international pole of attraction for chemicals and engineering • ICT development strategy can aim at building infrastructure to become a regional hub for informatics traffic, a cyber-port
Slovenia	• Proactive role of the government • Political and economic openness since early years of independence • Private sector promotional activities to build e-commerce • Well-developed telecom infrastructure • Appropriate regulatory framework for KE • Proximity to EU • Small population and territory • Technology park and incubators	• Small domestic market • Telecom market not fully liberalized	• Private sector should engage in promoting information society: private sector promotional activities are as important as governments' proactive role • Size does matter: small geographical extension and little population make infrastructure and awareness issues easier to address

Table 7.2 Country profiles: summary of findings for transitioning economies

Country	Strengths	Weaknesses	Knowledge gained
Argentina	• One of most educated populations in Latin America • National public university system well developed and provides sufficient number of graduates with high level of technical expertise • ICT market open to competition • Modern telecom infrastructure • Appropriate regulatory framework to attract foreign direct investment • Wide net of community technology centers with computers, fax machines, and Internet access • Local practice of sharing Internet subscriptions between multiple users, such as families or small businesses • Appropriate legal framework (digital signature in the Public Administration)	• Badly structured government fiscal policy • High level of public sector spending • Political uncertainty (power struggle between executive branch, legislative, and other agencies) • Negligible research capabilities of education system • Lack of funding opportunities, access to capital is major constraint to innovation • Lack of a comprehensive set of fiscal incentives for software and IT services industry development	• Argentina's story stresses importance of building e-Development on solid fundament of macro-economic stability; despite current implications of instability, Argentina implemented several original e-Development strategies: • To prevent high connection costs from limiting Internet development, Argentina established dedicated number for calls to ISPs with lower rates for dial-up Internet access • Provision of unified license for diversified telecom services; local phone service providers required to invest in infrastructure and to submit a technical plan consistent with level of demand • 1% of total telecom sales will be targeted to subsidize telephone services in non-profitable regions and to foster Internet development in schools
Brazil	• Brazil accounted for 88% of online sales throughout whole of Latin America	• Inadequate regulatory framework, lack of e-commerce legislation (still	• Strategic public–private partnerships helped Brazil to overcome internal digital divide

Continued

Table 7.2 Continued

Country	Strengths	Weaknesses	Knowledge gained
	• Universities lead R&D efforts • Early adoption of policies to promote the development of national enterprises in computer industry • Liberalization and deregulation of telecom market soon completed to spur development of the ICT sector	under approval) • High illiteracy rate, especially for IT skills • High costs for equipment • Lack of relevant ICT training programs and shortage of ICT qualified workers • Unfavorable tax and fiscal environment for foreign investors • Limited R&D funds and incentives for private sector • Low level of telephone line density (among lowest in Latin America)	• To promote local SMEs, government restricted import of technology where and when local capabilities were able to meet demand. This helped SMEs to develop and improve their own products and services • Privatization and deregulation in telecom sector brought accelerated growth in the ICT sector • Government strongly supports R&D potential of domestic academia, in effort to integrate universities into cycle of innovation led by private sector
Costa Rica	• Skilled workforce, educated society • Heavy investment in R&D • Public–private partnerships in fields of awareness, education, training • Institution building: Costa Rica created network of institutions devoted to sustainable development • Costa Rica sustained enabling environment for domestic SMEs (access to finance, administrative facilitations)	• State-owned monopoly in telecommunications • Limited domestic market • Internal divide between urban and rural areas	• FDI is not the only driver: sustainable development has to be supported by viable enabling environment for SMEs and local entrepreneurship • Costa Rica is focusing on ICT mainly as an export engine • Risk of tying the economy too much to a single foreign company (i.e. Intel)

	• Created one of the most attractive investment environments by providing incentives (fiscal, financial)		
Czech Republic	• Government as user and promoter of ICT and high-tech applications • S&T heritage • Skilled and qualified workforce • Strategic location • Capacity to attract FDI	• Telecom market still rigid • Lack of appropriate regulatory framework for infrastructure	• FDI alone not enough to drive growth in ICT sector; other factors play crucial role (i.e. telecom liberalization, regulatory framework) • Liberalization of telecommunication market essential to promote positive spill-over on ICT-related industry
Estonia	• Far-sighted approach of government • Government both user and provider of ICT • Comprehensive National Action Plan to develop Information Society, with realistic goals, specific target actions and timeline • Creation of appropriate institutional and regulatory framework • Proximity to IT leaders–Nordic countries • Liberalization of telecom market • Dynamic political class • Investment in human capital • Public–private partnership • S&T heritage	• Lack of financial resources • Small economy • Limited internal market • Lack of local language content • Brain-drain • Shortage of IT workers	• Public–private partnership not only viable but purposeful • The National Action plan to build an information society has to provide general framework of reference, specific measures and interventions, detailed timeline, and budgetary allocation • Realistic approach in setting goals of the strategy necessary to ensure success and focus of actions • Despite financial restrictions (small state budget), progress in KE possible through consistent and purposeful allocation even of a small budget • Institution building vital to ensure coordination of efforts and proper allocation of resources

Continued

Table 7.2 Continued

Country	Strengths	Weaknesses	Knowledge gained
	• High PC penetration		• Legal framework designed following international standards pivotal for development of KE

Hungary	• Overall strong economy by regional standards
	• A high standard of general and vocational education
	• Availability of comparatively cheap, technically skilled labor
	• Advanced banking sector – privatized and open to FDI
	• Comprehensive privatization policy
	• Attractive conditions for FDI
	• Active promotion of SMEs
	• Proximity of EU markets
	• Separations of operational and regulatory functions in telecom industry
	• Government-subsidized Academic Hungarnet network
	• Extensive net of telecottages (public telecenters)
		• High costs hinder Internet use in the country
		• Subsidizes access through telecottages and HungarNet reduces customer base for commercial ISP sector and internet cafes
		• Limited domestic market
		• Matav still maintains a monopoly over long-distance and international calls, and has market share of more than 75% over local services
			• Hungary's case highlights two potential trade-offs ECA countries may face:
			  • Between developing telecom industry and promoting Internet use in the country
			  • Between developing a web of free or heavily subsidized access centers and promoting commercial ISP sector
			• Hungarian government found creative way to support Matav's monopoly on long-distance calls; IP telephony providers are obliged to guarantee inferior quality of service: thus, IP telephony has potential for development while Matav preserves its monopoly

Malaysia	• Strong government vision on ICT development • Rapid industrialization with electronic goods production being most important category	• Shortage of skilled labor • Possibility of an emerging gap between the information-rich and those who do not have access to	• It is too early to draw conclusions about Malaysian e-Development experience. Final Report on Digital Opportunity Initiative states: it is not clear that the goal of entering

	<ul><li>The US$40 billion Multimedia Super Corridor, backbone for the country's information superhighway; attractive inducements to global and local capital through strong ICT infrastructure in major enterprise zones, improving business processes, and providing business incentives</li><li>Comprehensive policies to encourage ICT use in various sectors of the economy</li><li>Creative approach to addressing shortages in skilled ICT labor, such as Teaching Company Scheme (TCS): academics help companies with technical and managerial change strategies</li><li>Government grants to innovative ICT projects</li><li>Attractive environment to attract FDI to ICT development</li><li>Emphasis on telecom infrastructure</li><li>Fully liberalized telecom, computer and software markets</li></ul>	<ul><li>technology, notably because of the high cost of computers compared to average incomes</li><li>High dependence on exports, particularly electronics and electrical goods has made economic growth vulnerable to global fluctuations in the demand</li></ul>	the knowledge society is best served by a capital intensive focus on multimedia applications, as opposed to a strategy which is more focused on extending infrastructure, increasing ICT and general literacy, and focusing on SME and government usage of ICT so as to improve Malaysia's positioning through more widespread productivity gains and deeper access to global markets for local businesses
Poland	<ul><li>S&T heritage</li><li>Proximity to EU</li><li>Growing domestic market</li><li>Capacity to attract FDI</li></ul>	<ul><li>Rural vs. urban connectivity</li><li>Brain-drain</li><li>Rigid telecom sector</li><li>Weak R&D policies</li></ul>	<ul><li>Bridging the divide with EU countries not the only priority; attention should be paid to regional development within the country;</li></ul>

Continued

Table 7.2 Continued

Country	Strengths	Weaknesses	Knowledge gained
	• Awareness, especially among new generations	• Lack of appropriate specific actions within the policy statements	internal divide between rural and urban areas to be avoided • National action plan and policy strategies may be devoid of meaning if not accompanied by realistic timeframe and specific target actions
Slovak Republic	• Quite successful privatization and enterprise restructuring during last several years • Banking sector is almost completely in private hands and quite efficient and competitive • Telecommunication market in Slovakia has been liberalized except for basic public telephone service in fixed telecom network and operation of public telephone network • Competition in sector for Internet service providers (ISPs), which is dominated by foreign-owned firms • Educational attainment of labor force compares well to that of OECD countries, and is higher than in most ECA countries	• Booming unofficial or "gray" economy • Economy's reliance on large enterprises • High unemployment • Government currently does not have updated long-term strategic vision of development of information society in Slovak Republic; ICT regulations currently based on several isolated acts • Slovak Telecom's monopoly on basic public telephone service in fixed telecommunication network and operation of the public telephone network • Only partial privatization of Slovak telecom	• Even though Slovak government does not have strategic vision on ICT, sector developing quite successfully by regional standards. Lack of vision partially compensated by isolated, but mostly adequate regulatory acts. Especially important in this regard, openness of telecom market, especially ISP sector, to FDI. Even with absence of overall strategy, targeted policy interventions may have visible positive effect

South Africa			
	- South Africa is most advanced and productive economy in Africa region - Very well-developed financial, legal, telecommunications, energy and transport system - During last years, a significant percentage of university and technical-school graduates possess IT-oriented knowledge and skills (software development, network management) - Improvements of ICT infrastructure	- Low computer-literacy levels - Low computer penetration among society and schools - Low awareness of ICT opportunities among public sector - R&D spending budget being kept to low figures	- Limitations of monopoly in fixed-line telecom sector bypassed by full competition in vibrant mobile sector - Private sector has played crucial role in driving growth of Internet: supply and demand in financial sector leapfrogged to support and provide cutting-edge Internet services access, as well as offer full online services and to upgrade e-Commerce - Commitment of government to provide more IT-focused education and training led to restructuring whole educational system

Table 7.3 Country profiles: summary of findings for developing economies

Country	Strengths	Weaknesses	Knowledge gained
Bulgaria	• One of highest telephone line densities in ECA • Competition open in mobile and Internet sectors • High level of technical skill and general education, particularly in engineering and information technology skills • Relatively high-quality ICT products at competitive prices	• Slow privatization process • High connectivity cost and low computer penetration • Divide between rural and urban areas • Only during last few years government started making serious effort to use ICT for its economic and social objectives • Monopoly in telecom market • Unfriendly business environment for ICT • Limited domestic market • Access to finance • Lack of basic business skills (marketing, etc.) among local entrepreneurs	• Even though prior to 1989 Bulgaria had relatively strong electronics and communications industry; lost its potential due to general economic downturn and lack of government focus on ICT. Coherent government support to ICT industry essential for long-term sustainable growth of the sector
India	• Indian education system has strong emphasis on science and technology, resulting in large number of science and engineering graduates • Cheaper labor, Indian ICT professionals demand much lower wages and made India attractive source for global outsourcing • Qualified workforce is another strength of the country; Indian	• Overseas demand may be detrimental for India's economy in in case of global downturn • Poor Communications Infrastructure is creating internal digital divide between rural and urban areas. Given large population and territorial extension, India has very low teledensity. Communications infrastructure overall poor and out-dated; currently only 3 in 100 people have access to telephone	• Government played crucial role in realizing potential of India as major IT power. A set of policies to encourage FDI and promote ICT sector implemented in the last decade • Institution building is crucial element of e-Development. In India, Ministry of Information Technology very proactive to develop infrastructure supporting development of information technology

	programmers known for strong technical skills	line; computer penetration per family is fairly low as well • Overall business environment can be improved. Only recently country has changed policies to encourage private funding	
Latvia	• S&T heritage • Preexisting S&T sector • Human capital	• Late starter • Telecom sector not open • Lack of financial resources • Lack of specific actions to attract FDI (diverted in most cases to Estonia	• Building a favorable environment to FDI essential to retain capacity in ICT sector • Late starter can still play a role in KE and find niche markets and applications • Increasing competition among CEECs in attracting FDI; many countries have similar endowments (labor force and S&T heritage) but different strategies • Proximity to ICT leaders is not necessarily a driving factor. It can be a facilitator but only in case of appropriate policies
Lithuania	• Increase in R&D expenditure from government • Dramatic expansion of mobile telecom sector • Focused government strategy • National action plan to foster e-Business (e-Commerce and e-Banking)	• Lack of financial resources • Unattractive investment environment • Unable to attract FDI • Not reliable regulatory framework • Heavily affected by Russian crisis • Late starter	• Location can matter: in case of Lithuania, the proximity to Russia has played detrimental role in its economic development, due to Russian crisis, whereas promoximity to other two Baltic countries has generated positive regional spill-over • Progressive adjustment to EU standards (both in terms of

Continued

Table 7.3 Continued

Country	Strengths	Weaknesses	Knowledge gained
			regulation and economic policy) has boosted PSD • Regional and international cooperation can be crucial for transitional economies in fostering ICT development
Moldova	• Privatization almost complete • Basic macro-economic variables under control	• Limited domestic market • Incapacity to attract FDI • Rural *vs.* urban divide • Low ICT penetration • Limited access to financial resources	• Need for a strong regulatory and legal environment • Need for a friendly business environment
Romania	• The ICT sector has grown considerably by shifting from a dominance in hardware to that of software • High quality of government polytechnic institutions that produce graduates for ICT sector • Lightly regulated mobile telecom market grows very fast, partially compensating for lack of modern fixed line infrastructure • Incumbent operator has been prevented from directly participating in ISP market.	• Overall slow economic reforms • Lack of government vision on ICT development in country • No strategic plan for ICT use within government • Privatization proceeded slowly • Lack of properly functioning financial system • Low teledensity with wide disparity between urban and rural areas • Outdated communications network • Only initial phase of telecom market liberalization	• Absence of appropriate legal and regulatory framework is probably single greatest obstacle to adoption and development of ICT in country; thus, difficult economic conditions are no excuse. Politics or lack of ICT expertise among government officials, or both, are the cause

	This made data/Internet market open for competition • Government willing to implement advanced G2B applications such as e-Procurement	• Absence of appropriate legal and regulatory framework for ICT development • High Internet access costs • Brain-drain • Limited success with attempts at high-tech parks • Low level of ICT awareness among local businesses • Lack of business skills among local ICT entrepreneurs	
Ukraine	• Availability of vast human resources at comparatively lower costs • Tradition in ICT and science and technology • Younger generation is interested in new technologies and applications and is slowly developing entrepreneurship pointing at innovation • Telecommunications and Internet markets have great potential for expansion and growth • Government increasingly committing itself to developing an ICT strategy	• Questionable legal system • Communications systems inadequate • Low specialization of production and industrial policy • Education system declining and needs to up-graded; • General business skill level is quite low: English language, management, marketing and finance skills poor among entrepreneurs • Funding for innovation and R&D not available from neither public nor private sources; access to capital remains major constraint to innovation • Unfavorable environment for foreign investments	• Government transparency essential to promote innovation • A consistent legal system contributes to a transparent and vibrant economy • Political uncertainty may hinder social and economic development (especially when leaders not inspired to invest in innovation • Slow pace of the privatization process has limited technology potential of Ukraine

8

e-Development Profiles of Developed Countries

A Australia

Australia has only recently started investing in ICT development. The major investment started in the mid-1990s, when the government tried to cope with Australian external and internal gaps. Externally, Australia is remotely located from major economic centers, being left aside by the global markets. Internally, the island's territorial extension and its scarcely populated hinterland have the potential of creating an internal digital divide and isolation. To overcome the danger of internal and external divide, the government has heavily invested in building adequate infrastructure.

Despite the late start, the government has been able to draft a proper set of legislation to foster ICT adoption (see Table 8.1). From the liberalization of the telecom market to the creation of a plausible e-Strategy, the 1997 *Networking the Nation Initiative* first, and the 2001 *Backing Australia's Initiative*, the government has shown a very focused and precise approach. The holistic approach taken by the government, has implied harmonic investments both in infrastructure and human capital, facilitating the development of appropriate training and educational programs to foster ICT development.

The government is committed to providing a light-handed regulatory framework to support and encourage the development of electronic commerce. The introduction of the Electronic Transactions Act represents a major step in meeting this commitment. The Act had a two-stage implementation. Before July 1, 2001 it only applied to laws of the Commonwealth specified in the regulations. From July 1, 2001 it applies to all laws of the Commonwealth unless they have been specifically exempted from the application of the Act. The Electronic Transactions Regulations 2000 contain 158 items identifying 101 laws of the Commonwealth which are exempted from the operation of the Act. This includes both legislation and subordinate legislation.

The creation of dedicated institutions, or the restructuring of preexisting ones, has facilitated the institutional adjustment to cope with the renovated

Table 8.1   Australia's main ICT indicators, 2003

Fixed line and mobile phone subscribers per 1,000 inhabitants	1261.80
Mobile phones per 1,000 inhabitants	719.46
PCs per 100 inhabitants	60.18
Internet users per 1,000 inhabitants	566.66
Internet hosts per 10,000 inhabitants	1,428.07

Sources: adapted from World Development Indicators Online (2005) and International Telecommunications Union (2005)

challenges posed by technology development. At first, it expanded the responsibilities of the Department of Communications by including information technology and the arts within its umbrella.

Moreover, in 1997, the government established the National Office for the Information Economy (NOIE). The National Office helps Australian citizens and businesses create a world-class online economy and society through its work developing, overseeing, and coordinating Commonwealth Government policy on electronic commerce, online services, and the Internet.

An Electronic Commerce Expert Group was created in mid-1997 within the Attorney-General's office. The expert group includes representatives from business, the private legal profession, and government who design appropriate interventions and monitor e-commerce promotion activities for the public sector.

Australia's communications sector is undergoing rapid growth (almost 11 percent per year between 1995 and 2000) and substantial change. Until the early 1990s, Telstra – then a wholly government-owned business – was the sole supplier of telephone services in Australia. However, a second network was established by a privately owned telecom company, Optus Communications. This situation of duopoly terminated in 1997, which represents the main cornerstone for the liberalization of the Australian telecommunications market.

In addition, the Telecommunications Act 1997 was passed, regulating the telecommunications industry, particularly the licensing of and obligations on carriers and service providers.

Currently, the telecommunications market is growing, despite the global trend, as foreign investors have found interest in Australia. A majority stake in Optus, subsequently acquired by Cable & Wireless in March 2001, agreed to sell the company to Singapore Telecommunications (SingTel). Since mid-1997 other telecom operators have also been free to offer their services on the Australian market. Most of these have concentrated on international calls and mobile services.

The Australian government has supported various activities in response to the lack of adequate ICT skills among the citizens, such as Empower

Australia, which is a valid example of viable public–private partnership. The program, sponsored by Microsoft and managed by the Department of Communications and Information Technology, targets skills training for disadvantaged people and works through a network of non-governmental organizations (NGOs).

Digital Bridge is another initiative that targets mainly the young part of the population to ensure harmonic development of ICT skills among the future generation of workers and citizens.

Backing Australia's Ability is the innovation action plan launched by the government in early 2001 to "translate Australian ideas into local jobs." The action plan is organized in sub-categories programs aimed at fostering SMEs' capability and opportunity in e-Commerce and supporting R&D, education, and training in ICT-related sectors.

To increase awareness of the potential of the Internet and the social value and relevance of new technologies, the Reach Out Bush Network has been established. It is an awareness and training program that, using a train-the-trainer model, has provided Internet training to the young part of the population, who in turn have trained others in their local communities. Moreover, the Reach Out Bush Network has addressed connectivity issues, providing computers in twenty rural communities.

The public administration has also been very keen in the adoption of new technologies to foster efficiency and increase transparency. Most of the governmental agencies have their own dedicated websites to disseminate information and ease the relations with the civil and business communities.

Fiscal incentives in R&D and heavy promotion of private sector development, through facilitating policies, incentives, and training from the government are proving to be successful tools for fostering the ICT sector. Proper actions have been taken to support the R&D efforts of the private sector, particularly of SMEs. Moreover, the COMET Program aims to fostering cooperation among SMEs and their integration into the national and international e-marketplaces.

Australia has numerous strengths that facilitated the implementation of its e-Development strategy, among which are the facilitation of access to finance for SMEs, R&D incentives, investments in human capital, institutional and regulatory framework, and not least, public–private partnership.

However, it also has to deal with a few challenges, such as its location (Australia is remotely located from major economic centers), the territorial extension of the island, and its sparsely populated hinterland and its internal digital divide.

The Australian case shows that size does matter; reaching the dispersed population in rural areas has been a challenge for Australia, but it also shows that fiscal incentives are pivotal to facilitating R&D and fostering innovation.

Australia's experience is also useful for assessing the viability of public–private partnership. Many private sector entities have been involved in the support and creation of the research network. The investments in infrastructure have been accurately accompanied by support measures for human capital, by providing assistance in training and developing adequate structures and opportunities to prevent the brain-drain phenomenon.

B　Finland

Finland has had impressive economic performance since the mid-1990s. This was linked to the phenomenal success of the country's electronic equipment sector, which to a large extent can be attributed to a single company: Nokia. However, Finland has quite a remarkable record in other areas of e-Development as well. In many categories, such as Internet penetration, use of ICT by the business and banking sector, development and use of wireless-phone hardware and applications, Finland is one of the most advanced countries in the world (see Table 8.2).

Since the middle of the 1980s Finland has aimed at improving its telecommunications markets, increasing services, and lowering prices by increasing competition. The Finnish ICT legal and regulatory framework complies with that of the European Union.

The Finnish Government created appropriate institution framework with clear division of responsibilities between institutions. Finland also has several rather unique public institutions that increase the competitiveness of the local ICT sector:

- SITRA, the Finnish National Fund for Research and Development, is an independent public foundation that was created in the 1970s to address the lack of venture capital in the country. It acts as a think-tank and a private venture capital fund with "social conscience." The list of SITRA's Information Society projects portfolio contains a total of 142 information societies.
- TEKES, the National Technology Agency, provides funding and expert services for R&D projects in small- and medium-sized businesses seeking to develop specific ICT applications. Besides providing financial support

Table 8.2　Finland's main ICT indicators, 2003

Fixed line and mobile phone subscribers per 1,000 inhabitants	1401.55
Mobile phones per 1,000 inhabitants	909.59
PCs per 100 inhabitants	44.17
Internet users per 1,000 inhabitants	533.82
Internet hosts per 10,000 inhabitants	2,436.55

Sources: adapted from World Development Indicators Online (2005) and International Telecommunications Union (2005)

for R&D projects of particular enterprises, TEKES also has so-called "technology programs" that are used to promote development in specific sectors of technology or industry.

Finland has long had one of the world's least-regulated telecom markets, fostering a tradition of competition and innovation. Liberalization of telecommunications networks was completed far ahead of most other European countries. Today, Finland has one of the most competitive telecommunications markets in the world, which, according to OECD figures, has made Finland the cheapest country in the world in which to go online. Almost every Finn has access to broadband networks. Altogether, 98 percent of Finns live within a few kilometers from high-speed fiber-optic cable networks and all citizens have free access to the Internet at local public libraries, making public Internet access widespread in the country.

In Finland, the provision of the universal service is not tied to fixed networks only. A telecommunications company may also provide these services through its mobile networks. More and more Finns are preferring a mobile phone to a fixed line. Finland is one of the most advanced countries in the world in developing and using wireless-phone applications.

Finland invested massively in the technological infrastructure of its educational sector. The uniqueness of the Finnish plan was probably that it covered the entire school system as well as libraries, research institutions, archives, etc. This has generated major synergy effects.

Finland's system of higher education plays a very important role in advancing R&D activities. Universities have a degree of autonomy that gives them extensive latitude for independent research decisions. Plus, even though all Finnish universities are state-run, the government provides only about 70 percent of their funding. Thus, universities are encouraged to get involved in R&D for the private sector.

In general, the high level of public–private partnerships and cooperation in education and R&D is a prominent feature of the Finnish e-Development program.

The government ICT promotion campaigns have been quite modest in financial terms. Finns have been adopting ICT rather enthusiastically and little promotion from the government was needed.

Data sharing plays a very important role in the Finnish public sector. Electronic transactions within agencies as well as between agencies and customers are rather well developed. Business-to-Government (B2G) applications are popular, for example about 45 percent of Finnish SMEs use Internet in handling with administration. However, many existing government sites are not very informative. Moreover, not all public sector organizations have websites.

The Finnish government was the first to create a generic system for electronic identification, data transfer encryption, and digital signatures for electronic transactions: its electronic ID cards. These cards are not mandatory and have not yet become popular.

The Finnish electrical and electronic goods industries expanded rapidly in the late 1990s at an annual average rate of almost 34 percent. However, most of this impressive growth was attributable to one company: Nokia, the world's largest producer of mobile telephones and a leading supplier of mobile- and fixed-telecommunications networks.

Application software industry and content production are still relatively young in Finland. Finnish enterprises have made progress only in a few areas, such as imbedded software and data security.

Finnish enterprises have been engaged in electronic commerce for a long time by means of Electronic Data Interchange (EDI) and they enthusiastically embraced new opportunities opened up by the Internet. The situation is similar in the financial sector. Finnish banks have been providing their corporate and retail customers with online services for nearly twenty-five years.

Finland's rapid technological development can be partially explained by a traditionally high level of competition in the telecommunications field. In the 1930s, there were more than 800 local telephone companies and some 50 still existed in the mid-1990s. The large number of operators promoted fierce competition among equipment suppliers, which led to fast technological development.

In addition to the competitive environment, a high level of clustering promoted the growth of the ICT sector in Finland, especially its innovation system. The clusters include networks of large and small companies as well as research, training, and corporate organizations.

Innovation activities in SMEs are actively supported by the government, mainly by SITRA. The Finnish government plays a very active role in promoting clustering between the ICT sector and the "traditional economy." One of the most interesting of TEKES's programs is the Information Networking in the Construction Process Program (VERA) that supported electronic networking and cooperation between different actors in the construction business and ICT sector. However, the taxation is heavy on labor in the Finnish ICT sector, and conditions rather unattractive for FDI, which may hamper the optimal development of the Finnish ICT sector.

The success of Finnish ICT strategy can be explained by the following factors:

- Early deregulation of the telecom market and privatization of telecom operator;
- Low telecommunications access charges;
- Wide adoption of mobile technology; the provision of the universal service is not tied to fixed networks only; a telecommunications company may also provide these services through its mobile networks;
- Promoting a high level of competition in the ICT industry;
- Public–private investments and partnership in R&D;

- Support of R&D for SMEs;
- Access to finance for R&D;
- Promoting networking both within the ICT cluster and between the cluster and "traditional economy";
- Human capital and education;
- Connecting schools to the Internet;
- Introduction of electronic ID cards.

Nonetheless, Finland still has to face some challenges. Its ICT sector relies too heavily on only one company, Nokia, its e-Government is somewhat underdeveloped, and Finland is a rather unattractive FDI pole. In addition, the public sector plays too big a role in the national economy, data security problems are the biggest hindrance to the utilization of the Internet in business, the labor is heavily taxed, the population is small and the domestic market limited, and finally, the Finns show a low level of entrepreneurship.

Overall, the Finnish e-Development experience is rather unique. The country has several features that should have hindered successful e-Development, e.g. Finland has failed to create a favorable macro-economic situation or favorable conditions for inward direct investments. Thus, Finland's success cannot be explained only by technological and economic factors.

The building of the information society in Finland has some idiosyncratic features. For example, Finns are known for being creative, persistent, and hard-working people. They are very interested in all kinds of new technology and adopt it rather enthusiastically. These kinds of human and cultural factors can potentially contribute to a very large share of the Finnish e-Development success. The Finnish case study stresses the importance of "soft factors" for e-Development.

C   Ireland

Within a decade (1994–2003) Ireland transformed itself from a relatively undeveloped country to one of the fastest growing economies in the OECD. The growth was driven mainly by high-tech exports, particularly of computer hardware and software.

The e-Development record of Ireland may be considered in two dimensions:

(1) Production of ICT, for example development of software. Ireland is one of the world leaders in software exports. Inward investment by information technology companies has been one of the keys to Ireland's prosperity, and the country is now attracting large e-Commerce and other Internet-related investments. Low corporate taxes, competitive labor rates, a good telecommunications infrastructure, skilled labor, export-oriented economy, as well as responsive government, have been the essential drivers in luring business to Ireland.

(2) Consumption of ICT within the country. In this dimension Ireland is rather an advanced country, but not among the world leaders. For example, the number of Internet users per 1,000 people and level of ICT use in the banking sector are below the EU average (see Table 8.3). However, the country advances very fast (in 2004, 65 percent of Irish businesses conducted online banking) in this area, which shows that government efforts are effective.

There are several factors that may explain Ireland's success. The Irish economy has several characteristics that are prerequisites for the successful development of the ICT sector, especially in regard to attracting foreign investment in the sector, such as favorable macroeconomic conditions, an export-oriented economy (Ireland is one of the most trade-dependent economies in the world), a favorable taxation regime (Ireland has the lowest rate of corporation tax in Europe), and a highly educated workforce.

The Irish government has played a very proactive role in recognizing the importance of ICT for the economy. Major elements of the Ireland's e-Development program include:

- Maximum liberalization of telecom market;
- Promotion of FDI in the ICT sector, for example through favorable taxation regime and high international connectivity;
- Creation of favorable ICT-related regulatory environment;
- ICT skills training with heavy emphasis on introduction of ICT-related courses in the higher education system;
- Promotional campaigns;
- Maximum adoption of ICT by the government.

The government's approach to the regulation of electronic commerce activities was flexible and supportive of business. A public consultation process to outline legislative proposals was initiated (August 1999) with participants from business organizations and private individuals. Legislation regulating e-Commerce has been light and the government has as a specific policy goal the development of Ireland as an e-Commerce hub in Europe.

Table 8.3   Ireland's main ICT indicators, 2003

Fixed line and mobile phone subscribers per 1,000 inhabitants	1370.98
Mobile phones per 1,000 inhabitants	879.64
PCs per 100 inhabitants	42.08
Internet users per 1,000 inhabitants	316.67
Internet hosts per 10,000 inhabitants	399.19

Sources: adapted from World Development Indicators Online (2005) and International Telecommunications Union (2005)

The Irish government created an appropriate institution framework with clear division of responsibilities between institutions. It also established an overarching, umbrella agency that coordinates e-Development activities of different government agencies and other ICT actors in the country, the Information Society Commission.

Ireland's government was one of the first to understand that countries increasingly compete in the global economy. The National Competitiveness Council (NCC) was established in 1997 to report on the main challenges facing the enterprise sector in Ireland and to make recommendations to the government for the improvement of the country's international competitive position. The NCC coordinates its work with the Information Society Commission on issues of mutual concern.

An important element of Ireland's success is the adoption of a public–private approach to e-Development. A number of public–private organizations were created to help the government to invest in ICT promotion, training, and education, develop e-Commerce regulations, and solve connectivity problems. Such partnership benefits both sides.

A modern, liberalized telecommunications sector was determined as the most important prerequisite for successful development of the information society in Ireland. The Irish telecommunications market was dramatically restructured in the course of the 1990s, with a progressive liberalization of the sector culminating in the privatization of the state-owned monopoly operator. Ireland has also made rapid progress since 2000 in developing its broadband capacity, especially in the area of international connectivity.

The next most important priority of the government was ICT training and education to provide skilled labor for the industry. ICT-related courses were introduced in schools and universities and a special network connected educational entities to the Internet. Serious attention was given to ICT training of school teachers.

Ireland's government is very good at creating and satisfying demand for IT professionals in the country at the same time. The booming ICT production sector creates demand for skilled labor, government's heavy investment in higher education allows for the "production" of a great number of IT graduates, which, in turn, helps to creates favorable conditions for investment in the country's ICT sector. Two trends reinforce each other.

The Irish Government launched an extensive ICT awareness campaign that included specific programs targeted at the "enablers" of the information society, i.e. those who play the most important roles in the emergence of an information society in the country. One of the campaign's interesting elements is the e-Commerce Business Awareness Campaign, predominantly designed for SMEs. The Irish Business and Employers Confederation and the Information Society Commission jointly organized a nationwide series of seminars on e-Commerce. The seminars featured e-Commerce case studies and presentations by the leading service providers on how to develop and implement a successful e-Commerce strategy. e-Business best practice case studies were collected and widely disseminated in the business community by the Information Society Commission. The awareness campaign also included programs targeted at the late ICT adopter, such as non-office workers, the unemployed, and people working in traditional sectors.

The Irish Government also promotes the whole spectrum of e-Government activities: Government-to-Government (G2G), Government-to-Citizen (G2C), and Government-to-Business (G2B) projects. The last two types are aimed at making the life of citizens and businesses easier by allowing them to interact with the government online, for example to pay taxes and fees. This way government not only increases the efficiency of its own work, but also involves business and citizens in broadening the use of ICT. This represents true government e-Development leadership which should be replicated in other countries.

The government identified several priority sectors: e-Commerce services and utilities, business to business, retail and financial services. The government's strategy is largely focused on the creation of a favorable business environment and attracting inward investment. It actively promotes the development of the broadband networks and encourages Irish small- and medium-enterprises (SMEs) to adopt e-Commerce. Much attention is given to development of a strong local content industry, and an indigenous software industry competing in niche markets. The government actively promotes collaboration and strategic alliances between the sub-segments of the content industry, and software and electronics sectors.

The case of Ireland highlights a tremendous number of success factors needed for the successful implementation of an e-Development strategy, listed as follows:

- Favorable macroeconomic conditions;
- Export-oriented economy;
- Favorable taxation regime: Ireland has the lowest rate of corporation tax in Europe;
- Very highly educated workforce;
- One of the highest levels of PC ownership in the world;
- Proactive role of the government;
- Maximum liberalization of telecom market;
- Rapid progress since in developing broadband capacity, especially in the area of international connectivity;
- Creation of favorable ICT-related regulatory environment;
- ICT skills training with heavy emphasis on introduction of ICT-related courses in the higher education system;
- Government-supported promotional campaigns;
- Maximum adoption of ICT by the government;
- Adoption of public–private approach to e-Development.

Ireland's government is very good at creating and satisfying the demand for IT professionals in the country: a booming ICT production sector creates a demand for skilled labor and the government's heavy investment in higher education allows for "production" of a great number of IT graduates, which, in turn, helps to create favorable conditions for investment in the country's ICT sector. The two trends reinforce each other.

On the other hand, Ireland has to face a limited domestic market, a relatively underdeveloped banking sector with low use of electronic payments, and relatively high costs of Internet access and slow connection speeds available for residential Internet users. Moreover, conditions for producing ICT for export are better than conditions for their "consumption" within the country.

Ireland's focus on building modern infrastructure as a prerequisite for successful development of the information society pays off. The maximum liberalization of the telecom market helps the country to advance quickly to leadership positions in e-Development.

Ireland's e-Development experience is particularly relevant for small countries with a limited domestic market and skilled ICT labor force, such as Romania and Ukraine. The creation of an export-oriented ICT industry may benefit these countries greatly, including solving the huge problem of the brain-drain.

D   New Zealand

New Zealand is a small economy, still heavily reliant on commodity production in agriculture, fishing, and forestry. The New Zealand economy has been in recovery mode since encountering a brief recession over the first half of 1998. A major stimulus to the economic recovery since the end of 1998 has been strong growth from the primary production sector indicators, in the context of organizations such as the OECD. In response, the government has launched a massive campaign to deal with the situation, aiming to rank among the top half of OECD countries in the ICT sector by 2011 (see Table 8.4). A long-term strategy is in place that lays heavy emphasis on innovation, creativity, and workforce skills. There are signs that there is a need for intervention in the ICT sector, yet it is still unclear whether the government will be able to design and deliver the appropriate set of policies and interventions.

New Zealand currently displays a competitive deregulated telecommunications environment. The promotion of competition and market-led development is central to government policy.

The New Zealand Government passed a new Telecommunications Act Law at the end of 2001. This new law's main objective is to bring greater certainty, investment, competition, opportunity, and consumer benefit to the New Zealand telecommunications market. The establishment of the Telecommunications Commissioner is a landmark of this new legislation.

Table 8.4   New Zealand's main ICT indicators, 2003

Fixed line and mobile phone subscribers per 1,000 inhabitants	1096.73
Mobile phones per 1,000 inhabitants	648.26
PCs per 100 inhabitants	41.38
Internet users per 1,000 inhabitants	526.29
Internet hosts per 10,000 inhabitants	1,183.27

Sources: adapted from World Development Indicators Online (2005) and International Telecommunications Union (2005)

The Commissioner will reside within the Commerce Commission and will be responsible for resolving industry disputes over regulated services. The Commissioner will work with the industry to promote competition for the long-term benefit of New Zealand.

The government objective in introducing this new legislation is the restructuring and reform of the telecommunications industry in New Zealand to deliver a better deal for consumers. The new telecommunication law regime ensures a fine balance between encouraging further investment by existing players and lowering the barriers to investment by new players.

The Government of New Zealand started the deregulation and liberalization of the telecommunications sector in the late 1980s. As a result, a highly competitive telecommunications sector has been created in New Zealand. The telecommunications operator, previously part of the state-owned New Zealand Post Office, was privatized in 1987 and sold to US and New Zealand private interests in 1990.

Despite the fact that the telecommunications sector was fully privatized, the national government reserved the right to regulate certain parts of the telecommunication sector as part of the "Kiwi Share" agreement. This agreement obliges the privatized telecom operator to provide free local residential calls, not to discriminate between rural and urban customers in pricing, and to keep phone-rental cost increases at or below inflation.

The government introduced legislation in May 2001 for a new regulatory framework for the telecom sector. A telecom regulator will be established with the power to regulate prices and services access if other resolution procedures fail.

The following series of initiatives are a central part of the ICT strategy for schools launched in October 1998 with a total funding over 3 years of $16 m:

(1) The ICT Professional Development Schools: the intention is to develop throughout New Zealand, clusters of excellence, innovation and good practice in the use of ICT that will contract to provide professional development and support to other schools in their region and the rest of the

country. This project is part of the initiatives identified in "Interactive Education," an information and communication strategy for schools released on October 28, 1998.

(2) The ICT Principals Leadership: the initiative is a professional development program for all school principals across New Zealand to develop leadership skills in planning for the use and implementation of ICT in schools. The main phase of the program was completed in 1999 but there was also a small-scale program in 2000 and 2001.

(3) The On-Line Resource Center: the intention is to develop a central On-Line Resource center to provide all schools with a mechanism for the delivery of multimedia resources, including curriculum and administration resources, using the Internet.

The Government of New Zealand passed the Electronic Transactions Bill. This e-Transactions bill provides the legal foundations for e-Signature and public access to information in order to facilitate the use of electronic technology. Another main objective is to remove legislative impediments to dealing with government electronically, reduce transaction costs for business and the general public, and to promote consistency between New Zealand law and that of the country's major trading partners.

The government launched the e-Government strategy on April 26, 2001. The government's aim, under this strategy, is to create a public sector that is structured, resourced, and managed to perform in a manner that meets the needs of New Zealanders in the information age and which increasingly delivers information and services using online capabilities.

The e-Commerce strategy is an integral part of the government's broader policy initiatives to promote economic, innovative, and social development. Implementing the strategy is a shared responsibility. It requires a partnership between government, business, and the broader community and will require continuing close consultation between all parties, including with Maori.

The goals of the strategy are to capitalize fully on competitive advantages in a networked world, support enterprise by providing an environment that rewards innovation and entrepreneurship, and foster the highest quality e-Commerce skills to build innovation, and technical and management capability. The government's main target and objective through the implementation of the e-Commerce strategy is to deliver better-quality, cheaper, and faster services to its customers through the introduction of online services, and lead by example through e-Government and e-Procurement.

The Ministry of Research, Science and Technology (MoRST) policies and programs recognize that the most important international Science and Technology linkages are the researcher-to-researcher links, and that the primary role of government is to provide an environment which supports these links. According to this ministry's policy, international networks of the global knowledge age will provide the foundations of a successful national innovation system, hence the change of focus toward creating international linkages with other research institutions. Creating international linkages and partnerships is a process to adapt more effectively in the knowledge economy era, to understand the opportunities and challenges hidden behind a strong R&D policy, and to realize all the implications for the development of the country of New Zealand.

Technology transfer is a key component of government-funded R&D programs, whether through peer-reviewed papers, popular publications, workshops, conferences, demonstration projects, Internet websites, etc. Technology New Zealand helps businesses develop and adopt new technology by encouraging technological innovation in product and process development and strengthening technology management skills, by providing access to local and international technology information sources and advisory services and by funding people to research and develop new technologies within businesses.

New Zealand has a number of advantages to successfully implement its e-Development strategy. The small size of the country allows for the ability to respond quickly to the changes of the global environment to meet international standards, its regulatory environment is open and transparent, and its population is multicultural and well-educated. There is also a recognition of the opportunities and challenges in the ICT sector, an adoption of international standards in all the economic and social fields, and remarkable success during the first steps of e-Commerce policy adoption (2000).

New Zealand has an advanced technology and low cost-base that are attractive to foreign investors. The country has been in the top ten countries in the world for Internet access on a per capita basis since 1993, and has been amongst the highest spenders in the world on IT equipment per capita for the past two to three years. The country has strong foundations in quality and price-competitive infrastructure services in energy, transport, telecommunications, and professional services–by world standards.

New Zealand consumers and small businesses are comfortable with performing electronic transactions. The country has well-established e-Government services, including online customs services to importers and exporters and online company registration.

However, New Zealand also has to overcome some hurdles: a shortage of management, leadership, and entrepreneurial e-Commerce skills; a relatively low level of understanding of the opportunities afforded by e-Commerce and the information and communications technology (ICT) revolution; varying levels of ICT-literacy in the community as a whole; an uneven distribution of infrastructure capability at reasonable cost, particularly in rural communities; a lack of integration or connectivity to global business networks; the short supply of technical graduates from tertiary institutions; the emigration of skilled New Zealanders, particularly IT personnel with a high degree of technical skill who are attracted by the pay and opportunities overseas; the need to develop an innovation culture; and a lack of good-quality information to support policy formation.

To overcome the digital divide between rural and urban areas, the New Zealand government intervened actively in the privatization and deregulation process by reserving the right to regulate certain parts of the telecommunications sector. This involved the provision of free local residential calls and the non-discrimination between rural and urban areas as far as cost of communications is concerned. Despite the small and remote domestic market, the government of New Zealand has still been able to develop innovations in the ICT sector and to attract FDI from all around the world.

Instead of creating national standards that would apply to the ICT sector, New Zealand found it more appropriate to abide by preexisting international ICT standards. The government fostered an open and fully deregulated ICT market, which helped in attracting the interest of foreign investors and moving in faster pace toward the same regulatory framework as that in ICT-developed countries.

E   Singapore

Singapore is a very good example of the mix of policy and economic interventions designed by the government to drive and support the ICT sector. The Singaporean Government has understood the limited capabilities of the small island to compete in the global marketplace (due to lack of natural resources and a real industrial sector) and has focused on establishing the small country as a networked economy and society to become the main international hub for e-Business in the region. In pursuing such an ambitious goal, the government has undertaken major steps toward liberalization of crucial sectors, such as telecommunications, banking, finance, and insurance.

The continuous growth and development of Singapore hinges on the great commitment of the government to ICT. In fact, since the early 1980s the Singaporean Government has shown strong interest in the new technologies and has tried to take advantage of the new applications to drive economic and social development internally, and pave the way for the leadership role of Singapore in the Asian region.

The role played by the government to promote ICT development in the country is three-fold. First, as a user, the government has introduced ICT infrastructures and applications in the public administration since the early 1980s. Today, e-Government initiatives include a complete e-Procurement program and a specific e-Government portal for citizens. Second, as a provider, the government has always paid sound attention to infrastructure issues. Apart from speeding up the liberalization process of the ICT market, the government has promoted the creation of a valid network of communications and supported IT hardware adoption in public places, households,

Table 8.5   Singapore's main ICT indicators, 2003

Fixed line and mobile phone subscribers per 1,000 inhabitants	1302.75
Mobile phones per 1,000 inhabitants	852.50
PCs per 100 inhabitants	62.20
Internet users per 1,000 inhabitants	508.77
Internet hosts per 10,000 inhabitants	1,155.31

Sources: adapted from World Development Indicators Online (2005) and International Telecommunications Union (2005)

and firms. Finally, as a promoter, the government has tailored its services and policies to the needs of citizens and firms. The facilitation of training for the workforce and society has been vital in spreading the use of ICT (see Table 8.5).

In its efforts to foster innovation and move toward a knowledge-based economy, the government has been very active in the four main pillars of development. In terms of policy making, the government since the mid-1980s has set up national action plans and strategies for the computerization of the country, working in parallel on national IT plans and e-Government plans. In its latest IT plan, *Connected Singapore* (started in 2003), the government is now focusing its efforts on new areas that require creative input – education, design, the arts – and on potential new growth areas – value-added mobile services, infrastructure for wireless, and wired networks.

To ensure that all the different issues related to electronic transaction were properly identified and evaluated, the government in January 1997 created the e-Commerce Policy Committee to ensure that the legal and policy environment in Singapore was most conducive to e-commerce development. The Committee completed its work in the end of 1997. Following the recommendations of the committee, the Singaporean Government and Parliament worked together to respond properly to the needs of certainty and security in the e-Business scenario. In July 1998, the Electronic Transactions Act (ETA) was enacted to provide a legal foundation for electronic signatures. The act deals mainly with commercial code for e-Commerce transactions, the use of electronic applications and licenses for the public sector, and the liability of service providers.

The far-sighted approach of the government has been reflected in the creation of an appropriate institutional framework to set and support the policy and guidelines of ICT development. The various agencies coordinate their efforts to create opportunities for Singapore to become a logistics and information and communication (infocomm) hub, and an education center, by supporting the development of information communications and software businesses.

The strategy positions of the government were easily updated according to the changing needs and technologies thanks to the creation of appropriate institutions monitoring the development and implementation of the action plans. The National Computer Board (NCB) has been the overarching institution monitoring the implementation of the action plans and re-evaluating and up-dating the strategies. Moreover, the National Science and Technology Board (NSTB) develops Singapore's capabilities in science and technology to strengthen industrial and service sectors. The Economic Development Board has the responsibility of industrial planning, development and promotion of investments in manufacturing and services, as well as upgrading local business capabilities. The creation of dedicated institutions has supported the e-Development strategy of the government by efficiently allocating resources and creating institutional certainty and accountability.

The government has understood the importance of a liberalized telecommunications market to foster the whole ICT sector. SingTel, the state-owned operator, was partially privatized in late 1993 and 1996. Despite the relevant stake of the government in the incumbent operator, the market has been gradually opened to full competition, thanks to the licenses granted to two other fixed telephony service providers (Starhub and Singapore Cable Vision). Competition in the mobile services has been more active, since the end of SingTel's monopoly in mid-1997. Presently there are four mobile services operators that boost competition in the vibrant wireless sector.

The policy making of the government not only provided for strategy positions and action plans, but also included heavy investments in human capital. In fact, the government supported direct training for public officers and awareness campaigns to build confidence and usage of ICT. Investments have been, and still are, made in training and continuous education for citizens and workers. Apart from the e-Learning program promoted by the Ministry of Education, there are other significant and valuable examples of dedicated training and continuous education promoted by the government, either directly or through one of the specific e-Development agencies, mainly the IDA (Infocomm Development Authority).

The government, and related agencies, is committed to helping citizens familiarize themselves with ICT applications and services, so that the Internet and related services are gradually becoming an integral part of the daily life of most Singaporean citizens, workers, and students – what IDA calls the "e-Lifestyle." Most of the schools and universities are equipped with PCs. SingTel (the telecom operator) has provided all the residential phone subscribers with a free Internet account. In addition, to ensure harmonic and balanced appropriation of ICT the government has launched a program targeted at low-income households, different ethnic groups, and late adopters; the program includes donation of equipment, provision of free Internet access, and basic training to low-income households. Moreover, to overcome the divide within the nation that may arise given the four official languages (English, Chinese, Malay, and Tamil), the government is making strong efforts in promoting local language content.

Applications of advanced e-Government services have been early adopted in Singapore. The first applications involved G2G solutions, networking the Public Administration, and promoting informatization of the whole governmental process from the mid-1980s. G2B soon followed and today services to facilitate private enterprises (e-Taxation, e-Procurement and e-Registration) are widely offered. Applications to foster government–society relations are supported by a central portal, eCitizen, launched in 1999. eCitizen is the one-stop integrated portal for government services designed according to citizens' needs. The portal is a window to a wide range of services to guide the citizen through the host of services provided by the government and other governmental agencies around culture, recreation and sports, defense and security, education, learning and employment, family and community development, health and environment, housing, and transport and travel.

Development efforts help local companies acquire technical and business capabilities that allow them to compete in the world's infocomm markets. IDA supports local companies in building partnerships at local and international level through the Infocomm Local Industry Upgrading Program (iLIUP). The program helps local ICT companies improve their competitiveness and access global networks. It also connects multinationals with local companies that can share their experience and knowledge of local and regional markets.

Singapore's implementation of its e-Development strategy was facilitated by the very proactive role of its government, the far-sighted approach of the government, and a heavy investment in telecom infrastructure (almost 90 percent of household, academia, and public and private sectors connected). In the implementation of the strategy, institution building, creation of an appropriate legal framework, and gradual opening up of the telecommunications sector have been essential.

Moreover, Singapore faces only a few challenges, such as a small domestic market and the high interference of the government in the economy, deemed sometimes as over-regulation.

Singapore's e-Development case shows that e-Development is not only about infrastructure: human capital and awareness are crucial to ensure success. Singapore is now becoming an international pole of attraction for digital exchanges and positioning itself as a digital living lab.

F Slovenia

Slovenia has been active in the promotion and development of the information society since the early 1990s, and has successfully developed infrastructure for the information society (see Table 8.6). The government has been devoted to fostering the usage of information and communication technologies, and the proximity to European countries has always played a crucial role in easing the transition to an open market economy.

Its sound economic and political background has allowed Slovenia to be the only Eastern European country never to have had an IMF program. Without external pressures forcing Slovenia to push through structural reforms, it has been able to conduct a genuine public debate about the direction of economic policy. A strong culture of consensus-building has brought political stability, and has also meant that there have been no major reform reversals.

The science and technology policy of the Slovenian Government is defined in the following two documents: the National Research Program and the Technology Policy of the Government of the Republic of Slovenia. These policy formulations pave the way for the establishment of the Information Society in Slovenia that will bring the country to an even greater degree of integration within the European Union.

The government and the parliament have adopted and implemented relevant e-Legislation to increase trust and confidence in new means of conducting business and interacting with the public administration. In 1999, the Parliament adopted the Personal Data Protection Act, that is aligned with the EU Directives. The Intellectual Property Law is also harmonized with EU legislation. The Law on Electronic Commerce and Electronic Signature was adopted in 2000.

Slovenia's approach, in terms of institution building, represents an isolated case among the transitional economies. In 2000, the new government established the dismantling of the Ministry of Science and Technology and the subsequent assimilation of its constituent parts into the Ministry of Economy (Technology section) and the Ministry of Education, Science and Sport (Science section). Similarly, the Ministry of Economy has absorbed the Ministry of Small Business and Tourism, as well as the Ministry for International Trade and Development. A new Ministry of the Information Society has been formed. The Government Council for the Use of

Table 8.6   Slovenia's main ICT indicators, 2003

Fixed line and mobile phone subscribers per 1,000 inhabitants	1277.65
Mobile phones per 1,000 inhabitants	870.88
PCs per 100 inhabitants	32.55
Internet users per 1,000 inhabitants	375.75*
Internet hosts per 10,000 inhabitants	214.76

* 2002 data
Sources: adapted from World Development Indicators Online (2005) and International Telecommunications Union (2005)

Information Technology in State Bodies and Public Institutions has been established to deal with various aspects of informatics in government bodies.

Telekom Slovenije (TS, the public telecommunications operator) is still 74 percent state-owned, as plans for partial privatization have so far not been implemented, repeatedly postponed since 2001. TS's fixed-line monopoly officially expired at the beginning of 2001. Other telecom services, such as mobile telephony and Internet service providers, are in theory open to competition, although impediments to competition exist – for example, TS forces Internet service providers to use its own network. Both telecom privatization and tariff rebalancing are lagging behind schedule, but the infrastructure is well developed and Slovenia places itself among the middle ranking of the EU counterparts as far as telecom infrastructure is concerned.

The Young Researchers Program, launched by the Ministry of Education, Science and Sport to rejuvenate the human capital in S&T, and foster innovation and research, started in 1985 and is still ongoing. The program promotes R&D and sponsors all levels of higher education from undergraduate to Ph.D.

The main principles underlying the implementation of research policy are as follows: the training of researchers and other experts, the creation of a balance between scientific disciplines, the promotion of the application of scientific achievements in order to meet national needs, the promotion of international scientific and technological cooperation, and the encouragement of a broader and deeper public awareness of science.

ICT is becoming increasingly familiar to Slovenian citizens and entrepreneurs. Slovenians are particularly technologically savvy, and the geographical and cultural proximity to Western Europe has allowed the general public to develop a greater understanding of technology and its potential. The Slovenian Science Foundation's annual Slovenian Science Festival remains the main instrument in the popularization of scientific developments in Slovenia and abroad. The SSF program the "Public Understanding of Science and Technology" is one of the major tools used to increase awareness of ICT.

The Slovenian Government has understood the potential of ICT applications to foster efficiency and increase transparency in the work of public administration. This vision has allowed the government to play a crucial role both as ICT user and provider. As a user, the government has adopted a very sophisticated ICT system for cabinet meetings. As a provider, the creation of an e-Government portal http://e-uprava.gov.si provides e-Applications to citizens. Currently, citizens can apply, via the Internet, for copies from the registry of births, marriages, or the deceased. In the near future, more civic services will be available for citizens, and other services will be included for the business community. Data from the land register will soon be available, and for e-Taxation services it will be possible to submit one's personal income statement or data concerning VAT calculations.

Established in 1993, the Government Center for Informatics provides for a uniform data communication network that is primarily intended for the state but partly also for public administration (including the majority of government offices and agencies, some public institutes, and also major municipalities). In addition, the Center runs the computer center that is at the disposition of government bodies.

ICT adoption within the business community is quite encouraging: 100 percent of large, 98 percent of medium-sized, and over 91 percent of small-sized enterprises have access to the Internet. Electronic business in the sense of receiving orders online: 32 percent of large, 21 percent of medium-sized, and 12 percent of small-sized enterprises. The obstacles to a swifter development of electronic commerce and the use of the Internet are telecommunication costs, which are still relatively high, and the lack of adequate staff.

The government is providing adequate support to the creation of technology parks. The Ministry of Science and Technology subsidizes up to 50 percent of the eligible R&D costs of technology centers, 50 percent for consultancy services, and up to 25 percent of the R&D project costs linked with the infrastructure.

In 1994 the Ministry of Higher Education, Science and Technology harmonized R&D legislation and initiatives with EU standards. In 2004, the government spent 1.2 percent of GDP on R&D. The Ministry selects the projects to be sponsored, and the competition is based on a call for tenders.

Public–private partnerships for R&D are supported by the government through a measure launched in 2000 to strengthen company research and foster cooperation between researchers, universities, and companies.

One of the main success factors of Slovenia has been its openness even before independence. Many Slovene factories obtained Western technology in the 1970–80s through licensing agreements, which enabled them to become internationally competitive. By the end of the 1980s Slovenia was the richest republic of the Socialist Federal Republic of Yugoslavia. This openness has also always been reflected in the approach to international and regional trade. Given the small size of the domestic market, all but the smallest Slovene enterprises are reliant on export markets.

The proximity to European countries has always played a crucial role in easing the transition to an open market economy. Slovenia is firmly establishing itself as an open market economy and ICT is contributing to this transition by placing Slovenia among the leading countries in Europe to adopt, promote, and use new technologies.

Among the critical success factors of the implementation of Slovenian e-Development strategy, we note the proactive role of the government, political and economic openness since the early years of its independence, the existence of private sector promotional activities to build e-Commerce, a well-developed telecommunications infrastructure, an appropriate regulatory framework for the knowledge economy, the proximity to the EU, a small population and territory, and the existence of technology parks and incubators. However, we also emphasize that the Slovenian domestic market is small and its telecommunications market not fully liberalized.

Slovenia's case shows that the private sector should engage in promoting the information society; private sector promotional activities are as important as a proactive government role. Also, size does matter because a small geographical extension and small population make infrastructure and awareness issues easier to be addressed. Finally, location also matters. The proximity to Western Europe has played a crucial role in Slovenia's development and transition.

9

e-Development Profiles of Transitioning Countries

A Argentina

Argentina had many of the necessary elements for dynamic e-Development – a relatively modern telecommunications infrastructure (see Table 9.1), the highest per capita GDP and second-highest life expectancy in Latin America, high literacy rates, well-trained human capital, ICT market open to competition, and appropriate regulatory framework to attract foreign direct investment. The impressive growth of the ICT sector in the 1990s stumbled, however, due to current economic crisis, largely caused by badly structured government fiscal policy.

Even though the Argentine Government does not have a clear and proactive vision of ICT development in the country, it has been quite efficient and responsive to the ICT sector's needs. It privatized and deregulated the telecommunications market, lowered import barriers, and introduced a broad range of initiatives to increase Internet penetration and use of e-Business and e-Government applications. We noted the following government achievements:

- Reducing costs of ISP pricing for international connections by 50 percent;
- Establishing a dedicated number (0610) named "Call Internet" for telephone calls between the end-user and ISPs; and it seriously decreased the rates for dial-up access;
- Promoting non-profit Internet services; Argentina built over 500 community technology centers with computers, fax machines, and Internet access;
- Beginning of the development of a high-speed data network;
- Increasing Internet use and penetration in the educational system.

The Argentine telecoms were privatized in the early 1990s with the participation of foreign investors. In the same year, data services, including provision of Internet services, were open for free competition. Then, in 2000, the regulatory framework for fully opening Argentina's telecommunications

Table 9.1   Argentina's main ICT indicators, 2003

Fixed line and mobile phone subscribers per 1,000 inhabitants	396.43*
Mobile phones per 1,000 inhabitants	177.60*
PCs per 100 inhabitants	8.20
Internet users per 1,000 inhabitants	112.02*
Internet hosts per 10,000 inhabitants	200.75

*2002 data
Sources: adapted from World Development Indicators Online (2005) and International Telecommunications Union (2005)

market was established in every segment of the market, including local telephony, national and international long distance, cable, wireless, satellite, IP telephony, and the Internet. The market for telecommunications equipment imports also became open and competitive.

The Argentine Government was able to set an appropriate regulatory framework for foreign direct investment, promote creation of small- and medium-sized enterprises and implement privatization and deregulations programs. Foreign investors do not need to register or obtain permission to invest in Argentine companies. Complete foreign ownership of local companies is also allowed, which is a rarity in Latin America. Plus, there were no restrictions on movements of capital or repatriation of funds. This allowed for rather dynamic growth of the ICT sector in the country, by regional standards.

However, the government's decision to tie the peso to the dollar has created several problems for attracting FDI and promoting the growth of the local business. Long before the crises, business owners were very cautious of the devaluation, since 65 percent of private sector debt is in dollars. The government's irresponsible fiscal policy caused the 2001 crisis that brought progress in e-Development to a sudden halt.

The Argentine ICT sector suffers from the persistent power struggle between the executive branch, the legislative, and governmental agencies. The executive branch over-utilizes its power over the agencies it created, which makes the agencies' work less efficient and transparent. For example, the government created a regulatory agency Comisión Nacional de Telecomunicaciones (CNT), and then gradually took many of its responsibilities back, diminishing the agency's ability to regulate effectively. Thus, bureaucratic power struggles create hurdles for dynamic e-Development in the country.

In the early 1990s Argentina privatized its telecommunications sector. The state-owned provider was split between two companies – Telecom Argentina and Telefónica de Argentina – that got monopoly rights on basic telephony in their respective regions. To provide long-distance services throughout the country, a company co-owned by the two new telecommunications organizations was created. The new companies were obliged to meet various quality-of-service standards (QoS) as well as infrastructure expansion targets.

The privatization of the telecommunications sector and creation of the duopoly provided for a sharp increase in the number of telephone lines and a remarkable improvement in the quality of services. Wireless services have also expanded rapidly. However, the telecommunications infrastructure is heavily concentrated around the Buenos Aires area.

As a result of the deregulation, call rates and Internet access costs were significantly reduced. Subsequently, Internet use in the country has increased remarkably fast over the last ten years. For example, in 1993 the country had only 0.05 Internet hosts per 10,000 people, while for Chile the number was 1.01. By early 2003, however, the situation had changed dramatically. While Chile had about 138 Internet hosts per 10,000 people, Argentina boosted its internet use to over 200 Internet hosts per 10,000 people, enjoying the highest Internet host density among the large economies of Latin America.

Besides improving infrastructure, the local practice of sharing Internet subscriptions between multiple users, such as families or small businesses, also helped to increase Internet use in the country.

Argentina boasts one of the most educated populations in Latin America. The country has a relatively well-developed system of state schools with high enrollment in primary and secondary education. However, the quality of education has deteriorated somewhat due to lack of financial resources, aging infrastructure, poor training of teachers, and obsolete curricula. The majority of the schools were not connected to the Internet in 2003, but the Argentine Government has reactivated the educ.ar program, providing over 1,200 schools and education centers with computers and connecting at least 17 rural schools via satellite or broad-band Internet access. The program aims at providing another 4,400 schools with computer and connecting another 5,000 education centers to the Internet.

Even though Argentina has no significant government-sponsored ICT retraining programs, the national public university system is well developed and provides a sufficient number of graduates with a high level of technical expertise. On the downside, the university system is tilted too much toward training and has negligible research capabilities.

In 1994, Argentina's national universities were linked through a dedicated network and later the research centers also were interconnected. Members of the academic community represent the largest group of Internet users in the country. Promotion and awareness campaigns are limited in scope.

Even though Argentina has not yet developed a coherent strategy for its government's presence online, about 80 percent of central governmental entities and 10 percent of the local ones have websites. A governmental portal has been arranged to create a single gateway to all central governmental bodies.

The ratio of PC penetration in central government entities is estimated to be one PC to four employees. Computer-assisted networks for communication within the same government branch are well developed, but there is limited interlinking between local and central governments.

Argentina enacted legislation which provides for the use of digital signatures in the National Public Administration. A number of e-services are available to citizens and businesses, for example legislative process information, Social Security and financial status requests, tax transactions, and customs procedures.

e-Business and ICT sectors are relatively well developed in Argentina. Hoping to cash in on the Latin Internet Revolution, investors threw generous money at Argentine start-up companies. Argentina's ICT sector grew by a combined 6 percent in 2000, while other industry sectors experienced very little or no growth. Argentina's software and software services companies started to compete globally. For a while, there were more new Internet start-ups in Argentina than in all other Latin American countries combined.

Argentina had quite attractive conditions for international ICT companies – the highest per capita GDP and the second-highest life expectancy in Latin America, high literacy rates, strong infrastructure in the Greater Buenos Aires area that serves as the country's IT center. Plus, devaluation created financial incentives for Argentine ICT export. Thus, several corporations such as IBM, Microsoft, and Oracle have setup bases in Argentina. Argentine IT firms serve mainly as assemblers, integrators, or consultants to these companies. Most ICT companies are located in Greater Buenos Aires, within the sphere of influence on one another. Therefore, many argue that Buenos Aires is becoming one large technology park.

According to the Economist Intelligence Unit e-readiness rankings for 2005, Argentina is number 39, just below Brazil and above Lithuania. It is numbered 3 in Latin America, after Chile (31) and Brazil (38).

Argentina has great strengths with which to successfully implement its e-Development strategy, among which, having one of the most educated populations in Latin America, a national public university system that is well developed and provides a sufficient number of graduates with a high level of technical expertise, an ICT market open to competition, and a modern telecommunications infrastructure. It also benefits from an appropriate regulatory framework to attract foreign direct investment, an adequate legal framework (digital signature in the public administration), a wide net of community technology centers, the local practice of sharing Internet subscriptions between multiple users, such as families or small businesses, the creation of the "Call Internet" number for calls between the end-user and ISPs, which seriously decreased the rates for dial-up Internet access without reducing the high regular call tariffs necessary for self-sustainable growth of the telecommunications sector. It also provides a unified license for diversified telecoms services. In order to be able to supply local telephone services, companies are required to invest US$2 per person in the area and to submit a technical plan consistent with the level of demand. Finally, only 1 percent of total telecom sales are targeted to subsidize telephone services in non-profitable regions and to foster Internet development in schools.

Yet, Argentina has to deal with a badly structured government fiscal policy, a high level of public sector spending, political uncertainty (power struggle between the executive branch, legislative, and other agencies), negligible research capabilities in the education system, the lack of funding opportunities (access to capital is the major constraint to innovation) and the lack of a comprehensive set of fiscal incentives for the software and IT services industry development.

Argentina's sad story stresses the importance of building e-Development on a solid foundation of macroeconomic stability. In other words, e-Development interventions could serve as growth drivers and stability buffers to compensate (albeit only partly) fiscal and monetary policy errors as well as negative global economic conjectures.

B   Brazil

The Brazilian government has emphasized controlled privatization and deregulation in order to provide the business sector with an environment in which it can grow and adapt quickly to the changing economic and business climate, while at the same time still being subject to competition. The recently-launched Information Society Program is a first step in making technology-based services and job creation available to every citizen. Public–private partnerships are helping to identify innovative solutions to overcome barriers to universal access, such as the high cost of personal computers and lack of financing options for low-income citizens.

The Information Society (IS) program was launched in December 1999 by the president of Brazil. The Ministry of Science and Technology is responsible for coordinating the program, whereas the activities and focus are defined by a team consisting of members representing the private sector, the academic community, and representatives of the government. The IS

Table 9.2   Brazil's main ICT indicators, 2003

Fixed line and mobile phone subscribers per 1,000 inhabitants	486.46
Mobile phones per 1,000 inhabitants	263.55
PCs per 100 inhabitants	7.48
Internet users per 1,000 inhabitants	82.24*
Internet hosts per 10,000 inhabitants	179.78

* 2002 data

Sources: adapted from World Development Indicators Online (2005) and International Telecommunications Union (2005)

program allocates funding for the expansion of Internet infrastructure, the interconnection of all public libraries, and the creation of thousands of community access centers throughout the country.

The government of Brazil also expects that the country's main financial institutions will also understand the benefits and opportunities hidden behind ICT development and will become eventually not only partners but also catalysts and drivers in this effort in terms of funding, research, strategies, priorities, and policy making.

Strategic collaboration between public and private sector organizations has been instrumental in Brazil's IS program. For example, international computer manufacturers such as IBM, Hewlett-Packard, Compaq, and Acer are involved in the IS program. To support the program, the government will provide loans to lower-income households for purchase of the computers.

The Brazilian Congress, also responding to the changing global economic climate that was moving toward open markets and competition through privatization of state-run companies, as well as reduction of burdensome internal and external debts, decided to end the government's monopoly over telecommunications services in 1995 with the adoption of Constitutional Amendment No. 8, which authorized the entry of private, domestic, and foreign investment into the telecommunications sector.

At first, liberalization was extended only to specific market segments: those that were opened were the mobile services, satellite telecommunications, and value-added services. Then further legislation was passed to open the telecommunications sector fully. The Telecommunications Law of 1997 paved the way for a comprehensive sector reform.

The Brazilian Telecommunications Regulatory Authority (ANATEL) is an independent agency that is financed through license and spectrum fees as well as government appropriations. ANATEL's greater autonomy has increased both regulatory responsiveness to the sector, and investor confidence in the transparency and fairness of the regulatory process in Brazil.

Not only has Brazil the lowest levels of telephone line density of Latin America (see Table 9.2), but also the territorial extension of the country and the vast population have created a sort of internal digital divide. The new entrants into the telecommunications sector are to install digital technology systems and phone tariffs are expected to fall by 24.6 percent for national long-distance calls and by 66 percent for international calls by the end of 2005. The liberalization process is set to deepen still further. The sale of mirror concessions for fixed-line systems and one long-distance carrier took place in January and April 1999, earning a total of US$128 m. A number of new companies began operations before the end of 1999. Although these service operators will face the disadvantage of having no existing infrastructure or client base, they will not be expected to meet any government targets. Competition in the telecom sector has intensified further after 2002, since when any operator wishing to provide services is allowed free entry into the Brazilian market.

Due to low levels of general literacy and the prohibitive cost of computers, ICT literacy and technological skills are low. As such, technology training and skills development are priority areas for the Brazilian government. It is estimated that the availability of ICT, in relation to relevant IT training programs and the availability of new low-cost computers will inevitably promote more technology users among the general population. Moreover, Brazil faces another challenge, which is the shortage of ICT-qualified people.

The Brazilian government activities in raising awareness are quite limited in scope and scale. The research effort is still very limited in size, and will have to increase quite considerably if the ambitions of the National Policy for Informatics are to be met. Besides, tensions among these different research programs and support lines are likely to happen.

Uncertainty over regulation on taxes and other fiscal incentives is limiting the potential of Brazil to attract foreign investors and promote domestic entrepreneurship. Despite these difficulties, Brazil accounted for 88 percent of online sales in Latin America last year, with 45 percent of the region's online audience. Revenue from online sales in Latin America reached US$160 million in 1999. The two main factors that have set Brazil apart from its neighbors are the country's high rate of computer penetration and technically sophisticated banking system, making the switch to electronic banking and commerce more attractive. Among the Latin-American countries, Brazil dominates in such areas as online advertising, user numbers and e-Commerce is no exception. Books, magazines, and CDs are the most purchased products on the Web in Brazil. Growing e-Commerce (a 39.5 percent increase from 2003 to 2004, according to the Brazilian e-Commerce Chamber) prompted the Information Technology Law of January 2001 that provides numerous incentives to the computer industry. In 2004, Brazil ranked number 35 in e-Commerce.

The role of the state in promoting industrial development in Brazil has been a constant feature in the country's recent history, and has been subject to detailed scrutiny. The impact, results, challenges, and opportunities that have so far been derived from the implementation and execution of this promising IS program have not been officially published by the Brazilian authorities. The main issue is that the government has realized that the only way to remain a competitive economy throughout the world, to fight any poverty issue, and to foster better living conditions is to move toward the direction of ICT and to grasp all the benefits that such a sector could provide for Brazilian people.

It is also important to note that universities are leading R&D efforts. The early adoption of policies to promote the development of national enterprises in the computer industry and the liberalization and deregulation of the telecom market will also spur development of the ICT sector. Brazil is now the leading country in the enactment of e-Commerce laws.

Nevertheless, the high illiteracy rate, especially for IT skills, high costs for equipment, lack of relevant ICT training programs and shortage of

ICT-qualified workers, unfavorable tax and fiscal environment for foreign investors, limited R&D funds and incentives for the private sector, and the low level of telephone line density (among the lowest in Latin America) are all hurdles Brazil will have to overcome.

Strategic public–private partnerships have helped Brazil to overcome its internal digital divide. The government took action to promote local SMEs, by restricting the import of technology where and when local capabilities were able to meet the demand. This helped SMEs to develop and improve their own products and services.

Privatization and deregulation in the telecommunication sector brought accelerated growth in the ICT sector. The government strongly supports the R&D potential of domestic academia in the effort to integrate universities into the cycle of innovation led by the private sector.

C Costa Rica

Because of its stable political system, equitable income distribution, and widespread landownership, Costa Rica has long been considered among the most successful of the Latin American countries. For about ten years Costa Rica has experienced a silent digital revolution (see Table 9.3). This revolution has lacked the hype of the one in Silicon Valley but has been able to avoid the burning of investments in failed ventures. However, it has gained in strength over the past few years, and Costa Rica has become a center for software development in Central America.

Costa Rica has a fairly large amount of tech companies per capita: there are about 100 software companies, in a country of about 4 million inhabitants.

Costa Rica is pursuing a strategy focused on using ICT as an export engine, and it attributes much of its current economic growth to that strategy. The country's political stability, democratic tradition, and emphasis on the health and education of the population, have all contributed to relatively high standards of living.

Table 9.3   Costa Rica's main ICT indicators, 2003

Fixed line and mobile phone subscribers per 1,000 inhabitants	361.51*
Mobile phones per 1,000 inhabitants	110.97*
PCs per 100 inhabitants	21.81
Internet users per 1,000 inhabitants	193.10*
Internet hosts per 10,000 inhabitants	25.94

* 2002 data
Sources: adapted from World Development Indicators Online (2005) and International Telecommunications Union (2005)

Costa Rica has developed itself into a viable location for high-tech industries by providing not only an educated population and prime geographical location, but also by demonstrating the success stories of Intel, Microsoft, and others. To continue this ICT-led progress, the government is taking action to build technological skills in the population, develop strong partnerships between government and business, and further upgrade the already good telecommunications network.

Costa Rica offers a favorable environment for foreign investors, without performance requirements or minimum investment levels. Investment incentives are available for productive activities and for the export of services or goods from Costa Rica. The Free Zone System grants beneficiary companies the widest range of fiscal incentives and operational benefits currently available in Costa Rica, including: exemption from import duties on raw materials, capital goods, parts and components; unrestricted profit repatriation; tax exemption on profits for eight years and a 50 percent exemption for the following four years; and tax exemption on remittances abroad.

The National Council for Scientific and Technological Research (CONICIT) was created in 1974 with the assistance of the Inter-American Development Bank (IDB). Currently, this institute still contributes significantly to the training in higher level skill areas.

The primary reason for the government's desire to retain control of certain profitable state enterprises is that they yield a substantial surplus to the consolidated public sector budget. Without these profits, the government would be unable to finance itself without asking the legislative assembly for major new taxes. Any major reform in the new future is unlikely. However, awareness and need for competition is mounting and creating pressures. Rather than privatizing state-owned companies, the government is thinking of other ways of introducing competition, such as offering telecommunications services as concessions.

The telecom system, although better than elsewhere in the region, suffers from some inadequacies. As the sole provider, the ICE has struggled in particular to cope with the demand for new lines, both fixed and cellular, resulting in long waiting times. The telecommunications system, although better than elsewhere in the region, suffers from some inadequacies.

Use of the Internet and readiness for e-Business are advanced compared with the rest of the region. This is partly a result of the spread of high-tech investment in the economy, combined with high levels of technical education. In addition, Costa Rica is host to a number of e-Businesses, notably offshore Internet gambling operations. The government has strenuously promoted use of the Internet. In 2001 it announced the Agenda Digital program to extend Internet access to small businesses, post offices, and schools, drawing on the skills of volunteers from high-tech companies.

Costa Rica has taken an active stance in attracting foreign investment, recognizing it as a major contributor to the country's development. At the beginning of the 1980s, Costa Rica was the first country in Central America to make a conscious effort to attract direct foreign investment. Different incentive programs were enacted at the time as well as promotional programs to position Costa Rica internationally.

A critical element of Costa Rica's approach has been a focus on education. Not only does Costa Rica have high national standards of education, but it has also worked on ensuring that education institutions produce appropriately skilled workers and professionals. Given the limited number of engineers and technicians, the government has embarked on an aggressive campaign to transform the knowledge base of the country in alignment with the requirements of the high-tech sector. The Instituto Nacional de Aprendizaje (INA), an autonomous institution financed with public resources and private contributions, and the private Instituto Tecnológico de Costa Rica (ITCR) are the main providers of engineering professionals. Costa Rica has been supported in its efforts to upgrade its education system by the Inter-American Development Bank and private investor funding.

The Science and Technology Program (1990–1996), also partly financed by the IDB, funded 239 post-graduate scholarships, 90 research and development projects, and a variety of laboratory and computer equipment at 16 research facilities.

Promotional and awareness activities to increase the perception of new technologies and applications among the business and civic communities are funded by the government. Thanks to the focus on education, new technologies are increasingly becoming an integral part of everyday business and life for most citizens.

To expand ICT use, the Costa Rican government is creating and providing relevant and up-to-date content on the Internet. One of the best examples of this effort is www.costarricense.cr the national portal launched a few years ago, which made Costa Rica the first country in the world to offer all of its citizens their own email account in a centralized system. The portal also offers access to a wide range of government services, general information, and e-Commerce applications, including promotion of the eco-tourism industry.

A highly positive government attitude toward foreign investment, shared by all significant political parties and leaders, has led to specific legislation to promote this kind of investment along with new exports: creation of the first free-trade zone in 1982, promotion of exports since the 1990s.

The presence of major ICT global companies, such as Intel, has contributed to fostering the domestic private sector. In fact, a host of local SMEs are integrated into the supply-chain of the big companies and many spin-off activities are being generated by the presence of foreign investors.

Costa Rica's location in relation to the North and South American markets, its peaceful and stable political environment, the business-friendly policies it adopted in the 1980s, its excellent infrastructure, and its educated and skilled workforce have all made it an attractive location for high-tech, export-oriented firms and other IT-enabled industries.

Its skilled workforce and educated society is one of the advantages for Costa Rica. It also invests heavily in R&D, establishes public–private partnerships in the fields of awareness, education, and training, and focuses on institution building: Costa Rica created a network of institutions devoted to sustainable development. Costa Rica sustained an enabling environment for domestic SMEs (access to finance, administrative facilitations), and created one of the most attractive investment environments by providing incentives (fiscal, financial).

The main challenges facing Costa Rica are its state-owned monopoly in telecommunications and its limited domestic market. The case of Costa Rica shows that FDI is not the only driver; sustainable development has to be supported by a viable enabling environment for SMEs and local entrepreneurship. Costa Rica is focusing on ICT mainly as an export engine and risks tying the economy too much to a single foreign company (i.e. Intel).

D Czech Republic

The Czech Government seems to be fully committed in reaping the benefit of ICT to foster economic and social development in the country. The national strategy for an information society *The State Information Policy, the Road towards an Information Society* was launched in 2000, calling for specific actions within a well-defined timeline, such as IT literacy (through a reform of the educational and vocational systems for the civil society, and a program of IT literacy for public servants), ICT adoption by the business community, and e-Applications for the management of the health sector and other civil services, such as crisis management for environmental emergencies. However, the Czech Republic joined the *eEurope + Action Plan* in June 2001, and since then a few European Directives have become national legislations.

The establishment of an information society is already supported by an adequate regulatory framework to spur development through

Table 9.4 Czech Republic's main ICT indicators, 2003

Fixed line and mobile phone subscribers per 1,000 inhabitants	1324.94
Mobile phones per 1,000 inhabitants	964.64
PCs per 100 inhabitants	17.74
Internet users per 1,000 inhabitants	308.01
Internet hosts per 10,000 inhabitants	274.41

Sources: adapted from World Development Indicators Online (2005) and International Telecommunications Union (2005)

innovation: appropriate legislation, drafted along EU standards, was implemented on electronic signatures in late 2000, and on personal data protection and consumer protection in mid-2000. The Czech Republic has signed and ratified the European Convention for the Protection of Human Rights and Fundamental Freedoms. Moreover, it has adopted the OECD Guidelines on the Protection of Privacy and Trans-border Flows of Personal Data.

The Czech Information Society Forum was set up in 1999 as a consultative organ reflecting, in its orientation, technical and social aspects of the implementation of the national information policies and the development of an information society. The IS Forum works closely with the Specialist Working Group and the State Information Policy Council, established in 1998 to coordinate and manage the innovation and ICT policies of the Czech Government.

The Telecommunications Act of 2000 aims at terminating the incumbent's monopoly on voice services and opening the market to new entrants. Yet, the new Act does not eliminate significant entry barriers for new entrants. Moreover, local-loop unbundling is left to the telecom operators to agree upon. These agreements are very often impossible to reach given the incumbent position in the market.

Since the School Act was rejected by the Parliament in May 2001, no progress has been achieved in the field of legislative alignment to international standards in education and training, especially in the field of ICT. Yet, the new Governmental Information Society Strategy in Education was approved in May 2000. The budget (for IT-equipment of schools and training teachers) was CZK 7 billion over a five-year period. The main objectives are in accordance with the European Union *eEurope* initiative, that is every school would be connected to the Internet by the end of 2003 (Internet would also be available in all libraries and post offices), information technologies would be integrated into the education process and multimedia technologies would be widely used in teaching, all students leaving school would be fully IT-literate by the end of 2004, and all citizens should be IT-literate by the end of 2005 (see Table 9.4).

In the efforts to increase e-Government applications, the Czech administration is moving forward by setting up valuable information sharing mechanisms. The Ministry of Finance is publishing on the Internet ARES database (Administrative Register of Economic Subjects), which interconnects several databases: the Commercial Register (Ministry of Justice), the Register of Economic Subjects (Czech Statistical Office), the Trade License Register and the Register of VAT. The Ministry of Interior has made an interactive Internet application search of motor vehicles publicly accessible. This will allow those who purchase a used automobile to check whether the vehicle is listed on the database for vehicular theft in the territory of the Czech Republic. CzechInvest, an organization funded by the Ministry of Industry and Trade of the Czech Republic to facilitate FDI (by providing foreign investors with free services, such as the handling of investment incentives' applications), launched a database on the Internet in August 2000, which provides the names of more than 1,800 Czech companies that want to act as subcontractors to local manufactures, as well as database of industrial real estate.

The Ministry of Informatics was created in January of 2003 with the responsibility of developing e-Government, telecommunications, and promoting the information society (see Figure 9.1). In March 2004, the Czech Government adopted the State Information and Communications Policy (e-Czech 2006) that reflects the specificities of the Czech Republic while complying with the European objectives. It focuses on the following objectives:

- Affordable and secure communications services;
- Information literacy;
- Modern online public services;
- Dynamic e-Business environment.

In October 2004, the public administration portal http://portal.gov.cz was launched. It provides information to Czech citizens and allows them to complete basic transactions online. The latest goal the government has set for itself is presented in the January 2005 National Broadband Strategy: by 2010, 50 percent of the Czech population should be using broadband. The progress toward this goal should be monitored via the public administration portal previously mentioned.

To improve links between SMEs and industry, and R&D institutes and universities, the Ministry of Industry and Trade runs three specialized support programs for SMEs aimed at research, development, and innovative business (Technos, Transfer, and Park). The programs are designed to increase the technical level of SMEs. It focuses on research and development of new technologies, products, materials, and information systems.

The government being a user and promoter of ICT and high-tech applications, the country's S&T heritage, its skilled and qualified workforce, strategic location, and capacity to attract FDI are all important advantages for the implementation of the e-Development strategy. The full liberalization of the country's telecommunications market and the creation of an appropriate regulatory framework for infrastructure are key factors to the success of the *e-Czech* strategy.

FDI alone is not enough to drive growth in the ICT sector. Other factors play crucial role, such as telecommunications liberalization or an adequate regulatory framework. The liberalization of the telecommunications market is essential for promoting positive spill-over on ICT-related industry.

The Czech Republic, as many other transitional countries of Central Europe, has inherited a great science and technology system from the past. Czech governments should facilitate the development of the high-tech

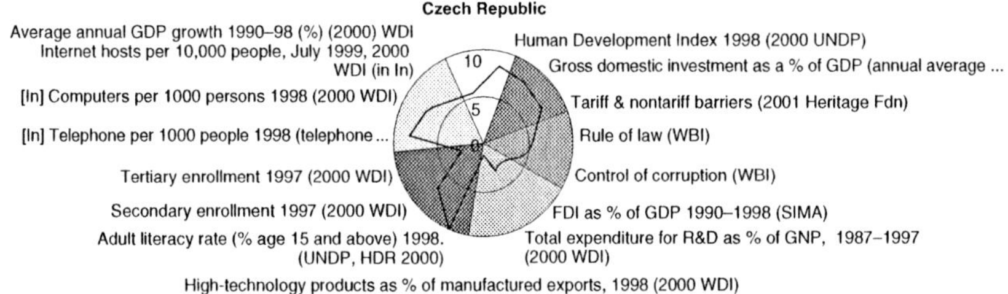

Figure 9.1   Czech Republic's knowledge scorecard

*Source:*The World Bank, Interactive Knowledge Assessment Methodology, KAM (2005)

sector to compete in hardware manufacturing. The lack of financing for research and development and of efficient business practices has hindered the development of this potential. Time will tell whether the initiatives recently undertaken by the government will generate positive spill-over effects in the domestic ICT sector.

E Estonia

Estonia is at the forefront of ICT development among the transitional economies of Central and Eastern Europe (see Table 9.5). The small Baltic country has in fact developed a strong ICT industry and has been very successful in developing an information society. New technologies and the Internet, along with Internet-related services, are increasingly becoming familiar to Estonian citizens and companies.

A very far-sighted approach on the part of the government has helped Estonia to become a regional leader in ICT. Since independence the small Baltic state has started investing in ICT, despite the lack of appropriate funding budget. Yet, the consistent and purposeful allocation of funds over the years has allowed Estonia to establish an informatics network for most public agencies, provide a set of advanced e-Government solutions, and promote a vibrant ICT sector.

The role of the government and the appropriate set of policies and measures implemented are key to this successful achievement. Moreover, the creation of specific institutions has facilitated ICT development in the country, also easing and speeding inflows of foreign direct investments.

The main act of policy making of Estonia on e-Development is the Principles of Estonian Information Policy, approved by the Parliament in May 1998. The information policy is an integral part of public policy reflecting the principles of the actions of the state in the creation of an information society for all in Estonia. The strategy and action plan provide for detailed proposals with timeframes, sources of finances, and responsibilities for the implementation of information policy programs every year.

Table 9.5   Estonia's main ICT indicators, 2003

Fixed line and mobile phone subscribers per 1,000 inhabitants	1118.61
Mobile phones per 1,000 inhabitants	777.38
PCs per 100 inhabitants	44.04
Internet users per 1,000 inhabitants	444.12
Internet hosts per 10,000 inhabitants	474.08

Sources: adapted from World Development Indicators Online (2005) and International Telecommunications Union (2005)

The government has understood the importance of an appropriate legal framework to complement e-Development strategy. As a result of this focused approach, the government designed and implemented a plausible regulatory framework not only to encourage ICT, but also to foster the areas interested by e-Development activities. To foster openness and transparency (supported by and functional to e-government initiatives) the government drafted the Freedom of Information Act that took effect in January 2001. Moreover, important legislations in support of e-Business services and applications were passed, such as the Personal Data Protection Act (approved in July 1996), the Databases Act (April 1997), and the Digital Signature Act (March 2000). The legislation takes into sound consideration the EU regulatory framework by which most of the transitional economies among the Central and Eastern European countries (CEECs) are abiding.

The creation of a dedicated body for IS strategy and policy, the Government Committee for Estonian Informatics Council reorganized in 1996, has supported the political vision of the government in creating an information society. The Council has the duty of setting the main general policy guidelines for ICT development for the country. Appropriate human and financial resources have allowed the Council to work as an effective catalyst for the establishment of an information society in Estonia.

Moreover, various programs have been launched to enhance the competitiveness of Estonia through supporting the start-up of high-tech SMEs and job creation, promoting innovation and the introduction of new technologies in the region. These programs are launched under the aegis of the Estonian Technology Agency (ESTAG). ESTAG promotes the competitiveness of the Estonian entrepreneurial sector and economy by supporting technological development. ESTAG also offers financial support for Estonian enterprises, R&D institutions, and universities.

Much progress has been made in the telecommunications sector over the last few years and the infrastructure's size and degree of modernization is a good achievement, particularly in the penetration of mobile and Internet services: in 2004, 89 percent of the Estonian population were mobile phone subscribers, and 52 percent were Internet users. Prices have been rebalanced to a considerable extent and the arrival of competition is reinforcing the process.

Early privatization enabled the telecommunications sector to benefit from foreign investment. In the period from 1991 to 1993, 49 percent of the fixed-telephony incumbent operator Eesti Telefon and its mobile counterpart Eesti Mobiiltelefon were sold to a consortium of foreign investors (Finnish Sonera and Swedish Telia). In 2001 Eesti Telekom lost its fixed-line monopoly, in line with EU Directives on competition in the communications market. Moreover, competition is present in the vibrant mobile communications market, where in addition to Eesti Mobiiltelefon, there two global systems for mobile (GSM) communications cellular operators: Radiolinja Eesti and Tele2.

Education and training have been the main component of the different actions of the program "Tiger Leap" for schools. For the implementation of Tiger Leap in the public administration and private sector, the government has created the Estonian Info College together with the universities and private enterprises. The program is helping to create favorable conditions for an IT-driven learning environment.

The Village Road project has attracted investments of private firms. Some firms have launched a campaign to provide farmers, teachers, and young families with cheap computers and Internet connection. For example up to 2,200 farmers have obtained a new PC and an Internet connection within the framework of the project, and all local governments have been connected to the Internet. The project has been such a success that its goals are periodically revised upwards, with the Village Road project 3 covering the 2005–2007 period.

ICT applications are becoming very popular in Estonia. e-Banking is the most popular application: in 2004, 68 percent of Estonian Internet users conducted their everyday banking via the Internet. e-Commerce is also expanding rapidly and e-Government is extremely advanced in the whole spectrum of applications – G2G, G2B, and G2C. As of today all governmental institutions have their websites integrated through one common window, the government portal "Sinu Eesti" ("Your Estonia"). For example almost all official forms have been available on the Internet for a number of years. All taxpayers in Estonia are able to file their tax reports electronically without leaving their computers.

The G2G applications are also very advanced in regard to the Internet-based environment for the government's everyday business. In fact, Estonian government sessions have been paperless since August 2000: all the ministers (even if they are not in the meeting room or in Estonia at all) are accessible through the Internet during government sessions and can contact their assistants and other officials during these sessions.

The Estonian Public Procurement Act (2000) requires that such procurement also be performed through the Internet. In addition, the government launched some WAP services (e.g. access to the business register) to facilitate private sector development.

The B2B sector is more successful: web-based ordering systems have been actively developed in many firms since 1997, and in 2003 about 15 percent of Estonians were purchasing products online. The most popular electronic service stays Internet banking: Estonian banks had more than 725,000 Internet bank customers in 2003.

Estonia has benefited from a number of positive factors contributing to the success of its e-Development strategy: the far-sighted approach of government; a government that is both user and provider of ICT; a comprehensive national action plan to develop the information society, with realistic goals, specific target actions and timeline; the creation of appropriate institutional and regulatory framework; the proximity of IT leaders, i.e. the Nordic countries; the liberalization of the telecommunications market; a dynamic political class; heavy investment in human capital; the realization of public–private partnerships; a strong S&T heritage; and high personal computer penetration (see Figure 9.2).

Nonetheless, it still needs to face the lack of financial resources, the small size of the economy, a limited internal market, the lack of local language content, the shortage of IT workers, and the never-ending brain-drain.

Public–private partnership is not only viable but also purposeful. The national action plan to build an information society has to provide for a general framework of reference, specific measures and interventions, detailed timeline, and budgetary allocation. A realistic approach in setting the goals of the strategy is necessary to ensure success and focus of actions. Despite financial restrictions (small state budget), progress in KE is possible through consistent and purposeful allocation even of a small budget. Institution building is also vital to ensure coordination of efforts and proper allocation of resources. Finally, a legal framework designed to follow international standards is pivotal for the development of KE.

Apart from a proactive government role and the good mix of policies in the promotion of ICT development, Estonia has benefited from some unique

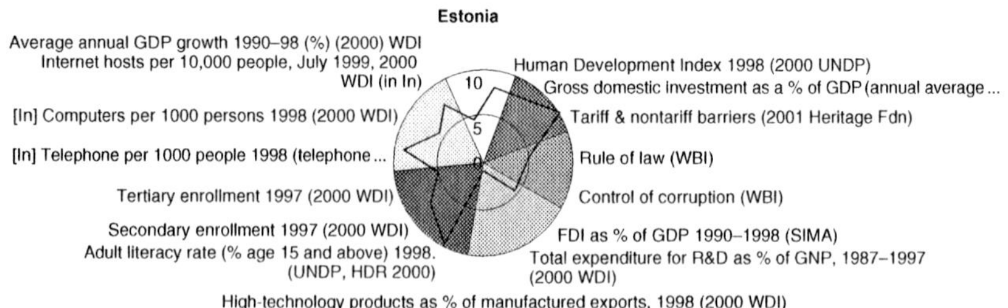

Figure 9.2 Estonia's knowledge scorecard

Source: The World Bank, KAM (2005)

strategic advantages compared to other transitional economies. First, the small population and territory have been advantageous factors in fostering connectivity and increasing awareness in both society and business. Second, the success story of Estonia is in part due to the latecomer's advantage. Linnar Viik, IT adviser to the Prime Minister, comments on e-Development in Estonia: "What good timing it was to get independence at the beginning of the 1990s. If we'd gotten independence in the 1970s, with an industrial economy and a mainframe IT environment, we'd be a very different country today." Third, the geographical location has helped Estonia's development: the proximity to the technologically advanced Nordic countries.

F Hungary

Hungary has become one of the strongest performing economies in the Europe and Central Asia (ECA) region with a dynamically developing ICT sector (see Table 9.6).

The government put an emphasis on self-sustaining development of the telecommunications industry. Some of the promotional measures included early privatization and market liberalization, an early and decisive move toward tariff rebalancing, making the telecommunications industry attractive for investors and creating conditions for self-sustaining network growth, and granting temporary monopoly rights for certain services to the incumbent operator, Matav.

Matav, was privatized gradually in the early-to-mid-1990s, with Deutsche Telecom being the main investor. Matav retained a monopoly in the provision of international and domestic long-distance services until at least 2002. In return for its monopoly rights, Matav was obliged to modernize the Hungarian telephone network rapidly, and establish the country as the leading telecommunications hub for Central and Eastern Europe.

Communications services in Hungary are divided between concession-based and competitive services, Public and mobile telephony as well as nationwide paging are concession-based. Other services, such as leased lines, data transmission, Internet services, and cable television are competitive and require a license from regional authorities.

Table 9.6 Hungary's main ICT indicators, 2003

Fixed line and mobile phone subscribers per 1,000 inhabitants	1117.41
Mobile phones per 1,000 inhabitants	768.77
PCs per 100 inhabitants	10.84
Internet users per 1,000 inhabitants	232.24
Internet hosts per 10,000 inhabitants	357.76

Sources: adapted from World Development Indicators Online (2005) and International Telecommunications Union (2005)

Hungary has 54 primary areas, each considered a concession unit. Matav holds concession rights in 36 primary areas and privatized local telecommunications operators operate in the remaining 18 areas. The concession agreements require LTOs to meet certain quantitative and qualitative targets for expanding and modernizing the telecommunications network. The mobile telephony market is fully liberalized. The government has issued national concessions to several mobile operators, and there are currently three main competitors.

The Hungarian government found a creative method for supporting Matav's monopoly on long-distance calls. IP telephony providers are obliged to guarantee inferior quality of service. Thus, IP telephony has potential for development while Matav preserves its monopoly.

At the end of 1980s, Hungary had one of the lowest teledensities in the region – less than 10 percent. Favorable business environment together with privatization and tariff rebalancing brought in much desired foreign investments in the sector and the density and quality of the cable telephone network has increased significantly since. Hungary had one of the least-developed telephone infrastructures at the beginning of the 1990s, with less than a million main lines and a penetration rate of only nine lines per 100 inhabitants. Today, Hungary counts over 3.6 million main lines, and at the beginning of 2004 had a penetration rate of 35.9 percent. The mobile telephone network has also expanded at an exceptional pace, largely due to the rather liberalized market and initial scarcity of fixed lines. For example, in 1994, the penetration rate of fixed lines was 17 lines per 100 people and the waiting period reached 10–15 years. For many people mobile telephony proved to be the quick-fix solution. The mobile phone penetration rate was 79.6 percent in early 2004.

It is important to note that Hungary, despite its regional leadership in terms of teledensity (the number of telephone lines per 1,000 population), is not among the top countries in Internet penetration. The main barrier to the development of the Internet in Hungary has been the high local call tariffs. As a result, Hungary had some of the region's highest Internet access charges. With tariffs lowering and the presence of alternatives (cable, ADSL) Internet penetration is slowly picking up (674,000 Internet subscriptions in late 2003).

Most experts name Matav's monopoly over long-distance calls together with its dominant market share over local services as the main hurdle for dynamic development of Internet use in the country. In the early 1990s, the monopoly brought improvement in the fixed-line network, but in recent years the fixed-line market has suffered from falling prices and prepaid packages in the mobile market.

About a half of Internet users in Hungary get free or almost-free connection through the Hungarian Academic and Research Network, HungarNet. It has about 1,000 institutional members – educational and research institutions, libraries, and museums. Institutional members contribute about 10 percent to the HungarNet's budget, the rest is provided by the Ministry of Culture and Education. On the downside, the availability of the subsidized access through HungarNet led to the relatively slow growth of the commercial ISP market: in early 2003 the network counted over 600,000 users through 700 institutions (6 percent of the Hungarian population). Another important barrier to Internet adoption is the low penetration of personal computers, caused largely by high customs duties on imported computers and other hardware. However, the government recently started providing subsidies for family computer purchases.

Another interesting phenomenon in Hungary is the widespread growth of telecottages (public telecenters). Since the first telecottages appeared in 1994, they have been steadily spreading all over the country. There were more than 400 telecottages in operation in 2003, and over 800 of them are expected to cover the entire Hungarian countryside. They serve almost a million people and cover most of the country, with at least one telecottage for every 50 kilometers. Telecottages are funded from local resources and with the help of various international donors, such as USAID.

The quality of education in Hungary is comparable to that in Western Europe. A high standard of general and vocational education has been important for attracting foreign companies to Hungary's ICT sector. The government spending on education is among the highest in the ECA region and universities are connected to the Internet through HungarNet. In 1997 the government started a USD15 m "Sulinet" program to provide Internet access for 1,400 schools. The Ministry of Education pledged that all schools (5,500) will have broadband Internet access by the end of 2005. Telecommunications costs of the schools' use of the Internet are covered from the central budget.

About 93 percent of the civil servants in Hungary use the Internet. Governmental entities of central Public Administration (PA) are interlinked through Internet/extranet networks. Intranet networks are also used within local public administration offices, but networks between central PA and local PA are rather scarce. All governmental bodies of the central public administration in Hungary have Internet websites, while only 40 percent of the governmental bodies of the local administrations have Internet presence.

In 2001 an e-Government program was adopted to provide various citizen-friendly e-Services and to improve the efficiency of internal government operations. From 1995, Hungary pursued an aggressive privatization policy in telecommunications, banking, utilities, and television sectors. Currently, the private sector accounts for more than 70 percent of GDP, one of the highest shares in the ECA.

Good infrastructure, pro-business regulatory environment, the availability of comparatively cheap, technically skilled labor, and adjacent EU markets has attracted a number of leading electronics and software firms to Hungary.

For example, Nokia, Ericsson, Motorola, and Microsoft have large software development centers in Hungary.

The country also has a large number of domestic start-ups in this area, some of which started to compete globally. Many Hungarian ICT companies are among the fastest-growing technology firms in the region. For example, Graphisoft is acknowledged as the world's number one provider of model-based software and services for the building industry.

The government actively promotes SME enterprises to expand their economic contribution to at least 50 percent – which they achieved in 2002. Among the promotional measures we count technical assistance, reduced taxation, tax exemptions, and subsidized loans. Special attention is given to helping SMEs to adopt modern information technology.

Internet services are an important component of the IT sector in Hungary. While the level of domestic Internet use is rather low, academic, IT, telecommunications, and financial sectors use the Internet extensively. A viable banking sector is an important basis for dynamic economic development in Hungary. Thus, the government invited foreign strategic investors to the privatization of its banking sector, which subsequently became one of the most advanced in the ECA region; 70 percent of the financial institutions are controlled by foreign owners.

The overall strong economy (by regional standards), the high standard of general and vocational education, and the availability of comparatively cheap, technically skilled labor made for the success of e-Development in Hungary (see Figure 9.3). The country also benefited from an advanced banking sector (privatized and open to FDI), a comprehensive privatization policy, attractive conditions for FDI, an active promotion of SMEs, the proximity of EU markets, the separation of operational and regulatory functions in the telecommunications industry, the government-subsidized academic Hungarnet network, the extensive net of telecottages, and the government's creative method of supporting Matav's monopoly on long-distance calls.

The main impediments to more successful e-Development in Hungary are subsidized Internet access through telecottages and HungarNet reducing the customer base for commercial ISP sector and Internet cafés, a limited domestic market, and Matav maintaining a monopoly over long-distance and international calls, with a market share of more than 79 percent over local services.

The country's high local call tariffs that hinder Internet use in the country are an undesirable by-product of the government's strategy on liberalization, however. Thus, the growth of the Internet has mainly been driven by demand in the academic sector, where the government-subsidized HungarNet network provides "almost free" access and now serves over half of the market. Hungary's is possibly the most impressive net of telecottages in Eastern Europe. However, availability of subsidized access led to relatively slow growth of the commercial ISP market. Hungary's case highlights two

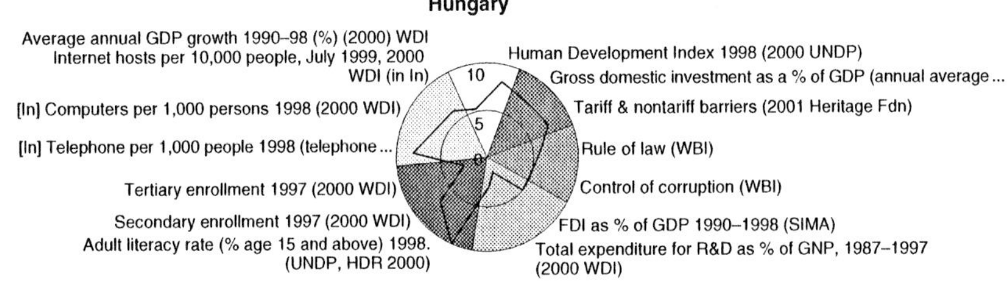

Figure 9.3   Hungary's knowledge scorecard
Source The World Bank, KAM (2005)

potential tradeoffs that ECA countries may face: (1) between developing the telecommunications industry and promoting Internet use in the country; and (2) between developing a web of free or heavily subsidized access centers and promoting the commercial ISP sector.

G   Malaysia

Malaysia is an example of a country that uses ICT as an enabler of socio-economic development process through focusing primarily on repositioning the country's economy to secure competitive advantage in the global economy.

The National IT Agenda (NITA) was launched in 1996. It provides the foundation and framework for the utilization of ICT to transform Malaysia into an information society, then a knowledge society, and finally a "values-based" knowledge society (see Table 9.7). In the same year, Malaysia launched a "Vision 2020" program with a comprehensive plan to build a fully developed, knowledge-rich society by the year 2020 through the development of the ICT sector and the adoption of ICT to increase global competitiveness.

The Malaysian government aims to build an export-oriented economy based on inward direct investment. The government introduced attractive policies for FDI, such as streamlining the investment approval process and unrestricted employment of foreign knowledge-workers. Comprehensive

Table 9.7   Malaysia's main ICT indicators, 2003

Fixed line and mobile phone subscribers per 1,000 inhabitants	623.58
Mobile phones per 1,000 inhabitants	441.95
PCs per 100 inhabitants	16.69
Internet users per 1,000 inhabitants	344.09
Internet hosts per 10,000 inhabitants	42.90

Sources: adapted from World Development Indicators Online (2005) and International Telecommunications Union (2005)

trade and investment policies, such as financial and non-financial incentives, a fair trade system, and import and export duties, promote local and foreign investment.

As one of the most important means for attracting FDI into its ICT sector, Malaysia has greatly improved its telecommunications infrastructure. Through the privatization of the government telecommunications department in 1987, and adoption of the National Telecommunications Policy in 1994, the telecommunications market has been fully liberalized. The computer and software markets have also been fully deregulated.

The National Information Technology Council (NITC) is a public–private think-tank that involves members of the public, private, and community-interest sectors and advises the government on ICT development strategy. It is chaired by the Prime Minister and has five thrust areas: e-Economy, e-Public services, e-Community, e-Learning, and e-Sovereignty. The last component is unique and focuses on "building a resilient national identity" for "integrity and societal stability in the face of borderless challenges to the nation."

The Multimedia Development Corporation (MDC) is a government-owned corporation, established in 1996 to spearhead the development of the Multimedia Super Corridor. It endeavors to cut through the bureaucratic red tape and serve as a "one-stop shop" for multinational and local companies wishing to relocate to the MSC. It markets the MSC, standardizes MSC's information infrastructure and urban development, and also advises the Malaysian Government on MSC-specific laws and regulations.

Malaysian Industry–Government Group for High Technology (MIGHT) is a partnership between the industry and the public sector in Malaysia. Its members include government agencies, multinational organizations, business, industry, and academic institutions. With experts from various fields of high technology, MIGHT provides various consultative and advisory resources. MIGHT has also compiled various publications ranging from directories to national action plans, to reports, speeches, and blueprints.

The Malaysian Government attempted to replicate the Silicon Valley model to attract domestic and foreign private investment to the technology sector. The US$40 b Multimedia Super Corridor (MSC) has become the backbone for the country's information superhighway. MSC embodies a 750 sq km area near Kuala Lumpur that is served by a state-of-the-art multimedia infrastructure. The superhighway provides quality access to global information as quickly and easily as possible. The network is supported by a high-speed link network which connects the MSC to Japan, ASEAN, the US, and Europe. The first phase (1996–2003) has exceeded all of its milestones. Malaysia has entered the second phase in 2003 which will see the creation of a web of similar corridors, the creation of a framework of cyberlaws, and connect four or five intelligent cities to other global cities worldwide. By 2020 the third and last phase should be completed, connecting all the intelligent cities and making Malaysia one single multimedia Super Corridor. Malaysia will also have an International Cybercourt of Justice and at least twelve intelligent cities will be connected to the global information highway.

The intent behind MSC is to create a high-tech environment and infrastructure in a certain geographic area of the country that can attract national and international investors and create spillover effects in the rest of the Malaysian economy. MSC is intended to support development of sophisticated public, education, and business multimedia applications.

The Multimedia Super Corridor incorporates two of the world's first "smart cities," Putrajaya and Cyberjaya, and will eventually lead to full electronic government, an automated hospital system, multimedia-rich schools, and R&D clusters consisting of universities and corporate centers. This corridor is also the focus of most of the measures regarding the promotion and awareness of ICT and the opportunities it offers.

Malaysia has also been developing its telecommunications infrastructure beyond MSC. The monopoly of largely state-owned Telekom Malaysia over the provision of fixed-line and cellular services ended in 1994 with the licensing of several competitors. Since then, the telephone penetration rate has been rising steadily both in urban and rural areas. Digital divide is still prominent, but it has been gradually decreasing.

The Malaysian educational system does not produce enough IT graduates. Skilled labor in ICT sector is in short supply. The Malaysian Government has started investing in building a high-quality, comprehensive higher education system. Computer illiteracy among the general population is viewed as inhibiting the diffusion of ICT. To address this issue, the government actively promotes computerizing the country's schools and ICT training for teachers.

Malaysia promotes a creative approach to addressing shortages in skilled labor in the ICT sector – the Teaching Company Scheme (TCS). The scheme operates through programs in which academics and students join with companies to contribute to the implementation of their strategies for technical and managerial change.

The government launched in 1997 the Electronic Government initiative to enable the government to become more responsive to the needs of its citizens. The government implemented its e-Government action plan in three steps, first focusing on basic e-Government transactions such as new business registration, then online tax payment and widespread information access, and finally electronic welfare benefits management and electronic voting. All the services for citizens, businesses and government are accessible online through the myGovernment portal (www.gov.my).

Malaysia aims at becoming a fully developed nation by 2020. The government set out to build up export-oriented manufacturing capacity based on inward direct investment. Electronic goods are the single most important category, growing at a double-digit rate throughout most of the past twenty-five years.

Well-developed infrastructure and administration are considered prerequisites for attracting FDI into Malaysia's ICT sector. Besides MSC, Malaysia created a rather strong ICT infrastructure in major enterprise zones and improved business processes. To foster local entrepreneurship, the government provides both financial and non-financial incentives to Malaysian businesses: zero income tax for a period of ten years, R&D grants, and 100 percent investment tax allowance on new investment in the MSC, unrestricted employment of foreign knowledge-workers, no restrictions on global capital, and limited restrictions on ownership. The computer and software markets have been fully deregulated. The computer services market develops dynamically and currently represents approximately 30 per cent of the current ICT market in Malaysia.

To support R&D activities in SMEs, the government introduced the Multimedia Super Corridor Research and Development Grant Scheme. It encourages creation of venture capital funds and promotes collaboration between Malaysian SMEs and world-class IT firms. Malaysia has a number of e-Commerce initiatives targeted at SME. For example MyBiz, an e-Commerce platform, helps increase efficiency of procurement and facilitate collaborative marketing by linking companies from over forty-three industry segments in a single business community network.

However, despite all the proactive government measures, Malaysia is not yet in the category of e-Business leaders. According to the Economist Intelligence Unit/Pyramid Research e-readiness rankings 2005, Malaysia is numbered only 35 in the world ranking. It has "begun to create an environment conducive to e-business, but [has] a great deal of work still to do."

To achieve its vision, Malaysia relies on a strong basis made possible by the government's strong vision regarding ICT development, a rapid industrialization with electronic goods production being the single most important category, and the US$40 billion Multimedia Super Corridor. It should attract national and international investors and create spillover effects in the rest of the economy. The network is also intended to support sophisticated public, education, and business applications. The country also benefits from attractive inducements to global and local capital through the creation of strong ICT infrastructure in major enterprise zones, by improving business processes, and by providing business incentives, comprehensive policies to encourage ICT use in various sectors of the economy, and a creative approach to addressing shortages in skilled ICT labor, such as the Teaching Company Scheme (TCS). The scheme operates through programs in which academics join with companies to contribute to the implementation of their strategies for technical and managerial change. It also counts with government grants for innovative ICT projects, the creation of attractive environment to attract FDI to ICT development, a strong emphasis on the expansion of telecommunications infrastructure, and fully liberalized telecommunications, computer, and software markets.

For Malaysia to follow the path of development it will have to overcome some hurdles, such as the shortage of skilled labor, the possibility of an emerging gap between the information-rich and those who do not have access to technology, notably because of the high cost of computers compared to average incomes, and its high dependence on exports, particularly electronics and electrical goods, which has made economic growth vulnerable to global fluctuations in the demand.

It is too early to draw conclusions about Malaysian e-Development experience. The major government initiative – MSC with its heavy emphasis on development of advanced multimedia applications – is yet to fully bear the fruit.

H   Poland

Information technology is growing rapidly in Poland, as users of the Internet have tripled from 2.5 million in 2000 to almost 9 million in 2003 (see Table 9.8). While business to consumer electronic commerce has developed recently, it is growing at a fast pace with US$280 m in Internet sales than in 2004, about three times the sales than in 2003. Electronic banking is the most developed activity with an estimated two million bank customers performing online banking. The B2B market has only begun to develop, but some e-Markets have been established for the trade of chemical and steel products.

The position document of 2000 "Aims and Directions of Information Society Development in Poland" has been prepared by the State Committee for Scientific Research and the Ministry of Posts and Telecommunications. The document paves the way for the development of the information society in Poland (see Figure 9.4 on p. 150).

In mid-1999 the Prime Minister appointed the Interministerial Group for Electronic Commerce to set up drafts for an appropriate regulatory framework for electronic commerce in Poland. The framework was set in 2002 with the Act on Providing Services by Electronic Means, the Act on Protection of Certain Services Provided by Electronic Means, and the Act on Electronic Payment Instruments.

Table 9.8   Poland's main ICT indicators, 2003

Fixed line and mobile phone subscribers per 1,000 inhabitants	769.65
Mobile phones per 1,000 inhabitants	450.91
PCs per 100 inhabitants	14.20
Internet users per 1,000 inhabitants	232.45
Internet hosts per 10,000 inhabitants	203.82

Sources: adapted from World Development Indicators Online (2005) and International Telecommunications Union (2005)

The Ministry of Science and Information Society Technologies is in charge of developing the information society in Poland and is leading projects such as the Polish Internet Library, ePoland, eEurope, etc.

Although Poland's communications infrastructure has improved since 1989, progress has been uneven. International telecommunications between business centers and in the largest towns are efficient, but domestic telephone links, particularly in the countryside, remained poor even in the late 1990s. However, this was in part compensated for by the spread of cellular telephones. Although expanding rapidly, fixed-line penetration is still low by European standards.

The telecommunications market is still dominated by the former state monopolist, Telekomunikacja Polska (TPSA), with almost 94 percent of the land lines in 2000. The company's reluctance to open its lines up to competition has provoked serious controversy, and also sparked off litigation. The market for local calls and inter-city business calls were liberalized first. The international calls market opened in early 2003. However, further liberalization seems inevitable, as a result of EU pressures combined with those of the domestic antitrust authority. TPSA is still the main player in the residential market, but much less so in the business market. The privatization of TPSA began in late 1998, with another wave of capital opening in mid-2000 and 2001. France Télécom bought some shares in 2004 and is negotiating for more, which would give it the majority holding.

Poland recently completed the reform of its system of education. It also developed a strategy of expansion of higher education to be completed by 2010. This strategy recognizes the importance of having a multi-faceted approach that trains the students in the use of ICT, connects the educational institutions to the Internet (all the Polish schools are connected), but recognizes that traditional schools are no longer the main way of learning, and therefore also develops a life-long learning and e-Learning approach to education.

The Ministry of Internal Affairs and Administration is also implementing a new Identity Card and Passport Issuing System. The modern, machine-readable identity cards will replace the current identity booklets by the end of 2005. In the future smart cards with microchips will be used which will extend their functionality. The Ministry also upgraded and integrated the local car registries into the unique Central Registry of Vehicles and Drivers (CEPIK). The new registry reduces registration costs, decreases the number of car thefts and driving license forgeries, and unveils vehicle owners evading the compulsory insurance.

A data transmission network PESEL-NET and e-mail system for public administration PEAR-2 have been successfully developed. Dedicated leased lines assure a high level of security for document exchange. At its start, the system covered merely the central administration level; however, in its ePoland Strategy (2004–2006), the Polish Government aims at increasing the capacity and coverage of PESEL-NET to include at least all the "poviats" (Polish administrative units).

In early 2001 the Agency for Enterprise Development was created to set the strategy and priorities for SME development and coordinate the National SME Services System, a network of over 150 SME-support institutions of various forms across the national territory.

Access to finance remains an important constraint on SME development. There has been an effort to improve the functioning of the loan guarantees system, including financing the advisory assistance for the six newly established loan guarantee funds and providing subsidies for local, sub-regional, and regional funds. €6.5 million have been allocated for this purpose.

Currently, there are no clusters in Poland. In the program "Increasing innovativeness of Poland's economy until 2006," the Ministry of Economy promises to support so-called "innovative local systems" but it is still unclear what the implementation of the policy will bring. At least, the technology parks and special economic zones have grown rapidly from a mere three around 2001 to about seventeen today. However, research and development in Poland may be hindered by the lack of significant cooperation between research institutions and the private sector.

Poland can count on a strong S&T heritage, its proximity to the EU, a growing domestic market, the capacity to attract FDI, and a great ICT awareness, especially among new generations, to successfully implement its strategy. Nonetheless, it will have to deal with the connectivity divide between rural and urban areas, a significant brain-drain, its rigid telecommunications sector, weak R&D policies, and the lack of focus of its policies (lack of appropriate specific actions).

Bridging the divide with EU countries is not the only priority. Attention should also be paid to regional development within the country and avoidance of an internal divide between rural and urban areas. A national action plan and policy strategies may be devoid of meaning if not accompanied by a realistic timeframe and specific target actions.

Poland ranks among the first tier of the countries that recently accessed to the EU, given the advanced status of the transition toward an open market economy. This leadership role has only lately been mirrored in the field of innovation and ICT. In fact, although the strategic government documents were growing in number, their value was sometimes doubtful when they are not based on legal regulations, not provided with suitable budgets and timeframes for their implementation. The recent strategy documents (ePoland, eEurope, etc.) finally show precise objectives, priorities, and adequate measures, as well as specific indicators to measure the strategies' implementation.

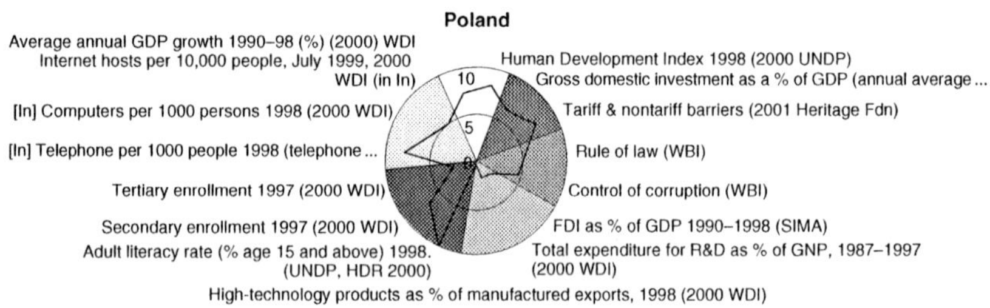

Figure 9.4   Poland's knowledge scorecard

Source: The World Bank, KAM (2005)

I   Slovak Republic

The Slovak Republic achieved significant progress in many areas of ICT utilization (see Table 9.9). Since 2004, Slovakia has developed a comprehensive e-Development framework. The country is neither a leader nor a laggard in e-Development among EU accession countries.

Slovakia's transition from a centrally planned economy to a modern market economy has been quite successful by regional standards. However, its government still faces many challenges, especially the maintenance of fiscal balance, the further privatization of the economy, reduction of unemployment, legalizing a booming unofficial or "gray" economy, and reduction of the economy's reliance on large enterprises.

The regulations in the area of the information society were established on several isolated acts but lacked a holistic vision, though most of them were adequate. For example, the Act on Telecommunications (2000) supports transparency, economic competition, and simplification of the regulatory environment, universal service provision and financing, and creation of a standard licensing system. The Act on Free Access to Public Information (2000) requires government authorities to provide certain types of information through the Internet. The Act on e-Signature was approved in 2002. It is only recently that the Slovak Government has started developing an

Table 9.9   Slovak Republic's main ICT indicators, 2003

Fixed line and mobile phone subscribers per 1,000 inhabitants	924.95
Mobile phones per 1,000 inhabitants	684.17
PCs per 100 inhabitants	23.62
Internet users per 1,000 inhabitants	255.87
Internet hosts per 10,000 inhabitants	212.18

Sources: adapted from World Development Indicators Online (2005) and International Telecommunications Union (2005)

information society framework, including the Competitiveness Strategy for the Slovak Republic up to 2010 (approved in 2004), the Strategy and Action Plan for Development of Information Society (2004), and the e-Government Roadmap (2005).

Slovakia is upgrading its telecommunications system and increasing its teledensity. However, in 2003, its teledensity was slightly lower than that of other transitioning countries of the region (31 lines for 100 people in 2003, while the Czech Republic and Hungary reached almost 40 lines per 100 people the year before). The telecommunications market has been fully liberalized since the beginning of 2003, but new fixed-line operators only entered the market recently because of the high connection rate Slovak Telecom was asking for. Because of the lack of competition in the sector, the infrastructure has been improving rather slowly. Fixed-lines teledensity is still well below the West European average. Plus, the quality of lines is unreliable and limits computer networking. As a partial compensation for lack of the modern fixed-line infrastructure, mobile telephony has been developing very fast and currently has almost 25 percent penetration rate.

The level of Internet usage by businesses is already almost as high as in the most advanced Central European countries, but Slovakia is behind in terms of usage by households and the education sector – it was only by the end of 2004 that all basic and secondary schools were equipped with computers and connected to the Internet. Nevertheless, the number of Internet users in Slovakia is expected to grow fast in the future. The growth is being driven by competition in the ISP sector that is largely owned by international firms, which in turn is driving down the costs of Internet access. Telecommunications fees for dial-up access did not fall as expected when the sector was finally liberalized in 2003, since the incumbent operator was charging extremely high prices for its "last mile" connection. However, connection agreements have been established since May 2005 with seven operators – which should finally bring down the prices and is likely to increase home Internet usage.

Slovakia has one of the most skilled labor forces among Central and East European countries. The educational system is well developed at all levels. The quality of education and training programs is generally high. Nevertheless, at university level student specialization occurs too early and is too narrowly defined, thus limiting flexibility and mobility within the labor market.

Universities and research centers in Slovakia are linked through SANET, Slovak Academic Network. In 1999, Slovakia started an ambitious project of gradual introduction of ICT in all basic and secondary schools. Over five years (1999–2004) all schools got modern multimedia classrooms, and thousands of teachers were trained to use the Internet and latest ICT applications.

Slovak society is rather conservative and shows a certain resistance to adopting novelties, including ICT. Private sector companies were first to seriously engage in ICT promotion and awareness campaigns; the government has been catching up only in the past few years.

Every official Slovak body has its own website providing comprehensive information on main and recent activities. Most of them have an English-language version. However, interactive e-Government services are not yet being offered. The www.obkan.sk portal (Citizen.sk) provides up-to-date information on public services provided by the state and local governments, and relevant independent organizations. This temporary solution will be replaced soon by a new and more complete (e-Services) public administration portal, currently in design.

The share of the private sector in GDP has grown steadily since 1991. However, for most of the 1990s the degree of state intervention in the economy was high and privatizations were often conducted through non-transparent management buy-outs.

Slovakia's policy towards SMEs is rather progressive and follows the approach promoted by the EU. Unlike large enterprises, many of which are still to be privatized or restructured, the SME sector of the economy is developing quite dynamically.

Privatization in the banking sector has made remarkable progress in the early-2000s. The banking sector is mainly in private hands and many of the major Slovakian banks were acquired by large international financial institutions. Credit cards started to be more widely used, but e-Banking developed faster, and most banks had started providing e-Banking services already by 2000. They support online payment for Internet shopping, and some banks even accept payment by mobile phone. As a result, the number of Slovaks shopping online has been growing steadily. The e-Retail industry is getting stronger and attracted a number of foreign investors. However, the e-Commerce market in Slovakia is behind that of the Czech Republic and Hungary, as it also suffered from the low penetration rate. Given the increased competition, the development of new services (DSL), the Act on Electronic Signature (2003), and the Act of Electronic Commerce (2003), online retail and online banking are expected to keep growing.

The online content industry in Slovakia is also developing dynamically. Many Internet start-ups attract strong local and foreign investors. ICT development and production sector is rather strong, but Slovakian technology companies are rarely named among the leaders in Central and Eastern Europe. As a general course, Czech and Hungarian technology companies develop more dynamically.

The quite successful privatization and enterprise restructuring that took place during the last few years has been a strength for the country, along with the fact that its banking sector is in private hands and quite efficient and competitive. The telecommunications market in Slovakia has been liberalized and there is also healthy competition in the sector for Internet service providers (ISPs), which is dominated by foreign-owned firms. Finally, the educational attainment of the labor force compares well to that of OECD countries, and is higher than in most ECA countries.

On the other hand, Slovakia shows a booming unofficial or "gray" economy, its economy relies mainly on large enterprises, and there is high unemployment. The government only very recently elaborated an updated long-term strategic vision of the development of the information society in Slovakia; the ICT regulations used to be based on several isolated acts. Finally the country will have to deal with the only partial privatization of Slovak Telecom – 51 percent belongs to Deutsche Telekom, but 34 percent belongs to the Ministry of Transport, Postal Services, and Telecommunications, and 15 percent belongs to the National Property Fund (FNM).

Even though the Slovak Government's strategic vision for ICT is recent, the sector has been developing quite successfully by regional standards. This lack of vision was partially compensated for by isolated, but mostly adequate, regulatory acts. Especially important in this regard is openness of the ISP market to FDI. The important lesson here is that even with the absence of an overall strategy, targeted policy interventions may have a visible positive effect. Active government promotional measures should help the Slovak ICT sector to reach leadership positions in the region.

J   South Africa

South Africa's vision for development encompasses the provision of affordable, high-tech, and high-level ICT services to remote and underdeveloped rural communities. The Telecommunications Act of 1996 set forth the foundations to establish the necessary policy framework and legislative reform to facilitate the development of all aspects of ICT infrastructure.

The ICT sector is growing significantly (see Table 9.10), with ICT spending accounting for 8 percent of GDP (2003). The government has implemented a number of framework policies for infrastructure, partnership and established task-forces that will help South African communities play a role in the global economy.

The South African Government also recognized the vital role of SMEs as an important component, complement, and driver in the nation's development, particularly through their ability to create jobs and sustain innovation.

Internet penetration in South Africa is by far the highest on the continent, with 3.1 million users in 2002 (31 percent of the total in Africa). This penetration is concentrated in urban areas close to major towns, yet penetration is low in rural and remote areas due to lack of infrastructure and the high cost of access and equipment.

South Africa's Government has placed a strong emphasis on ICT sector development through the implementation of a national ICT strategy. This plan proactively addresses ICT penetration, particularly for disadvantaged segments of the society. But its implementation may not be as successful as

Table 9.10   South Africa's main ICT indicators, 2003

Fixed line and mobile phone subscribers per 1,000 inhabitants	410.48*
Mobile phones per 1,000 inhabitants	363.64
PCs per 100 inhabitants	7.26
Internet users per 1,000 inhabitants	303.91*
Internet hosts per 10,000 inhabitants	62.25

* 2002 data
Sources: adapted from World Development Indicators Online (2005) and International Telecommunications Union (2005)

hoped for. According to a 2005 report by Research ICT Africa!, despite the ICT policy visions initiated by various departments, the presidential commissions, and the national strategies, there is no integrated ICT vision for the country, which makes the current ICT policy uncoordinated, and duplicatory.

The South African Information Technology Industry Strategy (SAITIS) is a bilateral project between the South African and the Canadian Governments and a private sector entity PriceWaterhouse Coopers, acting as the executing agency. This initiative sets out an Information and Communications Technology (ICT) Sector Development Framework for South Africa. The South African Information Technology Industry Strategy (SAITIS) and Info 2025 Vision include a focus on building infrastructure, especially within secondary towns designated as export zones for both ICT and non-ICT products and services.

The Telecommunications Act of 1996 brought about the licensing of a limited category of telecom service providers while providing for the retention of certain exclusive rights by Telkom South Africa, the state-owned monopoly telecom provider. Prior to 1996, Telkom was responsible for the regulation of the telecommunications sector. This situation changed with the passing of the Telecommunications Act, which provided for the establishment of an independent sector regulator known as the South African Telecommunications Regulatory Authority (SATRA) whose primary role was to administer the provisions of the Telecommunications Act.

e-Commerce and Internet-based businesses have grown rapidly in South Africa, but a legislative framework for e-Commerce is not yet in place. So far, the government has published a Green Paper on electronic law (1999), including e-Signature legislation and protection of personal information, and drafted an appropriate legislation, to build trust and confidence in e-Commerce. However, it does not seem that an actual legislation exists today.

Three important task-forces have been introduced to address the deployment of ICT as an enabler of social and economic development: (1) the Presidential International Task Force on Information Society and

Development to focus mainly on global ICT markets; (2) the National IT Task Force, which will deal with the issue of "brain-drain" and the deployment of ICT initiatives locally; and (3) the IT Council to handle local and provisional government IT functions.

In addition, the government has announced the establishment of the Investment Council, which will focus on positioning South Africa's imports and exports globally and also on generating foreign direct investment through international collaborations.

The government has also created the State Information Technology Agency to encourage the provision of information technology, information systems, and related services in a managed secure environment.

The Independent Broadcasting Authority (IBA) and the South African Telecommunications Regulatory Authority (SATRA) merged to form the Independent Communications Authority of South Africa (ICASA) in July 2000. The core responsibility of ICASA is to regulate broadcasting and telecommunications for the public interest. ICASA has been also assigned to control, planning, administration, management, and licensing of the use of the radio frequency spectrum, and to monitor the telecommunications marketplace to ensure that operators comply with their licenses.

South Africa's telecommunications industry is undergoing major restructuring, including significant privatization. South Africa was predicted to have one of the fastest-growing mobile-phone industries in the world, and an estimated 20 million users by now. However, this did not materialize because the privatization did not lead to lower prices.

Funds are currently being channeled into the field of telecommunications. Infrastructure is spread unevenly across the country. Unlike commercial zone development, there is a very low penetration of services in rural and remote areas. More investments are being made to bridge the internal connectivity gap.

South Africa's university system is the best in Africa, with a total of 36 universities and technical colleges (technikons). The educational system as a whole is experiencing a profound transformation, given the opening of formerly white institutions to all the members of the South African society. The larger, wealthier universities are battling to transform themselves, and previously non-white institutions are struggling with poor resources and plummeting student numbers. Literacy rates are increasing, but basic ICT skills remain limited across the educational offer.

South Africa is facing a significant "brain-drain" in technical and entrepreneurial ICT skills, with an estimated 200–300 ICT-skilled persons leaving the country each month. This is caused by the rapid growth in demand for ICT skills worldwide and little opportunity (jobs, remuneration, and innovation) in South Africa. Current unemployment rates are very high (30–35 percent), but it is also difficult to find a sufficient supply of skilled ICT workers to meet the rising demand.

The South African Government is undertaking a large series of initiatives in coordination with other African states, such as African Information Society or African Society initiatives, in an effort to promote ICT awareness even in the remote and rural areas.

The private sector and the "third sector" are actively involved in promotional measures to increase awareness of ICT and new applications at different levels of society. The National Information Technology Forum (NITF) is a non-government organization (NGO) composed of representatives from civil society, private sector, academia, and government. The NITF's main goal is to open the channels of communication and promote interaction amongst stakeholders in the ICT community and the broader public, and amongst policy-making bodies in the country.

All government departments and their ministries have established websites to disseminate information regarding their activities and are working to ICT-enable their constituencies. For example, in education, the Gauteng province developed the Gautengonline (GoL) program, and so far GoL laboratories have been installed in 1,100 schools, over 22,000 educators have received ICT training in their laboratories, and almost one million learners have access to ICT in schooling.

Despite the fact that the need to privatize – both for effective service delivery and to raise funds for the state budget – has been accepted by government, the slow pace of privatization has negatively affected investor confidence. Access to capital is becoming easier and fostering innovation and competition among South African entrepreneurs. Many South African businesses now have access to both international and local financial institutions. Black empowerment start-up organizations have access to financial means far beyond that available under the apartheid regime, and there is a vibrant and growing local venture capital market accompanied by inflow of foreign direct investment from ICT multinationals. A number of South African ICT-related businesses have obtained access to global markets through mergers and acquisitions with ICT companies in similar lines of business.

Free trade policies and tax incentives have allowed global ICT players such as Mecer, Acer, and Compaq to start assembling ICT hardware and network equipment locally, creating a pool of ICT-skilled technicians and programmers. There are also ICT tariff programs applied to the shipping of small units or parts that encourage value-added assembly to take place in South Africa.

The financial sector has been at the forefront of adopting ICT, contributing 50 percent of all ICT expenditure. Major banks operate their own regional networks, offering some websites with online banking services. Public enterprises are also being transformed and modernized in a widespread restructuring program. This movement has facilitated the development of an active entrepreneurial scene.

The South African Government has accepted certain driver issues to make the country internationally competitive and to fuel economic growth. Competitiveness needs to be increased in the energy, transport, and telecommunications sectors. Growth sectors that have been identified include exports of manufactures, tourism, agriculture, ICT, and cultural industries. To achieve economic growth and competitiveness, several issues cutting across the industrial sectors need to be addressed through knowledge transfer, training, investment, and management.

South Africa is the most advanced and productive economy in the Africa region, it has a very well-developed financial, legal, telecommunications, energy, and transport system. Moreover, during the last years, a significant percentage of university and technical-school graduates developed IT-oriented knowledge and skills (software development, network management). The country also worked on improving its ICT infrastructure.

However, the country still displays low computer-literacy levels, low computer penetration among society, low awareness of ICT opportunities among the public sector and the R&D spending budget is being kept in low figures for the last years, all of which are impeding South Africa's e-Development. In addition, the cost of mobile telecommunications is quite prohibitive and the household Internet penetration is low (3.5 percent in 2004) due to a low level of household PV ownership (12 percent) and high cost of fixed-line telecommunication infrastructure.

The private sector has played a crucial role in driving the growth of the Internet: supply and demand in the financial sector leap-frogged to support and provide cutting-edge Internet services access, as well as to offer full online services and to upgrade e-Commerce. Finally, the commitment of the government to provide a more IT-focused education and training has led to the restructuring of the whole educational system.

10
e-Development Profiles of Developing Countries

A   Bulgaria

Prior to 1989, Bulgaria had a relatively strong electronics and communications industry. Bulgaria was considered the technology center of the Soviet bloc with strong emphasis on software development. Yet, the general economic downturn of the former Soviet bloc undermined Bulgaria's traditional export focus on the ICT. In addition, lacking the capacity to compete on a global scale, the most talented ICT professionals fled the country. Only during the last few years did the government start making a serious effort to use ICT for its economic and social development goals, especially in light of the country's application for EU accession (see Table 10.1).

The government has adopted two framework documents on Strategy and National Program for IS development. A number of sector-specific strategies and programs have also been adopted: telecommunications sector policy, national strategy for ICT education, program on application of advanced information and management technologies in the administration, national strategy for promotion of small- and medium-sized enterprises (SMEs), strategy for development of high technology activities in Bulgaria. In 2000 a "National Strategy for e-Commerce" was passed.

Bulgaria has adopted some regulations necessary for successful e-Development, such as an e-Signature act. However, in general, the country does not have an innovation-oriented economic policy, which prevents the development of electronic commerce. More e-Government would also encourage the private sector to increase its investments in ICT to match the ones of the government. It would also allow businesses to do "e-Commerce" with the biggest economic player, the government.

Although the Bulgarian Government had already started paying special attention to the development of the Information Society in the early-1990s, the institutional framework has experienced several changes in the last five or six years – and it is still not very well defined. In spite of the creation of the Coordination Council on Information Society Issues (1998) and various

Table 10.1   Bulgaria's main ICT indicators, 2003

Fixed line and mobile phone subscribers per 1,000 inhabitants	846.86*
Mobile phones per 1,000 inhabitants	466.37*
PCs per 100 inhabitants	5.19
Internet users per 1,000 inhabitants	205.84*
Internet hosts per 10,000 inhabitants	66.57

* 2002 data
Sources: adapted from World Development Indicators Online (2005)
and International Telecommunications Union (2005)

national strategies, their implementation did not succeed because of a lack of political vision and leadership, financial resources, and unrealistic objectives. The current government – in place since 2001 – has adopted a more pragmatic approach, focusing on the ICT industry and the development of e-Government.

The market is more or less liberalized: 65 percent of the former state-owned Bulgarian Telecommunications Company (BTC) was finally sold in 2004 to a private investor; however, it will take time for other operators to enter the market. The use of the Internet started spreading, but is still low (in 2004, 26 percent of adult Bulgarians used the Internet), mainly because of the high cost of digital phone lines and the poor quality of the analogue lines.

Competition is open in the mobile and the Internet sectors. Nevertheless, while multiple Internet service providers (ISPs) compete with one another in urban centers, few even operate in small towns and rural areas. Moreover, where Internet access is available, the average cost for services is almost twice as high as in the cities. Thus, the country faces a serious problem of internal digital divide.

A national strategy for ICT education was adopted in 1998 by the Ministry of Education and Science. A state research and information services unit called "National Education and Research Network UNIKOM-B" was also established in 1998, which had the aim of coordinating, managing, and controlling all the computer communications and information services of the educational and research institutions in Bulgaria.

Government initiatives in the field of education are increasing, but these efforts are not deemed sufficient to foster the educational cycle for innovation. The lack of adequate training in information technologies, Internet, and multimedia remains the major constraint for the Bulgarian educational system. Information technology remains an unknown field to most of the teachers in primary and secondary schools: 25 percent of schools have no teachers with IT qualifications.

The situation seems to be better at the university level. The Ministry is currently exploring the potential of partnership with the private sector to foster education and training. In 2002, there were five Microsoft Academies, and in the past year we counted over 110 Cisco Academies for training in universities.

There are no specific and explicit activities promoted by the government to increase awareness among the public. The interest of the general public is nevertheless increasing, given the high attendance of many trade fairs and exhibitions. Mass media and private promotional campaigns are quite successful with a large number of the population and business community.

Steps towards e-Government in Bulgaria, albeit in their infancy, are producing results, but these are more adequate for businesses than for citizens. The services to businesses include the general tax directorate, the national company registry, the public procurement registry at the Council of Ministers, and the registry of small public procurement at the SME Agency. Some of the services directed at the citizens include social and health insurance data, reports to the police, notifications and job search at the employment agency, and online submission of income tax.

The innovation policy is still not a government priority, and there are no practical measures or incentives for companies to invest in innovation and technological development. The lack of favorable financing and crediting schemes remains the key problem for entrepreneurs. The law on high-tech parks and high-tech technology has been blocked in Parliament and is an evident sign of the political uncertainty on innovation.

Bulgaria can rely on some great strengths to implement its e-Development strategy, such as having one of the highest telephone line densities in the ECA region, the open competition in the mobile and Internet sectors, the high level of technical skill and general education, particularly in the areas of engineering and information technology skills, and the relatively high quality of ICT products at competitive prices.

Nonetheless, Bulgaria shows a slow privatization process, high connectivity cost and low computer penetration, and a divide between rural and urban areas. It is only during the last few years that the government started making a serious effort to use ICT for its economic and social objectives (see Figure 10.1). There is no longer a monopoly in the telecommunications market, but there are not yet many players to foster competition, the business environment for ICT is unfriendly, the domestic market limited, as is the access to finance, and a lack of basic business skills (marketing, etc.) among local entrepreneurs.

Even though prior to 1989 Bulgaria had a relatively strong electronics and communications industry, it lost its potential due to the general economic downturn of the early-2000s and lack of government focus on ICT. Coherent government support for the ICT industry is essential for long-term sustainable growth of the sector.

In the innovation policy field, the law on electronic documents and electronic signature passed in March 2001 are important signs of increased attention paid by the government to ICT. The updated program for

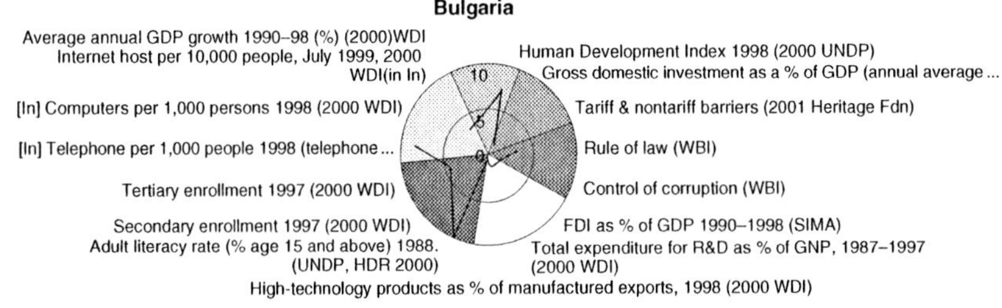

Figure 10.1   Bulgaria's knowledge scorecard
Source: The World Bank, KAM (2005)

development of the domestic information society determines the main activities of state institutions and sets performance deadlines. Yet, state investment on scientific R&D remains low. The number of scientific research projects, as well as of the persons engaged in scientific R&D, is steadily decreasing.

B   India

India has become an example for other developing countries of viable industrial policies to leverage information and communication technologies to foster economic and social development (see Table 10.2). After independence, India implemented a protectionist economic policy that was aimed at creating a solid industrial basis for the development of the country. In the mid-1980s and early-1990s, the government adopted a diametrically opposite approach, implementing a set of reforms that aimed at placing the country in the global economy and opening up the country to foreign investors. Notwithstanding the abundance of natural resources, the Indian government paid sound attention to the innovative segments of the economy, and has tried to move from an agriculturally based economy to a knowledge based one.

India's success in driving development through ICT has been accompanied by appropriate government measures. One of these has been the establishment of specifically dedicated institutions to help the technology sector improve its performance. Specific institutions have been created to support the potential of technologically savvy Indian entrepreneurs.

In mid-1998, the National Task-Force on IT and Software Development was set up by the Prime Minister's Office to formulate the draft of a national informatics policy, but the submission paper was not presented before mid-2002. The National Task-Force elaborates strategies to foster the ICT sector in India and set the strategies to sustain its development and competitiveness. The strategies are included in a precise action plan for ICT

Table 10.2   India's main ICT indicators, 2003

Fixed line and mobile phone subscribers per 1,000 inhabitants	71.03
Mobile phones per 1,000 inhabitants	24.75
PCs per 100 inhabitants	0.72
Internet users per 1,000 inhabitants	17.49
Internet hosts per 10,000 inhabitants	0.82

Sources: adapted from World Development Indicators Online (2005) and International Telecommunications Union (2005)

industry, with specific target, actions, and timeline. Attention is paid not only to software but also to hardware and other related fields of the ICT industry.

The establishment of the Telecommunications Regulatory Authority of India (TRAI) was a key step toward effective implementation of telecommunications reforms. In 1992, the mobile phone market was opened up to private operators, in 1994 the fixed services market followed, and finally in 1999, national long-distance operations were opened to private competition. Prior to these reforms, the Department of Telecommunications had been the sole provider of telecommunications services.

The introduction of competition in the telecommunications market has facilitated the rapid growth registered in recent years (41.4 m working connections installed by the end of 2003). Yet, given the large population, teledensity remains low (46 lines per 1,000 people in 2003). Mobile services have been liberalized since 1994, thus allowing greater expansion of cellular subscribers. Basic telecom services have also been liberalized but at a slower pace with private services offered in only six states. The establishment of an effective independent regulatory authority for the telecommunications and multimedia markets, to regulate, issue licenses, and police operators, was completed in 1997 with the creation of the Telecom Regulatory Authority of India (TRAI); but the creation of the powerful Communications Commission of India is still on hold.

The government is determined to increase teledensity and to promote a vibrant telecommunications environment. Internet connectivity remains low at 17 Internet users per 1,000 people in 2003, although penetration is expected to increase rapidly – up to 8m users in 2003 from 7m in 2001. As of 2004, there were over 180 Internet service providers (ISPs) in India, of which 41 were licensed to offer their services across the country (the remaining being state-specific).

India has some of the lowest human development indicators in the world (ranked 127th out of 177 in 2004), and the divide between rural and urban areas exacerbates the human capital issues. Yet, on the other hand, India also provides highly qualified professionals. Despite the low rate of literacy, the educational system of India is considered one of the strengths of the country.

The government has invested heavily in higher education, to ensure that Indian professionals can meet the increasing demand of technology companies, through the creation of the Indian Institutes of Technology. Yet, most of the vocational training is provided by the private sector, and wider reform of the educational system may strengthen India's social and economic development.

India shows great assets. The Indian education system has a strong emphasis on science and technology, resulting in a large number of science and engineering graduates. Indian labor is cheaper than elsewhere; Indian ICT professionals demand much lower wages and have made India an attractive source for global outsourcing. Its qualified workforce is another strength of the country; Indian programmers are known for their strong technical skills.

However, India also shows some weaknesses. Overseas demand may be detrimental to India's economy in the case of global downturn. Poor communications infrastructure is creating an internal digital divide between rural and urban areas. Given the large population and territorial extension, India has a very low teledensity. The communications infrastructure is over-all poor and out-dated. Currently only every 4.6 out of 100 people have access to a telephone line, computer penetration per family is fairly low as well (0.72 personal computer per 100 people in 2003). Finally, the overall business environment can be improved. It is only recently that the country has changed policies to encourage private funding (see Figure 10.2).

The government played a crucial role in realizing the potential of India as a major IT power. A set of policies to encourage FDI and promote the ICT sector has been implemented in the last decade. Institution building is a crucial element of e-Development. In India, the Ministry of Information Technology is very proactive in developing the infrastructure that supports the development of information technology.

Yet, despite developments within the Indian ICT industry, the government still has to face major issues to lead the country completely into the global economy. India is still plagued by a high rate of poverty and illiteracy. Moreover, infrastructures are very often inadequate: apart from roads and

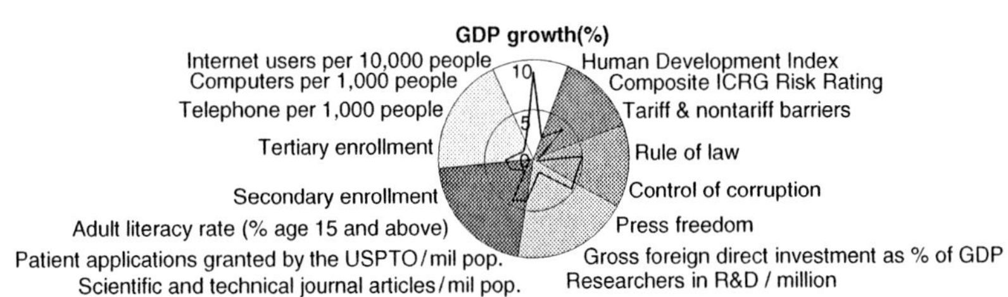

Figure 10.2 India's knowledge scorecard

Source: The World Bank, KAM (2005)

energy supply, India offers an unreliable information infrastructure and a widening internal digital divide. Rural areas are not fully served by telecom services and many villages have no telephones.

The export focus of the ICT industry can have a detrimental effect on the internal market. In fact, incentives for export have undermined the development of the domestic ICT market, and today India lags behind in terms of usage of ICT and related products in both business and society, especially in rural areas.

C   Latvia

Latvia inherited a strong science and research tradition from the time of the USSR. The development of an ICT sector, however, was not a priority for the government until the beginning of talks for accession into the EU. Latvia has currently adopted legislation that corresponds to EU legislation in the area of science and research.

The ambitious national program to build an information society, "Informatics," has encouraged dialogue and cooperation among the three sectors (public, private, and non-governmental organizations), especially between industry and academia. Latvia's geographical location – near the Nordic countries and Russia – has facilitated the inflow of foreign direct investment, which is essential to facilitate knowledge-transfer and foster innovation. The country's expertise in electronics and related industries, along with a growing interest among the younger generation in information services and Western technologies, is providing a qualified but relatively inexpensive labor force.

The national program "Informatics Action Plan for Years 1999–2005" was accepted by the Cabinet of Ministers in March 1999. Latvia is gradually moving to full adoption of a regulatory framework in compliance with international and European standards in support of an "information society." A draft information society program "e-Latvia 2005–2008" was presented early in 2005.

Table 10.3   Latvia's main ICT indicators, 2003

Fixed line and mobile phone subscribers per 1,000 inhabitants	811.23
Mobile phones per 1,000 inhabitants	525.85
PCs per 100 inhabitants	18.80
Internet users per 1,000 inhabitants	403.59
Internet hosts per 10,000 inhabitants	177.92

Sources: adapted from World Development Indicators Online (2005) and International Telecommunications Union (2005)

The Law on Personal Data Protection was passed by the Parliament in March 2000. Although the Law on Electronic Documents (including digital signatures) was passed in October 2002, two years earlier the Latvian Business Register chose to start a pilot project on implementation of e-Documents and digital signatures in state institutions. In the same period, two working groups had been established within the government to develop legislation in support of e-Commerce according to the relevant EU Directives, which led to the Latvian Parliament approving the Law on Information Society Services in November 2004. Moreover, the criminal law of 1998 has been amended to include computer crimes.

A coordination board for the national program informatics was formed in November 1997, as Boards of Informatics were put in place in all ministries between 1997 and 1998. The national program "Informatics" was approved by the Government of Latvia in March 1999. Information society projects were included in the Declaration (program document) of the Cabinet of Ministers in July 1999. Coordination of the State Investment Program for all information technologies and telecommunications-related projects has been performed by the Department of Informatics in cooperation with the Ministry of Economy since the fiscal year 1998.

Latvia started the transition process with a telephone penetration of 25 percent, one of the highest in Eastern Europe. However, further expansion has been slow since then, with teledensity reaching 29 percent in 2003 (see Table 10.3). Almost one third of the fixed-line network was digitalized at the beginning of 1999, and reached two thirds by the end of 2001. A fiber-optic cable has been laid to connect the Latvian network to those of Sweden, Finland, and Estonia. The monopoly telecommunications operator Lattelekom is controlled by the government by a 51 percent stake and involves a strategic investor TILTS Communications with 49 percent (TILTS is a joint venture of 90 percent Sonera Corporation and 10 percent IFC of the World Bank). Lattelekom was scheduled for full privatization in 1999. The sale has been held up by possible litigation between the government and TILTS communication on ending Lattelekom's monopoly status in 2003 – ten years earlier than originally planned – which was a condition for Latvia's accession to the World Trade Organization (WTO).

The number of Internet hosts in the country rose quickly after Lattelekom introduced a high-speed Internet connection. In 2003 about 40 percent of the population was using the Internet. Two mobile operators, Latvijas Mobilais Telefons and Tele 2, have been granted licenses to provide a global system for mobile communications (GSM) services. In 2003 there were 52.58 mobile telephone subscribers for every 100 people, or 64.8 percent of the total of telephone subscribers.

The multi-annual Latvian Education Informatization System project is being financed by the State Investment Program and implemented starting from 1997. Under the project, the creation of infrastructure, the training of trainers and users, the elaboration of education content, the computerized education system management, and different information services were being introduced and upgraded. As of 2002, the program had achieved the following results:

- Developed teaching aids: approximately 20 percent of the total amount of high school programs can be taught using information and communication technologies;
- Introduced school management software in about 1,000 sites;
- Trained 66 percent of all teachers on ICT usage;
- Connected 97 percent of schools to the Internet;
- Decreased the number of pupils per computer from 67 (year 1997) to 20 (year 2002).

In December 2000, the Law on Institutions of Higher Education was amended to provide for the implementation of higher education professional degrees and the possibility of students moving from academic to professional study programs. In addition, several legislative acts setting national standards for vocational training, vocational secondary education, and first-level higher professional education were adopted.

Promotional activities sponsored by the government and related agencies try to increase awareness in the civic and business communities on ICT and their beneficial potential. Most activities take place during conferences, seminars, and workshops specifically designed for the target audience, according to their different needs (i.e. business community, students, citizens, etc.).

In July 1995 the Latvian Government established the National Unified Informatics and Communications Center. Its purpose was both to manage the dedicated governmental communications systems and to promote development of information systems in government agencies.

Currently, the government is committed in the Latvian Association of Local and Regional Governments (LPS). The cost is estimated at USD30 million. Local governments will gain access to the system gradually. So far the association represents all the seven major cities, all the fifty-three towns, all the twenty-six districts, 388 rural municipalities (out of 444), and seventeen amalgamated municipalities (out of twenty-six) in Latvia.

Latvia's electronic industry was very important in the former Soviet Union, providing telecommunications equipment and electronics production for military needs at the time. The electronics sector of Soviet Latvia employed about 30,000 highly qualified specialists and the industry was dominated by five big state companies. Despite its importance in Soviet times, the Latvian electronics industry could not compete with Western companies when the markets were opened at the beginning of the 1990s. Low pricing strategy could not compensate for the poor service and quality of the products.

The restructuring process of the national enterprises was not very successful, and the companies' production fell in more than 90 percent between 1993 and 1997. The former electronics enterprises are still present but restructured into smaller units. The dismantling of the state enterprises has on the one hand facilitated the creation of a network of SMEs, and on the other has facilitated the process of the brain-draining of qualified and skilled labor.

Software design is the most significant segment of the IT sector in Latvia. Software maintenance, integration, consulting, and training are other rapidly growing areas. Outsourcing has become a core competence of Latvian software-development companies, which have gained significant experience from large-scale software-development projects undertaken for major international companies. There are a hundred or so software design companies in Latvia at this time, employing around 4,000 employees. Most are small companies that focus on the design of specialized software and on the provision of related services. Large software design projects are handled by some twenty or thirty companies.

Latvia's strengths lie in its S&T heritage, in its preexisting S&T sector and in its human capital. But it is a late starter, the telecommunications sector not open, and there is a lack of financial resources as well as a lack of specific actions to attract FDI (diverted in most cases to Estonia).

The Latvian case shows that building a favorable environment for FDI is essential to retain capacity in the ICT sector. Late starters can still play a role in KE and find niche markets and applications (see Figure 10.3). Many countries have similar endowments (labor force and S&T heritage) but different strategies. Proximity to ICT leaders is not necessarily a driving factor. It can be a facilitator but only in the case where there are appropriate policies.

Despite difficulties that arose through the lack of financial resources to drive the transition, Latvia is relatively well positioned to take advantage of its potential in ICT. The export volume of the IT sector to the West has grown from year to year: the Latvian Information System cluster created in 2001 (and that now counts about twenty companies) aims at exporting

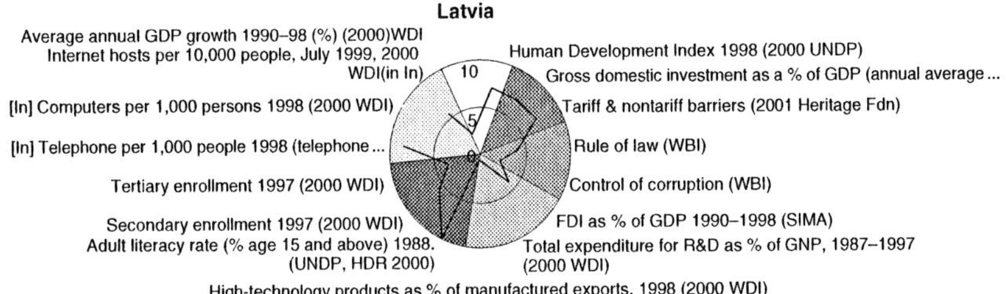

Figure 10.3   Latvia's knowledge scorecard

Source: The World Bank, KAM (2005)

between USD0.5m and USD1m per year (starting in 2010) in software, integration services, and outsourced services exports.

More than 300 companies work in computer manufacturing and servicing, as well as in computer and software maintenance, and in retailing of peripherals. These are small companies with no more than ten employees in most cases, although four companies have more than a hundred workers. Specialists have calculated that the market capacity for computers (both locally assembled and imported), software, and peripherals is around Ls 80–100 million per year.

D   Lithuania

Lithuania, as in the case of other Baltic transitional economies, has understood the importance of building an information society to take advantage of information and communication technologies as a driver for economic and social development. Yet, the lack of financial resources and other priorities identified in the first years of transition (democratization process, building a market-oriented economy, unemployment, etc.) have hindered the Lithuanian potential to build a viable and sustainable information society. Up to now, Lithuania had been remarkably unstable in regulating the development of an information society on the state level: in a relatively short period of time, institutions responsible for this area have been changed several times.

The Department of Information and Informatics under the Ministry of Public Administration Reforms and Local Authorities prepared the "Information Society Development Strategy." This three-year program was approved by the high level (inter-ministerial) State Information Policy Development Advisory Commission in 2001. According to this program, the Lithuanian Government was to support IS projects only in strategic areas and after approval by the Department of Information and Informatics.

The Lithuanian government announced the strategic directions of IS development: computerization of Lithuanian schools, modernization of science and the education system, and promotion and support of e-Business.

Table 10.4   Lithuania's main ICT indicators, 2003

Fixed line and mobile phone subscribers per 1,000 inhabitants	868.93
Mobile phones per 1,000 inhabitants	629.73
PCs per 100 inhabitants	10.97
Internet users per 1,000 inhabitants	201.90
Internet hosts per 10,000 inhabitants	192.63

Sources: adapted from World Development Indicators Online (2005) and International Telecommunications Union (2005)

The Ministry of Science and Education prepared the Strategy for Implementation of Advanced Information Technologies in Lithuanian Education in 2001. The Strategy describes the current situation, the future vision and goals of modernization, priorities, and ways of realization. The main purpose of the strategy is to provide the prospects and trends for integrating information and communication technology (ICT) into Lithuanian general education, to plan the stages of its implementation, to harmonize activities of various institutions, and effectively to use the funds allocated for the computerization of education.

In order to enter the EU market and to lay the foundations of an unprecedented and successful integration with the EU's regulatory framework and operations, the Lithuanian Government wisely chose to revise its existing laws and regulations and to set out the need for their necessary amendment.

The "Strategy of Development of Information and Communications for Lithuanian Education" plans to connect all schools in a single Educational Network, and to increase by a large amount the number of computers in schools. Today, the network connects the five major cities, and another twenty cities.

The government adopted e-Legislation consistent with international and EU standards, such as a law on legal protection of personal data (1996), a copyright and related rights law (1999), and a law of electronic signature (2000).

The Telecommunications Law, passed in mid-1998, on one hand establishes the telecommunications regulatory framework, but on the other hand has regard to the requirements of European Union law, as part of their obligation to comply with the EU standards. This law also regulates the relations between telecommunications operators and the users of their services and sets out conditions for promoting competition in the telecommunications sector. Lithuanian Telecommunications was gradually privatized in two different stages (1998 and 2000) to foreign investors.

The Information Society Development Committee, established in mid-2001, under the Government of the Republic of Lithuania, became responsible for the regulation of information technologies and telecommunications and the coordination of the development of an information society. The mission of the committee is to design, arrange, and coordinate processes aimed at the development of an information society alongside the creation of an open, educated, continuously learning society, members of which rely on knowledge in their activities, and have the opportunity and capability for making effective use of modern ICT means in every step of their life. Among the committee's goals are the following: (1) to participate in the process of shaping state policy for the development of information technologies and telecommunications and to coordinate its implementation; and (2) to coordinate planning, creation, and development of the ICT infrastructure complying with European Union standards.

The Lithuanian Development Agency (LDA) provides comprehensive information about investment opportunities, conditions, and procedures to foreign investors and private companies that are interested in setting up their businesses in Lithuania. Part of the LDA is the information center which is active in two major areas: on the one hand, it promotes Lithuania as an attractive place for investment and business and advertises the services that the agency offers to foreign investors, on the other hand it provides an actual information for local producers on export regulations, trade fairs, and general market conditions.

The telecommunications market in Lithuania has been liberalized, except for fixed-line telecommunications. In the last few years, the mobile telecommunications sector has experienced a dramatic expansion with a penetration rate of 87 percent in 2004 – up from 47 percent in 2002. In fact, there are currently three mobile operators. Moreover, the Internet market is also experiencing impressive growth with 202 users per 1,000 people in 2003 up from 61 users per 1,000 people in 2000, and there are presently about fifteen Internet service providers (ISPs) (see Table 10.4 on p. 168).

Telephone access is close to the regional average, with teledensity of 239 for fixed-line phones and 630 for mobile phones in 2003. Lietuvos Telekomas (Lithuanian Telecoms, the fixed-line operator) lost its monopoly at the beginning of 2003, but although there were twenty-one international fixed-line operators in 2004, Lithuanian Telecoms had an overwhelming 97 percent of market shares.

The Lithuanian governmental decree of July 2, 1998 stimulated state research institutes to participate more actively in the research and development programs of the European Union, and NATO. Additionally, the Lithuanian Government promoted an R&D initiative, the Program on Innovations in Business, intended to be one of the first and main elements in national innovation system. A revised program was adopted in July 2003 with measures for the 2003–2006 period. The long-term goal of the program is to increase international competitiveness of national businesses promoting R&D innovation, modernize existing businesses, and foster the creation of modern start-ups using Lithuanian and international scientific and technological potential.

During 2000, the Lithuanian Government funded investments, in the amount of MEUR2.5 (more than MLt6) for the renovation of computers and other equipment in universities and the modernization of research equipment in state research institutes. Another important project, the integration of Lithuania's Academic and Research Computer Network LITNET in the European Academic Network TEN 155 (LITNET-GEANT), is supported by Lithuanian government.

Another major task of the institutions dedicated to ICT is to increase ICT awareness in public opinion and to promote the national IS strategy program. The Lithuanian Computer Society and INFOBALT, the association of the largest IT companies, are the most active in promoting the information society, supporting the efforts of the public sector in shaping ICT policies, and increasing understanding among the general public. The practical activities aimed for support and promotion of the development of IS started in the middle of 2000. In the context of the European Commission's e-Europe initiative, the Lithuanian government announced a plan to establish e-Vyriausybe (e-Government), which it approved at the end of 2004 as part of the "Programme of the Government of the Republic of Lithuania for 2004–2008."

Lithuania formed its principles of commercial law based on EU Directives. It is developing and establishing favorable conditions for electronic commerce that promote its wide spread use and development. Seimas, the Lithuanian Parliament, adopted the Law on Electronic Signature (2000) and the Law on Electronic Commerce (2002). The Lithuanian Government supports the development of e-Business. The special working group to prepare proposals to the government for the promotion and support of e-Business was established.

The special portal http://www.infocom.lt for promotion and support of business was established under the support of PHARE and the INFOBALT Association. Lithuania has made some further progress in developing its enterprise policy. There have been positive developments in terms of an increase in the budget for SME promotion and a progressive rationalization of business support schemes. The budget for implementing SME policy has increased four-fold and is now secured through a direct allocation from the state budget.

The network of business centers has further expanded and several initiatives such as subsidized advisory and training services and a pilot supplier linkage program were successfully implemented by the SME Development Agency (SMEDA) at the end of 2000. These latter activities were, however, discontinued at the beginning of 2001 because of uncertainties about a merger of SMEDA with the Regional Development Agency. This is now resolved, but negatively affected the credibility of state-sponsored programs. A new trend in Lithuanian SME policy is decentralization.

Even though Lithuania had to struggle to overcome all the impediments set by the huge impact of the Russian financial crisis, the country has managed to keep up with its goals. By revising its existing legislative infrastructure, by implementing the IS program, and by giving birth to institutions responsible for fostering and driving the national ICT strategy, Lithuania is on the right path for reaching a Knowledge Economy (see Figure 10.4).

Lithuania benefited greatly from the increase in R&D expenditure by the government, the dramatic expansion of the mobile telecommunications sector, the focused government strategy, and the national action plan to foster e-Business (e-Commerce and e-Banking). But the country has yet to face the lack of financial resources, the unattractiveness of its investment

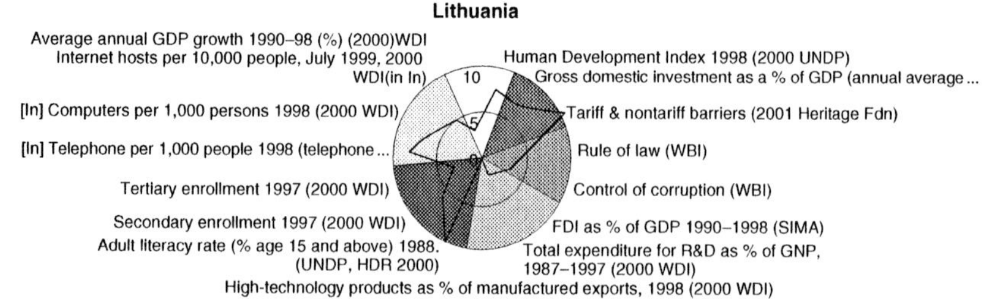

Figure 10.4   Lithuania's knowledge scorecard

Source: The World Bank, KAM (2005)

environment, its inability to attract FDI, and its unreliable regulatory framework. The Lithuanian case shows that location can matter: in this case, the proximity to Russia has played a detrimental role in its economic development, due to the Russian crisis. By the same token, though, the proximity to the other two Baltic countries has generated a positive regional spillover. The progressive adjustment to EU standards (both in terms of regulation and economic policy) has boosted private sector development (PSD). Finally, regional and international cooperation can be crucial for transitional economies in fostering ICT development.

E   Moldova

Real GDP grew by 6.3 percent year on year in 2003. Moldova's economy also benefits from relative macro-economic stability and generally solid import demand in Russia that accounts for almost 40 percent of export sales.

Markets in the Commonwealth of Independent States (CIS) have traditionally accounted for two-thirds of Moldova's total export revenue since independence. Entering other markets, especially in Western and Central Europe, proved to be very difficult for Moldova.

Moldova is largely ignored by most rating agencies such as the Economist Intelligence Unit/Pyramid Research or McConnell International.

There have been some negative developments since the Communist Party of Moldova assumed power in 2001, including the exclusion of opposition press representatives from the presidential inauguration and the removal of the heads of national television and radio. In Transdniestr, censorship is exceptionally heavy (as it is in Gagauz), owing to the effective functioning of the government's propaganda machine, although some independent print and television media have survived.

Trade barriers for ICT equipment have been reduced. Foreign direct investment is allowed in network sectors. There has been some opening up in service sectors related to electronic commerce and ICT networks.

Table 10.5   Moldova's main ICT indicators, 2003

Fixed line and mobile phone subscribers per 1,000 inhabitants	351.30
Mobile phones per 1,000 inhabitants	131.96
PCs per 100 inhabitants	2.13
Internet users per 1,000 inhabitants	79.85
Internet hosts per 10,000 inhabitants	33.23

Sources: adapted from World Development Indicators Online (2005) and International Telecommunications Union (2005)

Cumbersome technical standards or licensing requirements present a barrier to trade in equipment for information and communication technologies. Service sectors are not open to trade, creating a barrier for electronic commerce and the implementation and operation of ICT networks.

However, the Moldavian Government is moving forward to liberalize the telecommunications sector. Progress is being made in achieving universal access, but there are many obstructions to implementation. Services such as data, paging, and mobile telephony are available from competing private providers. Alternative carriers compete for private network services, leased lines, and other telecommunications services for businesses, and the incumbent provider networks are being opened up to competition through interconnection and/or unbundling obligations.

An independent regulatory body (Non-governmental Agency for Regulations in Telecom and Informatics) was established according to the amendments to the Law of Telecommunications approved in May 2000, whose main target is to separate the regulation in ICT sector between the national state policy and the regulations (taxes, licenses, etc.) for ICT sector.

Moldova has a telephone density of around 22 lines per 100 inhabitants (see Table 10.5). Telephone line provision in rural areas remains poor. In May 1997 the government awarded the first global system for mobile communications (GSM) mobile phone license to Voxtel, a consortium consisting of Moldtelecom (Moldova Telecommunications), France Télécom, Moldavian Mobile Company, Romania Mobil Rom, and the International Finance Corporation. A second license was awarded in November 1999 to Moldcell, a Turkish–Moldovan joint venture, and now a third one was awarded to the state telecommunications enterprise Moldtelecom.

The number of students studying for vocational qualifications has declined substantially as the courses have proved increasingly outdated, while enrollment in universities has increased. ICT training has greatly improved through the introduction of the State Register of Population (SRP) of the Republic of Moldova.

Moldova is also part of the Internet Access and Training Program (IATP). It is a program of the Bureau of Educational and Cultural Affairs (ECA), US

Department of State, funded under the Freedom Support Act (FSA) and administered by the International Research and Exchanges Board (IREX). IATP is an innovative program that utilizes the Internet to encourage information sharing, network building, and collaboration among alumni of ECA-sponsored exchange programs and other targeted constituencies in these eleven countries of the New Independent States (NIS). IATP currently maintains a network of 160 Internet access sites throughout the region. These access sites typically contain between three and fifteen computers and serve as the primary means of IATP service delivery. They average 39,300 users and 7,600 people trained per month.

Moldova's privatization record is mixed. Privatization of small- and medium-sized enterprises is virtually complete, but the sale of larger enterprises has proved more difficult and highly politicized. Many large enterprises are still under government control. Plus, mass privatization has led to widely dispersed ownership, even in SMEs. Significant blocks of shares are held only by the state and by investment funds, which were initially permitted to hold a maximum 20 per cent stake in any one enterprise.

The new initiative, put in place since December 2000, represents a business-model of free access to the Internet with a base for e-Commerce development. This model is operating via the portal Moldova Cyber Community and is encouraging the use of new technologies for payments. Within the portal an International e-Commerce Center has been created, which is aiming to promote e-Commerce in Moldova and its use in transactions with foreign partners.

Some local businesses operate websites. The basic information they provide is static and infrequently updated. Some businesses accept orders placed by telephone or fax. Some businesses distribute hard-copy catalogs for remote browsing of goods and services. B2B interactions remain inefficient with little transparency. Faxes and telephones are commonly used to facilitate orders or for remote client support, although some paper-based transaction (e.g. signature) is required.

The Moldovan case stresses again the need for a strong and transparent legal and regulatory framework. It also highlights the importance of foreign direct investments to boost the national economy, a task in which Moldova has failed so far, unlike the Czech Republic. The government does not seem to be firmly committed or willing to lead by example. Implementing a firm e-Government strategy may have a positive impact on the private sector's catching up with the use of ICT.

F   Romania

Romania lags behind most of the ECA countries in e-Development because of overall slow economic reforms and lack of Government vision on ICT until recently.

Table 10.6   Romania's main ICT indicators, 2003

Fixed line and mobile phone subscribers per 1,000 inhabitants	523.61
Mobile phones per 1,000 inhabitants	324.22
PCs per 100 inhabitants	9.66
Internet users per 1,000 inhabitants	184.05
Internet hosts per 10,000 inhabitants	21.82

Sources: adapted from World Development Indicators Online (2005) and International Telecommunications Union (2005)

Economic reforms in Romania have proceeded substantially slower than in the majority of Central and East European countries. The government was late to implement the structural changes in private and financial sectors. Privatization was also painfully slow. As a result, Romania ranks third in GDP per capita at purchasing power parity (USD7,277 in 2003) among the EU acceding countries (Bulgaria and Romania) and the EU candidate countries (Croatia and Turkey).

The Romanian telecommunications market was fully liberalized at the beginning of 2003. Since then, over 2,000 providers have registered with the National Regulatory Authority for Communications (ANRC), 700 of which are operating on the market.

Romania had a history of national ICT development plans that have not been translated into real actions until recent years. e-Commerce, e-Business, and high-tech parks legislations are progressively being introduced. Romania also has a high tax rate (25 percent) that impedes investments and growth of the ICT sector.

The area where Romanian regulatory framework is rather advanced is the data/Internet market. It is open for competition, and Romania counted 410 registered ISPs in 2003. This has allowed for the dynamic growth of the market and active use of various means to deliver bandwidth to the end-user: cable, VSATs, private networks, leased lines, etc. Internet connection s through cable grew by 50 percent in 2003, but the cost is still prohibitive for most Romanians. Actually, Internet penetration is relatively low (3.5 m users in 2003) – but growing rapidly – mainly because of the high cost of Internet connection (see Table 10.6).

During most of the 1990s, Romania had rather weak government telecommunications regulatory and management institutions and a confusing division of responsibilities among them. Recently, the Ministry of Communications and Information Technology was created to address the problem. It "regulates, coordinates and controls activities for the IT&C sector and establishes the development strategy for Romania in these domains." Its mission is to ensure a solid basis for Romania to transit smoothly to the information society, one of the goals of the Romanian Government's 2004–2008 program.

The telecommunications market was liberalized at the beginning of 2003, and the Greek company OTE took a 53 percent share in the national company RomTelecom. Since then, significant progress has been made, whether in basic telephony, mobile telephony, the Internet, or IT.

The liberalization of the telecommunications market has led to intense competition. Resulting falling prices spurred an increase in the number of phone lines and in the quality of the lines. There were 5.4m fixed phone lines in 2003, a penetration rate of 58 percent.

The mobile market is also competitive with four operators, two of them not only covering Romania, but also offering roaming in a number of other countries. The mobile phone penetration grew even faster than the fixed-line penetration and reached 32 percent in 2003.

Internet access is low, due in part to the high costs of PCs and ISP charges relative to the GDP per capita. About 20 percent of Romanians used the Internet in 2004, but the estimated number of personal computers per 1,000 people at the end of 2003 was 97. This suggests an important use of the Internet at work and in schools. We note, however, that computer sales are rising fast – 40 percent in 2003 and 50 percent in 2004 – and could improve Internet penetration shortly.

Romania has a very high literacy rate and good quality technical and engineering education. The education system underwent a radical restructuring and adaptation to the market economy realities. Serious emphasis was being placed on ICT-related education. The government-run Polytechnic Institutes produce high-quality IT graduates and are considered to be one of the richest of Romania's assets. This strategy has paid off since Romania has now the highest density per 1,000 people of IT graduates in Europe (and ranks sixth in the world, before the US or Russia). However, many of the graduating students are leaving for higher-paid jobs in Western Europe, the United States, and Canada. The brain-drain is a very serious problem without an easy solution in the near future.

In 2001 Romania had 36 commercial banks, 32 of which had private capital and 21 some degree of foreign ownership. The sector is rather poorly regulated and supervised, which led to a number of big financial scandals, particularly in the mutual funds and savings sectors. Commercial credit in Romania is expensive and hard to obtain. Lack of a viable banking sector limits the growth of private enterprises, ICT sector included.

During the 1990s, the ICT sector in Romania shifted its focus from hardware production to software development. Availability of high-quality ICT specialists produced by the Polytechnic Institutes allowed the sector to develop rather dynamically and even gain some global reputation. Currently, there are more than 2,000 software firms in Romania, many of which have partnerships or are even owned by foreign companies. Oracle, Cisco, IBM, Compaq, Motorola, and others have already established their presence in Romania.

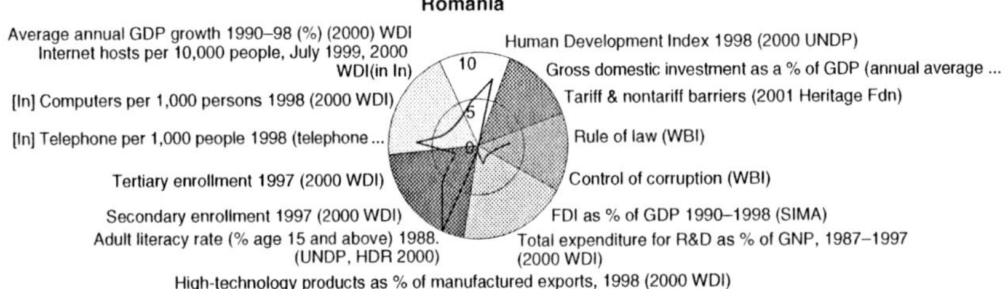

Figure 10.5   Romania's knowledge scorecard

Source: The World Bank, KAM (2005)

The Romanian IT market is one of the fastest growing in Europe. IT services yielded USD230m in revenues in 2003. Romania has established a solid reputation in the software market, especially for anti-viruses and anti-spam software. But piracy is rampant in this sector, and if piracy were to decrease by only 10 percent, the income of the Romanian ICT industry would grow by USD21m.

Romania has great strengths. The ICT sector has grown considerably by shifting from a dominance in hardware to a dominance in software. The high quality government Polytechnic institutions are producing graduates for the ICT sector. The lightly regulated mobile telecommunications market is growing very fast, and so is the Internet market.

However, the country faces a great number of challenges. The government vision of ICT development in the country is fairly recent. Privatization has proceeded slowly and the financial system is not functioning properly. The high tax rate impedes investments and growth of ICT sector and the attempts at high-tech parks has had only a limited success (see Figure 10.5). The level of ICT awareness among local businesses is slowly picking up. Finally, Romania also faces a significant brain-drain problem.

G   Ukraine

The Ukrainian economy during the Soviet era relied on heavy industry and technology that had largely been superseded in the West: steel, chemicals, shipbuilding, coal, machine-tools, and weaponry. Ukraine's main challenge since independence has been to diversify its industrial policy, previously based only on government subsidies, to overcome the collapse of traditional export markets. However, the difficult task of dismantling the centrally planned system has been exacerbated by the complete lack of consensus among political and business leaders over the trajectory for reforms.

The lack of consensus and the political uncertainty have slowed the privatization process. Moreover, Ukraine seems to have been the least pro-Western of the former Soviet countries. The skeptical and suspicious

Table 10.7   Ukraine's main ICT indicators, 2003

Fixed line and mobile phone subscribers per 1,000 inhabitants	299.84*
Mobile phones per 1,000 inhabitants	135.85
PCs per 100 inhabitants	1.98
Internet users per 1,000 inhabitants	18.75*
Internet hosts per 10,000 inhabitants	19.19

* 2002 data

Sources: adapted from World Development Indicators Online (2005) and International Telecommunications Union (2005)

approach toward Western investors has prevented foreign capital inflows and the development process has been hindered by state interference and over-regulation. Ukraine does not have a very proactive environment to encourage entrepreneurship and the business environment in Ukraine is, in addition, affected by heavy taxation and high levels of red tape and corruption. In the wake of the recent change of government, the business environment is expected to become friendlier.

The Government of Ukraine has stated its interest in the use of ICT to support the transition and improve efficiency of economic and social development actions. Yet for a long time, the only relevant policy position concerning ICT and the information society was the National Program of Informatization adopted by the Parliament in 1998. The program brought about a set of ambitious tasks for Ukraine, such as the adoption of ICT for public administration and the support of innovation across the business and social environments.

The next set of information society-related laws were approved by the Ukrainian Parliament in late 2003. These were the Law on Electronic Digital Signature and the Law on Electronic Documents and Electronic Document Circulation. These two laws are supposed to foster the development of e-Commerce in the country. In 2003, the Ukrainian Government also launched the Web-Portal of the Ukrainian Government (http://www.kmu. gov.ua). The portal provides information and services for Ukrainians, businesses, civil servants, and the international community.

There are institutions in place that deal with particular policy issues for the development of an ICT policy. The Ministry of Science and Technology is responsible for fostering innovation and adoption of new technologies both in the private and public sector. Moreover, the State Committee of Information Policy assists the government in drafting strategies and preparing legal drafts to support e-Development. Yet, the lack of coordination and financial resources undermines the effectiveness of these institutions.

Ukraine's telecommunications sector has an important growth potential largely unrealized and Ukraine ICT scenario is characterized by an internal digital divide. The dominant player, UkrTelecom, has been reorganized in light of its privatization (which has been repeatedly postponed since the late 1990s), which was again delayed at the end of 2004. Ukraine's fixed-line density is very low – 24 lines per 100 people in 2003, compared to an average of above 50 in the EU – but the government plans on bringing the penetration up to 40 percent by 2010 (see Table 10.7). Despite a low income level, the growth of the mobile phone market has been exponential. The number of subscribers grew from 6.5 m at the beginning of 2004 to 10.6 m in the third quarter of 2004. This is not only the result of a growing middle-class, improved payment schemes, and lowering costs due to the fierce competition of the two largest mobile operators, but also because of the poor quality of the fixed-lines.

Despite the high rate of literacy, the educational system in Ukraine lacks human and financial resources to meet the increasing demand for greater education. The curricula at the different levels of education, from primary to tertiary schools, seem to be insufficient and out-dated. Additional decrees have been adopted in 2000, but they yet have to generate significant results. The private sector has often lamented the poor level of ICT education. Most of the ICT training is provided by private institutions and/or in-house by the companies who hire inexperienced university graduates. Intel has established an Internet laboratory at Ukraine's Taras Shevchenko National University. Equipped with basic infrastructure, the $30,000 lab is part of a global Intel initiative to support the development of e-Commerce software.

A program of "informatization" for educational institutions and the computerization of village schools has been set up. The Ministry of Science and Education planned to connect more than 200 village schools to the Internet in 2001, and around 3,000 over a period of four years. More than 240 schools in Kiev now have access to the Internet.

In general, Ukraine offers a difficult business climate, and the business environment for ICT products and services is less encouraging. Regulatory uncertainty and lack of entrepreneurship have hindered the development of innovation.

The Ukrainian institutional and regulatory framework lacks effective measures to sustain a viable economic and social development policy. Despite the interest of the government in leveraging ICT to sustain and promote social and economic development, the fragile political balance hinders the adoption of a viable strategy and policy.

Notwithstanding the many difficulties – political and legal uncertainty, slow economic progress and unfavorable business environment – Ukraine remains a very interesting country for its core characteristics. This is confirmed also by the fact that Ukraine has been chosen by the UNDP and the World Bank as a test-ground for e-Development interventions, namely, the UNDP Innovation Springboard project and the e-Development Technical Adjustment Lending project of the World Bank Group.

Ukraine's e-Development strategy can pivot on some strengths of the country, such as the availability of significant human resources at comparatively lower costs and a tradition in ICT and science and technology. The younger generation is interested in new technologies and applications and is slowly developing entrepreneurship pointing to innovation. The telecommunications and Internet markets have a great potential for expansion and growth, especially since the government is increasingly committing itself to developing an ICT strategy.

However, some important elements are hindering this process. Ukraine's legal system is questionable, its communications systems inadequate, and there is a low specialization of production and industrial policy. The general level of business skill is quite low, i.e. English language, management, marketing, and finance skills are poor among entrepreneurs. Moreover, the funding for innovation and R&D is available neither from public nor from private sources. Access to capital remains one of the major constraints to innovation, along with an unfavorable environment for foreign investments.

Ukraine's case shows that government transparency is essential to promote innovation and that a consistent legal system contributes to a transparent and vibrant economy. Political uncertainty may hinder the social and economic development (especially when leaders are not inspired to invest in innovation), and the slow pace of the privatization process has limited the technology potential of Ukraine.

Part IV

From e-Development toward the Knowledge Economy: Analysis of Evidence from the Case Studies

11

Revisiting the Basic Concepts of e-Development and the Knowledge Economy

There are no well-articulated or established definitions for either *e-Development* or the *Knowledge Economy* and that often has been a source of confusion.

We define *knowledge-based economies* as those which are directly based on the production, distribution, and use of knowledge and information (OECD, 1996).

What is the knowledge economy? A *knowledge-driven economy* is one in which the generation and exploitation of knowledge play the predominant part in the creation of wealth (UK DTI, 1998).

For countries in the vanguard of the world economy, the balance between knowledge and resources has shifted so far toward the former that knowledge has become perhaps the most important factor *determining the standard of living* – more than land, than tools, than labor. Today's most technologically advanced economies are truly knowledge-based (World Bank, 1998).

Our working definition for the Knowledge Economy is as follows:

> The Knowledge Economy is a state of economic being and a process of economic becoming that leverages intensively and extensively knowledge assets and competences as well as economic learning to catalyze and accelerate sustainable and robust economic growth.

We review the economies of nations within a spectrum of possible states of development as follows and we relate those to development pathways (see Figure 15.1 on p. 237):

- *Subsistence-focused*: where survival is the issue – i.e. Afghanistan today.
- *Commodity-based*: where commodities are the dominant means and goal of economic production and exchange and within that category there are barter-based economies up to some transitioning economies.

- *Knowledge-based:* where knowledge is one of the key means and goals of economic production and exchange and one of the key economic resources with a high degree of utilization and sharing (OECD, 1996).
- *Knowledge-driven:* where knowledge is the major means and goal of economic production and exchange and the most valuable economic resource under continual renewal, sharing, and utilization; technological innovation and economic learning are key modalities of economic development and growth (UK DIT, 1998).

A country's or community's ability to benefit from the knowledge revolution was studied comprehensively by the Bank in its 1998 World Development Report *Knowledge for Development*, and by the OECD. The World Bank Institute subsequently developed a framework for analyzing the various policies and institutions required to develop a knowledge economy. It found that there are four critical requisites for a country to be able to participate fully:

(a) A regulatory and economic environment that enables the free flow of knowledge, investment in Information and Communications Technology (ICT), and encourage entrepreneurship;
(b) An educated and skilled population to create, share and use knowledge;
(c) A dynamic information infrastructure ranging from radio to the Internet, in order to facilitate the effective communication, dissemination, and processing of information;
(d) A network of research centers, universities, think-tanks, private enterprises, and community groups to tap into the growing stock of global knowledge, assimilate and adapt it to local needs, and create new knowledge.

The demand side is as important as the supply side in developing a knowledge economy. Knowledge for development is mostly, though not exclusively, used by the private sector. The private sector also is likely to demand new knowledge as to when the investment climate is good, when the economy is growing and new market opportunities are opening up, and when the profitability of investment is high. All of the traditional macro-economic prerequisites of growth are therefore also prerequisites for private individuals and firms to demand new knowledge. Demand and supply of knowledge for the private sector spill over into societal demand for public sector knowledge. Societies which share knowledge on science and technology tend, over time, to insist on greater government transparency and better government service as well.

The need for e-Development interventions is stressed also by the development of the e-Economy and the increased competitiveness and openness that it brings about. The Knowledge Economy is fostering market transparency, integrating separate geographical markets, and facilitating integration into innovative global markets.

Without appropriate actions and interventions, such as the proposed e-Development ones, the transitional and developing countries may exacerbate the risk of being left behind and become victims of the digital divide and even the abyss rather than reaping digital dividends.

Moreover, the need for standardization, of both processes and policies, calls for the action of an overarching organization that can provide appropriate guidance and advisory services to transitional economies willing and able to take advantage of the Knowledge Economy. The benefits for transitioning and developing countries in engaging in the Knowledge Economy development framework are those generally predicted for the intra-industry integration and commerce, with generally greater efficiency and cheaper and faster ways to conduct business.

We now expand on the four main pillars of development we introduced in Chapter 3: (1) policy making; (2) institution building; (3) investment making; and (4) capacity building.

Below we provide additional examples of e-Development interventions aiming to advance developing and transitioning economies toward the Knowledge Economy level organized across the four main categories as listed above.

A   Policy making

The scope of the Knowledge Economy encompasses a wide range of issues, and a programmatic approach is needed to make sure that all e-Development activities are consistent and coordinated. Education, infrastructure, public sector reform, private sector development, and legislation – just to mention a few – are fields in which different governmental agencies should coordinate their policies and operate in a systematic manner to pave the way towards the Knowledge Economy.

Policy making has a rather mixed record. On the one hand, most of the countries that recently joined the EU have already started defining national strategies to meet the challenge of transiting toward a knowledge-based economy, for the most part reflecting the wording used by the European Union for the Information Society. On the other hand, a number of countries not involved in the EU-accession process still lack a long-term vision on ICT in support of their social and economic development.

A similar progress is underway for the relevant enabling regulatory and legal environment: it has been gradually improving in recent EU countries reflecting the process of harmonization to international standards – especially in reference to the World Trade Organization and the EU. In the CIS countries, the legal and regulatory frameworks for e-Development are far from perfect, with problematic areas in telecommunications market regulations, legislation on electronic documents, and intellectual property rights.

Most of the countries share some common characteristics in their quest for e-Development: their national strategies often lack realistic goals, target actions, timeline, and mechanisms of implementation. Policy statements often remain on paper. Legal and regulatory frameworks are still generally inadequate in the areas of R&D promotion and support of high-tech SMEs. Finally, few among even the most advanced countries have a strategic plan and appropriate regulatory framework for ICT use within the government. Consequently, e-Development policy making needs improvement in the several areas listed below.

Adopting comprehensive national e-Development strategies

The strategy should be developed and adopted at the highest government level. This is the first and probably single most important step for successful e-Development. All stakeholders, such as government agencies, private sector, local authorities, citizens' groups, and academia, should be actively involved in developing and implementing the strategy.

The strategy should also be an integral part of the national development process. Experience from advanced developing countries and newly developed ones shows that ICT can be utilized for development purposes in three distinctive, not mutually exclusive ways: (1) as a sector of the economy; (2) as a means to increase efficiency in both public and private sectors; and (3) as a tool to achieve specific economic and social goals. It is important to understand the benefits of these e-Development modes and create a strategy that combines them in a way tailored to the specific needs and conditions of a given country.

(1) The first and most narrowly defined approach is developing ICT as a sector of the economy. The ICT sector includes the telecommunications and broadcasting, as well as information technologies – hardware and software production, Internet service providers, application service providers, data storage centers, etc. There are several reasons for a country to be interested in developing its ICT sector. It is a very profitable, high value-added business with strong export potential. Plus, this sector may serve as a locomotive that accelerates the development in other sectors of the economy.

Many countries have already greatly benefited from utilizing the full potential of their ICT sector. The most notable success stories include the software development industry in Ireland, hardware production in Costa Rica, and use of ICT to create regional communications hubs in Singapore and Malaysia. In the ECA region, countries such as Armenia, Estonia, Bulgaria, and Hungary are trying to pursue a similar path.

(2) e-Development can utilize the whole range of technology applications – networking and clustering, process acceleration and automation,

information dissemination and knowledge sharing – to increase the efficiency of the government and the business sectors, thereby accelerating the economic growth in a country. e-Government applications such as e-Taxation, e-Registration, e-Procurement, etc., increase the transparency and efficiency of both public and private sectors. In the private sector, ICT can create new business opportunities, drastically reduce barriers to entry, and lower trade and transactions costs by creating digital marketplaces to manage supply-chains, automating transactions, allowing local businesses to access to global markets, and improving intra-firm communications. According to Goldman Sachs, estimated cost savings through e-Commerce even in "traditional" economy sectors often exceed 10 percent (Brookes and Wahhaj, 2000).

Success stories include public e-Procurement systems in Romania, Chile, Mexico, and Korea which, on average, reduced acquisition costs by about 30 percent and significantly increased SME participation in the bidding process. An ICT-based system for import procedures in the Philippines greatly increased the speed of services for businesses: cargo is released in four hours to two days, as opposed to eight days with the earlier system. Governments in many ECA countries have also started actively employing ICT to improve their services to businesses, for example through e-Taxation in Romania and Armenia. However, in most cases, the stage of development of such projects in the region is too early to allow a full evaluation of results.

(3) Finally, ICT can be used as a flexible and versatile tool to achieve specific economic and social goals, such as improving healthcare management, or better targeting poverty in rural areas. In rural areas, e-Development applications can also be utilized to increase dynamism, profitability, and overall competitiveness of rural enterprises. Several projects of this type have been recently implemented in India and Africa. For example, Drishee is a platform for rural networking and marketing services in India – the localized Intranet between villages and a district center provide access to various services, including online land records, registration and applications of income and residence certificates, and crops market information. In the ECA region, interventions of this kind have so far been limited to promoting rural telecenters.

Adopting a detailed action plan

The e-Development strategy should be more than just a political vision that provides for a general framework of reference. It must contain an action plan with comprehensive policies to encourage ICT use in various sectors of the economy, society, and government, with specific measures and interventions, detailed timelines, and relevant budgetary allocations. Realistic goals are necessary to ensure the strategy's success.

Creating a favorable legal and regulatory framework

A legal and regulatory framework needs to be designed according to the goals specified in the country's e-Development strategy. For example, if a country decides to focus on creating an export-oriented ICT industry, it would need to develop a set of regulations to insure access to finance for high-tech SMEs, promote links between private sector and universities, simplify export procedures, etc. Instead, if the government priority is to use ICT to increase the efficiency of the government and the business sector, a different set of regulations and laws is required, focusing on the adoption, rather than development, of technologies.

There are also universally important laws and regulations dealing with the sustainability of electronic transactions. Major issues include contract enforcement, consumer protection, liability assignment, privacy protection, intellectual property rights, process and technical standards, security, authentication, encryption, digital signatures, and connectivity protocols. EU legislation can serve as the best practice for a number of transitioning and developing countries (especially, ECA countries), in particular the e-Signature Directive 1999, e-Commerce Directive 2000, Copyright Directive 2001, and Data Protection Directive 1995.

B   Institution building

Some countries have a history of unsuccessful attempts to deliver on their e-Development strategies or initiatives, largely because they lacked adequate institutional mechanisms for their implementation. Few countries have a functioning umbrella agency for the coordination of e-Development activities within the government. Also, lack of clear division of responsibilities and power struggles between different branches and agencies of the government create political and bureaucratic obstacles for e-Development and inhibit proper allocation of resources within the public sector.

To successfully implement e-Development projects, the institutional framework should be designed to perform the tasks listed below.

Assigning clear responsibilities to the agencies involved

Lack of clarity at the institutional level heavily affects the efficiency of the public administration and decreases accountability. The national strategy and action plan should set clear guidelines on institutional responsibilities within the public administration. Particular institutional structures will vary, but there are several common key points. First, one institution has to be in charge of developing e-Government standards, both technological and administrative, to insure compatibility of IT systems and processes in different ministries and agencies. This will allow seamless and effective integration of various government services for the private sector. Second, it is very desirable to make the Ministry of Finance actively engaged in e-Development to insure proper and timely financing of e-Developing activities.

Coordinating e-Development activities

The establishment of an overarching umbrella institution for coordinating and monitoring e-Development activities is highly desirable to avoid inefficient projects that overlap across multiple government departments. In general terms, a good format for such an institution would be a council or commission, broadly representative of all the major actors involved, including ministries and agencies, private and educational sectors, and civil society. This helps to build a broad-based support for e-Development and avoid hijacking of the agenda by a single agency or ministry.

Providing the highest level of political support

The institutional framework should provide for the highest level of political support to e-Development activities. Ideally, the Prime Minister or another high-ranking executive should chair the umbrella e-Development body. In many instances, the presence of an effective "champion" within the government spurs the whole e-Development process.

Due to their nature of streamlining administrative procedures and increasing transparency, e-Development projects may face strong political resistance from particular groups who rely upon vested interests. Therefore, the strong initiative of high-level politicians is crucial to implement e-Development projects smoothly. Plus, it is often easier to secure political support and find an efficient e-Development champion at the highest political levels than among mid-level bureaucrats. Lower-level officials tend often to be less receptive to ideas that require changes in the way they do everyday business.

Box 11.1   Ireland: public sector institutions at the heart of e-Development Information Society Commission (ISC)

Ireland established an overarching agency, ISC (http://www.isc.ie), to shape and manage the strategic framework for the Irish Information Society as well as to coordinate e-Development activities of different government agencies and other ICT actors in the country. It is an advisory body to the Prime Minister and includes representatives of the private and public sectors, relevant government departments and social partners throughout the country. The functions of the ISC include:

- To monitor the implementation of major e-Development activities by the key actors;
- To drive awareness campaigns targeted at the enterprise sector and the general public;
- To establish and monitor the key benchmarks for the development of an information society in Ireland;

- To encourage and support local and regional information society initiatives;
- To identify and oversee the establishment of flagship projects to demonstrate the benefits of the information society and win support for an Irish information society.
- To establish advisory groups for further study of potential information society benefits and actions required in individual sectors of the economy.

C   Investment making

The technology infrastructure is the main hard component of and contributor to the Knowledge Economy since it allows for sharing of knowledge and information among various actors in the society. Computers, telecommunications, and digital technologies have become the backbone of the Knowledge Economy as railways and roads were to the industrial economy.

Privatization and liberalization are essential for the development of an affordable and modern telecommunications infrastructure. Privatization of the incumbent operators has begun in a number of countries. In some countries, telecom deregulation is complete, while in others it is only partial but progressing at a rapid pace.

The ISP and mobile telephony markets are usually more open to competition than the fixed-line market. The mobile communications sector has been booming, partially compensating for the lack of modern fixed-line infrastructure. On the downside, there are serious regional disparities in infrastructure development both within and between the countries. The digital divide between urban and rural areas remains a serious problem.

Several measures can be designed to address the infrastructure problems in the transitioning and developing countries.

Improving universal access to telecom services

Improving the telecom markets in "laggard" countries requires large investments that can often be found abroad. Thus, it is essential to create a favorable environment for investors, both foreign and local, and strengthen the regulatory capacity of independent authorities to police and regulate the telecommunications market properly. For instance, in exchange for lucrative licenses in urban areas, telecom operators can be encouraged to meet specific quality and connectivity criteria, such as service standards and infrastructure expansion in rural areas.

Promoting affordable Internet access

Policies targeted at self-sustainable growth of fixed-line infrastructure may, in the short term, contradict those promoting Internet use, thus undermining the design and development of effective telecommunications policies. Allowing

---

Box 11.2   Finland: promoting universal service through flexible telecom market

Finland has long had one of the world's least-regulated telecom markets, fostering a tradition of competition and innovation. Liberalization of telecommunications networks began in 1985 and was completed in 1994, far ahead of most other European countries. Today, Finland has one of the most competitive telecommunications markets in the world, which, according to OECD figures, has made Finland the cheapest country in the world to go online.

In Finland, the provision of the universal service is not tied to fixed networks only. A telecommunications company also may provide these services through its mobile networks. More and more Finns even prefer a mobile phone to a fixed line. In addition, all citizens have free access to the Internet at local public libraries. Public and research libraries have been networked and will be connected into the ATM network to provide multimedia services.

---

tariff increases is often necessary to make the telecommunications sector more attractive to investors. This brings an increase in call rates in the short term, thus inhibiting Internet adoption. However, once market liberalization is completed, competition brings both lower costs and higher quality of Internet connection. This however requires time, which few countries can afford. To obviate this problem, the following methods can be recommended:

- Establishing a dedicated number for calls to ISPs, with lower rates for dial-up Internet access.
- Promoting subsidized Internet access for the least affluent groups of users, through community telecenters.

While these are viable solutions, if a significant portion of Internet users has access to subsidized networks, the customer base for commercial ISPs is weakened, which in turn may dampen growth and even indirectly increase ISP prices for general users. Similarly, widespread availability of subsidized access through community telecenters blocks the development of commercial Internet cafés. The government must then find a way to incorporate subsidized networks into the commercial ISP market and gradually commercialize community telecenters.

Providing Internet access for selected groups of users through dedicated networks

While providing universal access to modern ICT should be the ultimate goal of infrastructure development, it is vital to insure access for the most important groups of users – i.e. those who can significantly contribute to economic growth and benefit the most from using ICT, such as education and R&D institutions, private enterprises, and government entities. The following measures can help improve access to modern infrastructure for the above-identified groups:

- Creating "centers of infrastructure excellence" in major enterprise zones or special telecenter services for SMEs to boost local companies and attract FDI to the country.
- Expanding academic networks to cover the entire educational and R&D system, including schools, universities, libraries, research institutions, and archives. Such networks can create major synergy effects that otherwise would not be possible.
- Developing government networks to interconnect offices of central and regional governments for efficient data exchange and functioning of the Public Administration.

Centers of infrastructure excellence have been implemented in a number of Asian countries, but they have not become a popular idea in every transitioning and developing country yet. Government-subsidized academic networks, however, have been developing fairly quickly. Most countries have also made conscious efforts to improve the ICT infrastructure for the public administration. However, networking among local public administrations and between central and local public administrations is still limited.

Improving telecom infrastructure in rural areas

The digital divide between urban and rural areas is a serious problem in numerous developing and transitioning countries. The underdevelopment of telecom infrastructure in rural areas deprives vast segments of the populations of access to the latest government and business services driven by ICT, and represents a significant impediment to the developing of rural enterprises.

ICT kiosks and smart subsidies can be utilized for rural infrastructure development at comparatively low cost. In many Indian states, for example,

---

Box 11.3   Hungary: academic and research network

About half of Internet users in the country get free or almost free connection through Hungarian Academic and research Network, HungarNet (http://www.hungarnet.hu). It has 900–1000 institutional members – educational and research institutions, libraries and museums. Institutional members contribute about 10 percent to the HungarNet's budget, the rest is provided by the Ministry of Culture and Education. As a result, the growth of the Internet in Hungary has mainly been driven by demand in the academic sector. A high level of connectivity in academia contributes to the increasing quality of research and education in the country.

Box 11.4   Chile: rural telecommunications infrastructure building

In order to improve telecom infrastructure in rural areas, the Chilean government established a special fund in 1994. The fund was financed by the government budget, and managed by a council of the Telecommunications Minister. Based on geographical proximity and technical solutions, the councils' secretariat, the sector regulatory Subsecretaría de Telecomunicación (SUBTEL), decided on annual projection, which was publicly announced to telecom companies. Then, through public tender, each project would be awarded to the bidder who asked for the lowest subsidies. Such a system greatly contributed to the reduction of government subsidies on rural telecom infrastructure development. In 1995, US$2.1 million subsidies generated US$40 million of investments, and 1,285 rural phone lines; for comparison – in the 1980s, $30 million subsidies created only 300 lines. The fund supported establishing lines to more than 6,000 rural localities with about 2.2 million people between 1995 and 2000; the proportion of Chile's population without access to basic voice communication reduced from 15% to 1% between 1994 and 2002.

ICT kiosks are run by local entrepreneurs and provide connectivity as well as e-Government and e-Business services to villagers. In Chile, the government was successful in drastically increasing teledensity in rural areas using "smart" subsidies to telephone companies.

Promoting alternative means of communication

Developing telecom infrastructure should not focus solely on fixed-line services. One of the main advantages of e-Development is the flexibility to use various technologies. Wireless communication, for example, becomes increasingly popular. In many cases, it provides better and more cost-efficient solutions, especially in the remote areas with poor fixed-line infrastructure. The use of the Wireless Application Protocol (WAP), for instance, allows access to specific services of the business registry from virtually anywhere in the country.

There is a number of emerging wireless technologies that have promising e-Development potential. For example, the United Nations has already recognized Wi-Fi (Wireless Fidelity) as a powerful tool to narrow digital divide and bolster economic development in rural areas. Wi-Fi provides broadband Internet access to specially outfitted PCs and laptops within a certain distance from the transmitter. This allows for creation of so-called "hot spots" virtually anywhere – in homes, airport lounges, libraries, or villages. Wi-Fi equipment can deliver connection from about 80 feet within buildings to up to several kilometers in open space.

Wi-Fi presents many advantages that make it a suitable solution and valuable tool for supporting e-Development agenda: Wi-Fi is comparatively cheap (less than USD250 for a small installation), fast and reliable, easy to install, and has low maintenance requirements. It operates on the unlicensed airwave spectrum, so there are no extra monthly costs on top of the charge for a broadband connection that is shared among the users.

Promoting the wide adoption of IT hardware

Personal computers are an essential part of the modern ICT infrastructure. However, prices for computing equipment remain too high for the majority of the population, especially in rural areas. Government credits and/or tax breaks for buying computers to households may help to accelerate technology adoption among the population. For instance, in the Czech Republic the first USD200 of expenditure on hardware and software for personal use of households is tax-exempt.

D   Capacity building

Capacity building covers a wide range of issues related to the overall capacity of the public and private sectors to implement e-Development: ability of entrepreneurs to operate within a vibrant innovation system that drives growth and employment; and capacity of the government to take advantage of technology applications to improve transparency and efficiency of governance, as well as to create a favorable environment for the dynamic growth of the private sector.

In practical terms, capacity building focuses on "soft" human capital issues such as awareness, education, training, and technological innovation. These interventions, however, will not produce a desired result unless they are supported with "learning-by-doing" activities. In other words, it is essential to supplement "soft" capacity building interventions with pilot projects and applications in major areas such as government-to-business (G2B), e-Government, and innovation. Thus, applications and pilot projects are a vital part of capacity building agenda.

To build human capacity of the public and private sectors for successful e-Development implementation, the measures listed below can be undertaken.

Raising awareness on ICT potential

One of the serious problems for e-Development in developing and transitioning countries is low awareness of ICT opportunities among government officials and enterprises. Increasing ICT awareness among the business community is essential to let the private sector play the role of catalyst and accelerator of innovation. The need to increase awareness among political actors is exacerbated by the political nature of ICT interventions. The government authorities in a given country are the *porte-parole* of e-Development, and their support is crucial in fostering ICT initiatives.

While designing awareness-raising activities, it is vital to advertise not ICT for itself (a very common mistake), but its ultimate benefits. For example, in promoting use of ICT for agri-business or rural enterprise, it is better to frame it not as an "e-Agriculture," but as "promoting efficient market access for small farms" or "promoting sustainability of entrepreneurs in rural areas by establishing a local market information network." The primary focus should always be on the target users' problems and objectives. Technology should remain just a tool, and as such, it has a secondary importance for the user.

Improving quality of education and training

The educational system at university level in most of the countries needs to be updated to become more responsive to the ever-changing demands of the Knowledge Economy, especially in the fields of business education, innovation and technology, and focus on applicability and commercialization of new products and processes. University–industry and other types of public–private partnerships can be utilized to increase the quality, reach, and relevance of formal education curricula and specialized training.

International experience shows that heavy investment in knowledge-intensive and ICT-related education helps to create a positive spill-over effect on the whole economic system. For example, Ireland has succeeded in creating centers of excellence in the domestic educational system that have attracted foreign investors to the ICT industry and supported growth and employment.

Governments must clearly define the training needs of their employees and incorporate best practices from around the world into the training programs. Curricula must encompass basic ICT training along with specialized skills necessary for each target group to perform his/her duty. Finally, governments should also invest in vocational training for the private sector through different co-funding schemes. Enterprises should be encouraged, through tax allowances, for example, to participate in the vocational training process.

Supporting technology innovation/R&D

Innovation is a driving force of the Knowledge Economy and essential for the countries' capacity to compete. A proactive government approach in

---

Box 11.5 Malaysia: public–private partnership in human development

Malaysian SMEs experienced difficulties in their research and training activities due to a lack of skilled labor in the country. The Teaching Company Scheme (TCS), a concept introduced in the UK, was employed to tackle the issue. The program creates partnerships in which academics and students join with companies to contribute to the implementation of their strategies on the technical or managerial side. In this way, TCS supplements SMEs' financial and human capital, while allowing students to get valuable hands-on experience and improving the links between public and private sector in the country.

promoting ICT-related R&D contributes to the establishment of a technology-oriented National Innovation System (NIS), in which public R&D institutions and private ICT sector interact with each other and the educational system to sustain growth and employment. Governments should strive to establish an environment which facilitates the creation of commercially oriented R&D networks.

Many problems limit the capacity of local ICT industries to support a virtuous circle of technological development. Investment climate problems include: limited access to financial resources, especially for new entrants; a generally inadequate regulatory framework for SME development, with high taxation, strict labor regulations, and choking red tape. ICT industry-specific problems include: limited R&D incentives for the private sector; unfriendly regulatory environment and policies on technology parks; lack of ICT training programs for professionals; and shortage of a skilled IT workforce. A very common problem is the lack of entrepreneurial skills among ICT professionals.

Promoting technology-oriented innovation in developing and transitioning countries may include:

- University–industry funding of ICT research programs, with government money typically matched by companies in cash and/or in-kind contribution.
- Increased government R&D-related funding, not only to academia and national research institutions, but also to the private sector, introducing useful competition to encourage practical and effective innovations (see Box 11.6).
- Development of capital markets to support long-term financing of ICT companies and risky R&D projects. For example, 30 percent of startups of ICT businesses were financed through venture capital funds in the 1990s in Finland (see Box 11.7).
- Development of favorable regulatory framework to protect owners' rights and promote commercialization of R&D, which are essential elements to facilitate the innovation and commercialization of inventions.
- Improvement of R&D networking through introduction of industry clusters, particularly relevant to link innovative SMEs with other players, such as large private enterprises.
- Promotion of incubators and technology parks, in close proximity to universities, to attract high-tech industries and foster linkages between industry and academia for joint R&D development. Incubators endeavor to reduce the risks confronting start-up enterprises, create new businesses, and assist the innovation firms by providing favorable working environment and conditions. The services include assistance with business planning, raising finance, and marketing.

Box 11.6   Czech Republic: SME and R&D policies for innovation

The Czech government launched the Technos Program in 1997 to increase the technical level of SMEs. It focuses on research and development of new technologies, products, materials, and information systems. SMEs can apply for the subsidy and demonstrate the financial ability to cover at least 50 percent of the project costs. http://www.unece.org/indust/sme/ace.htm

---

Box 11.7   Finland: supporting commercialization of R&D

The Finnish government plays a very active role in supporting innovative small- and medium-sized enterprises in ICT cluster. The government-run Tekes Foundation (http://www.tekes.fi/eng) gives grants and loans to SMEs seeking to develop specific applications. Tekes' funding is targeted at projects that produce know-how and bear high technological and commercial risks. The projects to be funded promote sustainable competitiveness, commercialization of research results, and emergence of new business activities. Besides providing financial support for R&D projects of particular enterprises, Tekes also has so-called "technology programs" that are used to promote development in specific sectors of technology or industry, and to pass on results of the research work to business in an efficient way.

SITRA (http://www.sitra.fi/eng/index.asp), the Finnish National Fund for Research and Development, is an independent public foundation created in the 1970s to address the lack of venture capital in the country. Since it was created and supervised by Parliament, it acts as a private venture capital fund with "social conscience." Lately, when more private venture capital funds appeared in Finland, SITRA added think-tank-like activities to its portfolio.

SITRA's funding covers not only the provision of venture capital but also follow-on investment, the commercialization of technology and management activities. Companies that have received funding for their product development get a strong equity position that makes it possible for them to grow and go international.

12
Knowledge Economy Policies and Practices: Learning from the Experience of Diverse Countries

As developing countries join the global information infrastructure era, each country will need to find effective ways of moving to knowledge-based environments, maximizing the benefits and controlling the risks from ICT expansion. This would involve coordinated action through national ICT strategies encompassing the new technologies and services as well as many aspects of the institutional environment. Strategies are needed which would help to build the necessary human, scientific, technical, and innovation fundamentals, as well as the management techniques and institutional and economic incentives that are consistent with creatively using ICT to reap the potential social and economic benefits.

Priority needs to be given to policies, regulation, education and training, and technological assessment programs to enhance the capacity for creatively producing or using ICT. The role of government is very important in supporting new forms of market facilitation and private sector development, introducing effective regulation and promoting stakeholder synergies.

A China

In the Middle Ages China was the most technologically advanced country in the world, creating the earliest mechanized industry and advancing to the experimental investigation of nature. The period was the climax of many centuries of scientific and technical progress. Then in the fourteenth century a new climate deterred further progress. Many techniques remained close to the imperial court, almost exclusively for the pleasure of the ruling class. This new climate developed due to a lack of resources. China also closed itself to the outside world, cutting off competitive pressures and new ideas, two essential factors in progress. There was, in addition, a tendency to stay away from experimental science, decisive in the development of Western technology. Reinforcing all this were bureaucratic structures and social tendencies to preserve the status quo. China, though remarkably positioned, missed the industrial revolution and entered the industrial age only half a century ago with the ascension to power of the Communist regime.

Today again technological disparities throughout the economy are enormous, and if the climate for innovation is not significantly improved, China risks another technological standstill, like the one several centuries ago. The industrial performance of enterprises across provinces, especially the profit-asset ratio, shows considerable dispersion between the best and the rest. And the performance of foreign-funded enterprises appear to be about twice that of the domestic firms, all across the country, both in profitability and productivity. (This statistic confirms what foreign enterprises can contribute to modernizing the economy.) There has also been a recent decline of industrial competitiveness, with the specialization of manufacturing remaining a problem. Comparative advantages remain in labor-intensive industries (textiles) and mass high-tech industries employing skilled, but cheap labor (color TV). But standard consumer electronics, about 35 percent of China's exports, are produced almost entirely under foreign licenses and by foreign-owned firms. Some sectors requiring somewhat sophisticated technologies – such as automotive, where there are too many producers (more than 140) – are being hit hard by entry into the WTO. The gaps between Chinese industries and foreign competitors are enormous in certain sectors. For instance, in iron and steel, productivity is a sixth of the world average – a twentieth of that of the best world performers.

In agriculture the dispersion of productivity in cereals production among the different provinces reaches more than a factor of two between the best performing provinces and the worst. Moreover, the progress in agriculture productivity in GDP per capita has been slower than in other countries, an effect of deteriorating extension infrastructure and of the nature of the property structure, favoring the individual but hampering intensive cultivation. Throughout the country, the strong S&T infrastructure contributes little to the economic development, evident in remarkably low correlations between them. This is clearly demonstrated by a recent statistical study (Guisheng, 2000) covering the whole set of economic development (GDP, per capita GDP, exports, total factor productivity) and correlating it with S&T inputs (funding and personnel), outputs (patents and scientific publications), and potential (education expenditures and students enrolments).

The government, aware of current limits and drawbacks, admits that "the problem of science and technology divorcing from the economy has not been solved thoroughly. A major obstacle restricting China's economic development is the poor capability of transforming scientific and technological advances into practical productive forces, the low level of applying new and high technology to production, and the poor capability of enterprises in technological innovation" (Guanhua, 2000).

To improve the situation the government is increasing its effort in science and technology and notably in R&D programs for new and established industries and for agriculture ("863" and Key Technology Programs). But raising the technological level of the Chinese economy depends first on well-functioning market structures throughout the economy. New and improved technologies diffuse throughout an economy under the pressures of competition. It forces firms to adopt innovations, modify their products for better serving their clients, and change their processes to improve productivity. Least efficient enterprises are deemed to follow best performers rapidly or to disappear. Main diffusion agents are providers of these new technologies and related services – large as well as small firms. Customers, well informed on goods' prices and quality, play an essential role too.

The primary measures to be taken to strengthen markets should be to foster a more open trade among Chinese provinces, allowing economies of scale and scope, and facilitating the diffusion of best products through price- and quality-based competition. Eliminating tariff and non-tariff barriers between provinces – erected to protect local enterprises and related interests – is essential. Competition can be improved by establishing and enforcing appropriate laws, and eliminating privileges from personal and political connections (see Figure 12.1). Support to small firms providing services, consulting, technologies, and seeds to producers, farmers, and local communities should also be considered. This requires adequate incentives and removing regulatory and bureaucratic obstacles to their establishment and operation. Finally, China needs to improve its system for technical norms and standards. China's exceptionally poor technical regulations and standards – such as product quality, work safety, and environmental protection – are a major obstacle to proper diffusion of modern technology and know-how in China.

The mediocre diffusion of modern technology and related management methods owes much to the ways technology and industry policies are conceived and implemented. There has been an over-concentration of attention, support, and incentives on designated industrial zones and high-tech parks, conceived to attract foreign firms and domestic firms for exports. This policy has been successful in many respects, but parks are a small part of the economy. China also suffers from an excessive fascination for high-tech production, without using high technology in the modernization of agriculture, manufacturing, and services, and together with neglecting the policy instruments that could increase the receptiveness to, and adoption of, new technologies in the industrial and rural issues. Technology push in R&D projects is too important: the projects are supported by government funds, designed by government institutes, with little involvement of users. And finally, there is disproportionate focus on large firms, even though smaller ones are a major source of technological dynamism and renewal.

A new mindset is needed in the design and implementation of the government promotion of technology. Priority should focus on the following four aspects: (1) the technology fertilization of the "average industry" over "high-tech" productions; (2) the technological culture over advanced research;

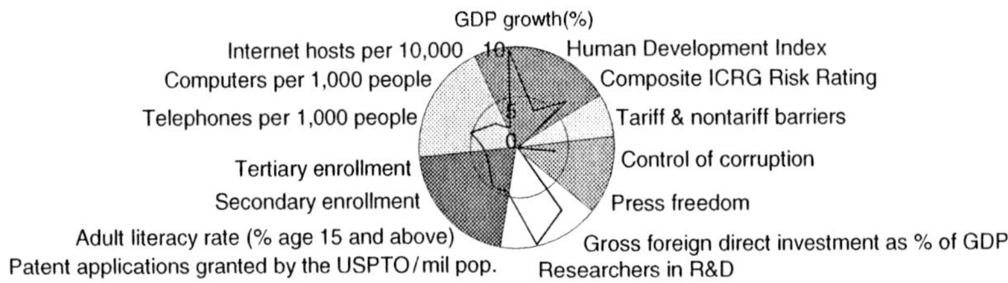

Figure 12.1   China's knowledge scorecard

Source: The World Bank, KAM (2005)

(3) bottom-up initiatives over top-down interventions; (4) the support to smaller firms over larger ones. To achieve this, the government needs to redeploy its programs for technology diffusion, stimulate innovation in enterprises, and promote innovation sites and clusters. These principles should inspire Chinese policy makers, both at the local and central level. They might find difficulty in applying such principles, which go against traditional tendencies to push new technology undertakings from scratch, in a context where business activities and political networks are still strongly intermingled.

B   Korea

The level of development now attained by Korea, coupled with rising competition in high-volume, standard products and international technological and economic developments, make it essential for Korea to exploit knowledge effectively in economic activity. Part of the challenge is to raise its competitiveness in knowledge-based activities and industries – areas where a genuine capacity to innovate is vital. Over the past decades, Korea's industrial profile has moved towards what can be viewed as typical for an OECD country. Currently, knowledge-based industries, as estimated by the OECD, account for 50.4 percent of value added in the business sector, ranging from a low of 31.4 percent in Iceland to a high of 58.6 percent in Germany (former West Germany). These industries have in fact grown more rapidly than the average for the total business sector in practically all OECD countries. In Korea, knowledge-based industries account for 40.3 percent of business sector value-added. Whereas knowledge-based manufacturing accounts for a relatively large share of GDP, the share of knowledge-based services is unusually small. On average, services now account for over 70 percent of economic activity in the OECD economies, compared to less than 20 percent for manufacturing.

Furthermore, based on productivity and trade statistics, many knowledge-based industries seem to exhibit a quality gap relative to other industrialized countries. Korea is well placed internationally in several of these industries, despite problems with respect to innovation capability, access to skilled personnel, and value-added content. This situation reflects the Korean emphasis on mass production and price competition as means to expand market share, rather than on innovation and product differentiation to increase profitability through enhanced productivity and value-added.

The government seeks to champion a triangular relationship in the Korean economy – one in which: (1) the reformed *chaebol* would focus on their core competencies, becoming world-class, competitive conglomerates; and (2) knowledge-based high-tech SMEs and suppliers of parts would form a supporting pillar; while (3) foreign companies would invest in Korea, contributing with advanced manufacturing and management skills. These three functions are likely to be important for maintaining or developing competitiveness in the knowledge-based economy. More fundamental, however, is the task of strengthening the mechanisms for spontaneous development and use of Knowledge in the Economy. Throughout the OECD area, there is a similar ongoing shift in industrial policies away from defensive support of specific firms and industries toward building institutional conditions and policies which strengthen the capacity of industry to do so in response to changing consumer demands and market opportunities.

There are at least five key sets of industry-related issues that require special government action in Korea as the country seeks to strengthen a knowledge-based economy. Unless they are properly addressed, the presence of these issues will limit the pressures for change and the responsiveness of the private sector to new opportunities, and thus serve to preserve outdated industrial structures at the expense of knowledge-based activities: (1) the dominating position and limited responsiveness of the *chaebol*; (2) the untapped potential of SMEs; (3) remaining barriers to contributions by foreign firms, including inward FDI; (4) impediments to high-value-added services; and (5) inadequate incentives for firms to invest in intangible assets.

The Korean Government should continue to press for efficient resource allocation and higher profitability in the *chaebol*, but should do so primarily through the financial channel and through corporate governance reform. Meanwhile, competition policy should be clearly separated from structural, or interventionist, policy. Conditions for start-up and growth of SMEs should be improved through a consolidation of existing support programs backed by more critical evaluations and an increased emphasis on the diffusion of technology and the upgrading of workforce skills. Furthermore, the government should follow up on the liberalization of inward FDI with measures that can induce foreign firms to transfer more skills and technologies to Korea, including improved intellectual property rights and the removal of barriers to labor mobility. It should dismount the remaining barriers to service-sector development, e.g. through continued regulatory reform, and develop a comprehensive strategy for improving the conditions for investment in intangible assets.

C Lithuania: innovation profile

There is a widespread consensus that innovation has a significant effect on productivity at the level of the firm, industry, and country and is thus a key element leading to economic growth. Originally, innovation was primarily defined in terms of technical change and product development, but has become more widely interpreted and applied. Organizational change and process renewal have been important improvements that also have had their effect on productivity gains and economic growth.

Mere existence of knowledge-creating organizations, however, is not enough. Effective use of high innovative technologies and processes throughout the economy is essential. The second component of this chapter deals with transfer of technology in the economy through supportive government policies, incentive, and institution framework, including business incubators and technology parks.

Lithuania has made a lot of progress in recent years to modernize many of the institutions and organizations related to science, technology, and innovation. In the early years of independence since 1990 Lithuania was left with an over-large and over-specialized research system cut off from its former users and sources of funding. This posed a number of acute problems and big challenges, which have had to be faced within an environment of seriously reduced funding. Nevertheless, much restructuring has been achieved with considerable talent and research capacity being retained in Lithuania.

A great number of analytical reports have been written by Lithuanian and foreign experts on the state of the art of science, technology, and innovation in Lithuania and the need to develop these basic elements of a knowledge-based society. The reports and their recommendations have been widely accepted among politicians, civil servants, members of research communities, industrialists, etc. Analytical reports have lead to White Papers and action plans, and again, these papers have received positive and almost unanimous support. However, only a few of the recommendations have been implemented, or they have been implemented only partly.

Even if the real level of resources devoted to R&D in Lithuania can be larger than official data suggests, the level of Lithuanian R&D expenditure is much lower than that of the EU or OECD average. Another problem is that the quality of spending has not adapted to the requirements of a market economy. A major part of government financing has been defined as institutional funding of R&D institutions, i.e. subsidies provided on a per capita employment basis designed to maintain existing staff, facilities, and equipment. Only a small fraction of government financing has been allocated to support what the government itself has defined as its priority objectives, and also financing to be distributed on the basis of competitive selection procedures have been modest by any standards.

Difficulties in increasing investments in R&D and in the implementation of action plans reflect a low awareness of the significance of R&D and innovation among politicians, industrialists, and high-level civil servants. What is mostly and most urgently needed in Lithuania is that science and technology, research and development, and innovation be given a strong priority at the highest political and societal level. This level should also openly commit itself to comprehensive development processes that require time and patience over more than one or two electoral periods. If Lithuania is really aiming at developing as a knowledge-based society it has to take good care of developing and upgrading its education and science. This is a very demanding task for politicians and administrators, because development of education and science set special requirements to perseverance and stability of policy. For economic reasons it is more than obvious that this can not be done without changes in the present division of resources in different fields of education and science.

The basic elements of the Lithuanian innovation system are, as in all market economies, R&D carried out in business enterprises, government research institutes, and universities. Many changes have been made in recent years in these organizations, but many of the current organizational structures tend to follow and even reinforce the old practices of separating the basic elements from each other. When compared to Western European countries, the Lithuanian R&D system is inflexible in the sense that practically all public resources are fixed with existing institutes. Naturally, this kind of system is more than inclined to resist any changes in priorities, division of resources, and ways of working. Cooperation and interaction of companies with research institutes and universities is modest and occasional. The same is true of cooperation and interaction between research institutes and universities, among research institutes, not to mention programs and schemes where companies, universities, and research institutes join their resources and competencies.

Different societies value and accept the role of government quite differently which is partly based on traditional relationships between citizen and government, cultures of trust and distrust and emphasis that is put on private initiative. Economic literature and experiences of most market economies give justification for governments to be active in starting and coordinating development processes. However, it is just as important to recognize and acknowledge the following fundamentals of advanced and advancing market economies:

- Technical change occurs by profit-motivated firms which try to appropriate the economic benefits of their innovations.
- This means that a major part of innovations are initiated and created by firms, and it also implies that a major part of R&D is carried out or should be carried out in companies.

- However, the market mechanism is not able to guarantee the optimal allocation of R&D resources and the widest possible diffusion of knowledge because of high costs and risks, etc. Consequently, there is a need for government intervention.
- On the other hand, there is a danger of "government failure," too. There are numerous examples where the government has failed in picking winners and losers.

The big challenge for R&D policy is to find out the functional division of labor between government intervention and self-management of companies. To present knowledge and experience, intervention is desirable and necessary, but the closer you go to direct operational activities of companies, the more important it is to consider the costs and benefits of government intervention. However, there is a lot that universities and government research institutes as well as public research programs can do to catalyze and leverage private sector resources and activities, and to diminish the innovation risk, but first of all, the government sector should be capable to use market forces to stimulate innovation.

Not only are performers of R&D fragmented and isolated in Lithuania, but this applies also to the public administration dealing with R&D and innovation. In government R&D the dominant player in Lithuania is the Ministry of Education and Science. It controls a major part of financial and other resources and is responsible for a large part or the entire chain of policies for R&D and their implementation. Through innovation, and particularly industrial innovation, the role of the Ministry of Economy and some other ministries has been growing, but so far this has not come true in an increase in inter-ministerial cooperation and interaction. The important lesson to be learnt from the experiences of more advanced countries is that the number of policy issues that have strong connections innovation is increasing, and the boundaries between policies aiming at promoting innovation become and must become vague. This is why in many countries the old term science and technology policy or research policy has been replaced with innovation policy. Consequently, Lithuania has a growing need to redefine and clarify the division of existing tasks and responsibilities between the key ministries in science and technology, and to increase by all means connectivity between various actors.

Regions and localities within countries have become more and more important platforms for innovation policy. This is true of Lithuania as well. The main idea which has already been applied, e.g. in the Vilnius and Kaunas regions, is that measures are adapted to the specific structures and potential of individual regions. The concepts of clustering and science parks, technology centers, and incubators are good examples of regional development approaches. The Lithuanian Government and the regional and city authorities have taken first steps in the direction of regional development of innovation with fairly good results. This policy should be intensified with the aspiring aims to stimulate economic growth on the basis of unique features and resources of each region, in order to contribute to a larger number of growing enterprises and to an increase in employment. The EU structural Funds Program can also serve in Lithuania as a model and source of funds for the structure of the action program, which constitutes the basis of regional innovation policy. Particularly, in Ireland, Finland, and Sweden, EU structural funds have had a very important role in shaping and renewing innovation policy.

In recent years governments in most EU countries have shifted their attention toward funding more application-oriented activities. In Lithuania, it is unquestionable that the focus of science and education should be changed from basic research more toward economically relevant applied research. However, also in small countries like Lithuania there is a need for public investments in basic research, and also in industrial sectors and technologies. Development of basic research can and must be target-oriented, toward economically and socially potential fields of technology, and toward the building up of creative research capabilities and securing the basis for technology innovation. Also in bigger countries, this has required that investments in basic science are associated with stricter conditions and more concrete performance measures.

A natural consequence of growing resources and increasing impacts of individual policies, organizations, programs, and structures is that governments express their increasing need to evaluate the effectiveness of the behavior of the mechanisms more clearly. Until now, in Lithuania R&D evaluation has been minor, and the country has been very dependent on foreign evaluators. R&D evaluation should be raised as an important issue, and evaluation practices developed on a more permanent basis. In addition, the increased complexity and the dynamics of the innovation system requires better understanding of major developments and trends in the national innovation system, and in its environment. This requires focused attention from policy makers and their contributors, and a sufficient number of specialized actors studying and producing information and data on a national innovation system for the use of policy making.

There are very positive signs of a proactive role and approach for the adoption of KE in Lithuania, by the various actors involved. A lot of background information has been compiled and analysis made by national and international experts. A great number of plans and other preparations have been done in various parts of the public and private sectors. There is a fairly wide consensus among political decision makers on the guidelines for development, and resources as well as actions, which are needed. The foundation has been created. In the coming months and years two things are most important: clarifying the major aims and means of the "National Development Project", and intensifying policy measures for the growth and effectiveness of the national innovation systems, and particularly its vote, the national R&D system.

A number of recommendations can be made for the further development of the Lithuanian R&D system. The basic idea behind the recommendations below is to focus on issues which can be considered to be of central importance in the current situation, and which might already in the short-term increase awareness of the role of science, technology, and innovation in national development, increase commitment to the basic aims and operations, and to shake up traditional structures, organizations, and practices in order to increase dynamics in the system.

As mentioned in various contexts, Lithuania has an increasing need to coordinate activities related to science, technology, and innovation, to forcefully direct science and technology policy, and to increase the visibility and priority of these mechanisms. The experiences of several EU countries, including Ireland, Finland, Sweden, and of the candidate countries, Estonia, prove that formation or strengthening of an advisory council on science, technology, and innovation at the highest political level is an effective and surprisingly lean mechanism for these purposes. This comes close to the proposal of the Lithuanian Science and Technology White Paper on the Science and Technology Board.

One of the central problems in Lithuanian R&D is the fact that only a very small fraction of government financing is distributed on the basis of competitive selection procedures. Usable and effective instruments to increase flexibility and generate positive changes are even easily available, as the experiences of big as well as small EU countries demonstrate. This can be applied at the level of institutes and universities by changing the principles and practices of their (basic) funding. The other and even better way is to establish a specialized public agency or public agencies for this purpose. There is some variation in the practices of EU countries, but basically most countries have a dual system: a special agency for technical research and development work under the Ministry of Economy, and a corresponding agency (usually a system of research councils) for basic research under the Ministry of Education. Because the experiences of practically all countries have been positive, it is recommended that these new mechanisms for R&D funding be seriously considered in Lithuania, too. One of the latest encouraging examples is the Estonian Technology Agency (ESTAG), which started to operate as a completely new organization at the beginning of 2001.

The establishment of the Agency would be a very good instrument to design, implement, and coordinate and to act more generally as an agent and spokesman of technical change. As part of the establishment of the new agency, also new financial instruments should be developed (in the form of grants, loans, seed money, etc.) especially for SMEs and start-up companies, but even for bigger companies to reduce the risk inherent in R&D. In addition, it is important to give all support to such new establishments as technology centers and parks, incubators, and other arrangements to intensify technology transfer from universities and research institutes.

In principle, the operations related to R&D at the ministerial level can be organized in three ways. The dominant player model is characterized by one organization being responsible for a large part of the entire chain of policies (Ireland, Sweden, and the United Kingdom are examples). Some countries follow a model in which there are two separate systems existing next to each other, supporting innovation from different perspectives. One system focuses on education and research, while the other is oriented toward technology and economic development (e.g. Germany, Netherlands, and Finland). The third model, the polarized model, represents a very focused approach on the different aspects of innovation-related policies. An extreme example is South Korea, where the national innovation system is split into strongly separated pillars.

The situation in Lithuania resembles the dominant player model with the Ministry of Education and Science as the dominant player. Broadening of the scope of the policy for science and technology from R&D to innovation necessarily increases the role of the Ministry of Economy. To make sure that the two new organizations, the Science and Technology Policy Council, and the National Technology Agency, work well requires that governance at the ministerial level is developed from the dominant player model more toward the division of labor model.

Reorganization of the system of state research institutes should be seriously considered. This cannot be seen as separate issue, but it should be seen in the wider context of development of universities on the one hand and corporate R&D on the other hand. There are several possibilities in the reorganization or restructuring; abolition of some institutes; combining of institutes; combining of institutes with universities; combining of institutes with relevant sectoral ministries; privatization of institutes; establishment of a research centre for applied and contract research (VTT in Finland, Sintef in Norway, TNO in the Netherlands, Fraunhofer Gesellschaft in Germany). There is no reason to avoid considering this complexity of issues, which is central to the whole R&D system.

D   The case of Sri Lanka[3]

Sri Lanka has the potential to spark a new era of ICT growth in a way that generates near-term and wide-ranging benefits for the country. Expectations are growing of tangible progress as Sri Lanka moves into a new social and economic era.

Recent trends in ICT markets make it possible now for Sri Lanka's public and private sectors to deliver results with unprecedented speed (see Figure 12.2). The scale of job creation in coming years for developing countries can surpass what software and related services have been able to deliver to India.

Beyond software-related opportunities, immense new markets are today opening for call centers, image-processing operations, secretarial services,

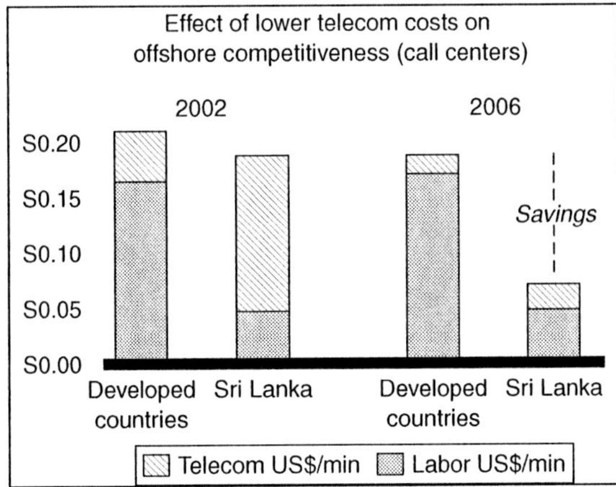

Figure 12.2   ICT-related potential savings for Sri Lanka

remote security monitoring, and online tutoring. Millions of jobs will be created in countries that have affordable talent and conducive economic policies. These opportunities are now accessible to developing countries because of a convergence of four forces:

- *Plunging costs of international telecommunications* enable individuals and firms in competitive markets to directly do business around the globe;
- *e-Government innovations* enable companies to obtain approvals and conduct operations in a fast and transparent way;
- *New electronic marketplaces*, such as e-Bay's professional services market, allow micro-entrepreneurs as well as larger firms to rapidly build global reputations; and
- *"Anytime, anywhere" learning* lets individuals and companies acquire new skills at exceptional speed and savings.

Countries that encourage their entrepreneurs to harness these forces can now grow more quickly than nations that seek growth through investment by (slower-moving) multinational corporations. This is particularly true for countries that have extensive networks of expatriates with global experience and/or capital to share in building new ICT ventures.

No country has yet systematically put in place all of the essential conditions for breakthrough growth by its entrepreneurs in the global information economy. Sri Lanka could be the first one to do so, surpassing India and Singapore in the creation of a world-class package of reforms. It could become the standard of success by which other countries will be measured in the next era of the information economy, given commitment by leadership to economic reforms that provide conditions for growth and ensure a sharing of success throughout the country.

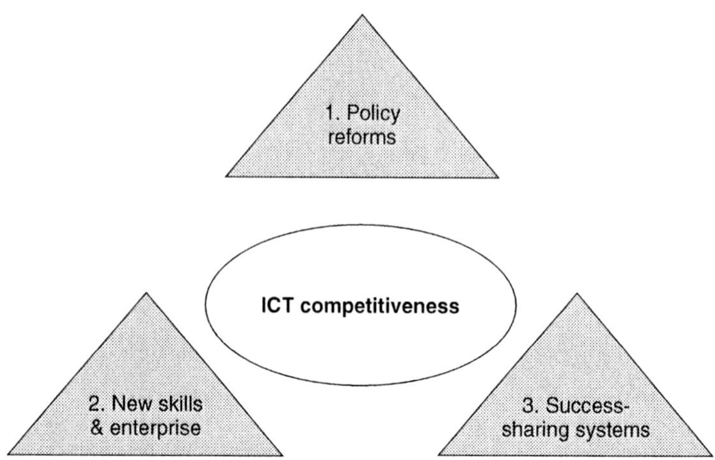

Figure 12.3   Complementary areas of action for ICT competitiveness

New revenue-generating reforms and ICT cluster initiatives introduced in the coming year could provide the springboard for sustained economic growth, and a model of entrepreneur-led success for many other countries in turn to view and follow. A concerted, near-term campaign could put in place a foundation of sustained competitiveness for Sri Lanka in immense new global markets, through complementary initiatives in three main areas (see Figure 12.3). Sri Lanka could offer a climate second to none in the world for both resident and non-resident ICT export firms. Key elements of reform could include:

- Relief from telecommunication monopolies and cumbersome regulations;
- e-Government, e-Commerce, and legal reforms to automate incentive approvals, online contracting, and payments;
- Fast, affordable online incorporation of ICT-related export companies;
- New freedoms to invest with and do business in foreign currencies, including e-Currencies;
- Tax-free "Technology Visas" whose fees fund Sri Lankan skills development;
- A national voucher/scholarship fund for ICT skills formation (including e-Learning and short courses);
- Binding arbitration and strengthened intellectual property rights.

Targeted, fast-track reforms could be applied to promote Sri Lanka's leadership in linking local firms and institutions to emerging information industry opportunities. An opportunity is at hand to initiate public–private partnerships that can improve lives around the country, by stimulating entrepreneurship and learning opportunities leading to productive futures in the

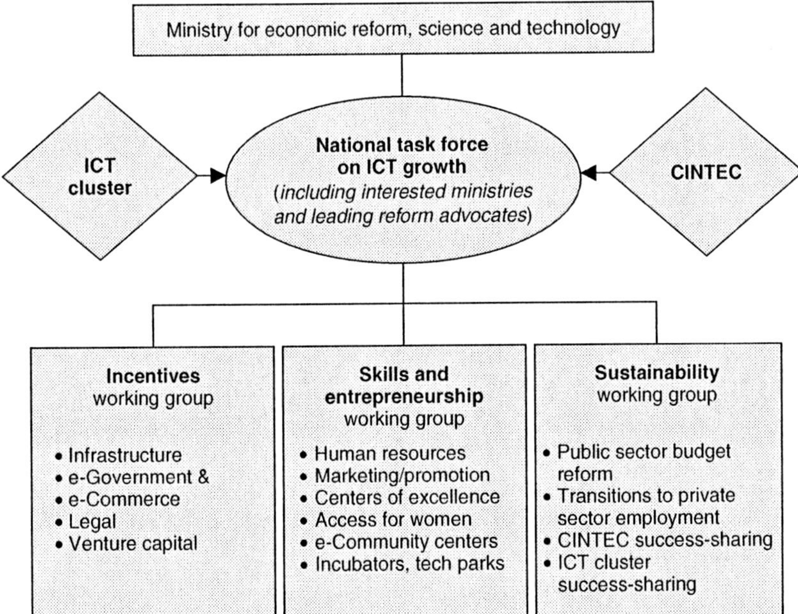

Figure 12.4   Public–private sector interaction framework

global information economy. The ICT cluster will welcome an opportunity to work closely with the Ministry for Economic Reform, Science and Technology in refining the roadmap. The roadmap should bear in mind the following objectives:

- Stimulating jobs and exports;
- Accelerating rural access;
- Generating revenues for government, cluster activities;
- Enhancing scholarship and training opportunities;
- Implementing e-Government systems;
- Creating links to leading overseas technical institutions;
- Expanding opportunities for women;
- Engaging ICT diaspora;
- Winning market leadership recognition.

A National task-force on ICT reform could take responsibility for the implementation of the roadmap under the supervision of the Ministry for Economic Reform, Science and Technology.

Finally, we suggest the following framework (see Figure 12.4) to promote public–private sector consensus and coordinated action in support of reform initiatives for ICT success.

Part V

Recommendations and Conclusions

13
Recommendations: Policies and Pilot Best Practices

In this section, we present the key findings of our work, along with a set of recommendations we believe are critical for the successful implementation of an e-Development strategy and optimizing the use of ICT in the Knowledge Economy.

Our key findings can be summarized as follow:

- e-Development can serve to *support business (and especially SMEs) creation on a larger scale and scope and at a faster rate* leveraging ICT as well as changes in mindset and regulatory/business environment.
- e-Development necessitates and facilitates *innovative thinking* in designing development interventions as a result of the challenges and opportunities associated with the use of ICT and related market, knowledge, and network spill over effects.
- e-Development necessitates *enhanced knowledge generation and sharing policies, institutions and infrastructures* and in that sense serves as a driver and bridge towards the Knowledge Economy.
- e-Development necessitates *an enhanced, deeper and broader networking of people and companies* in order to cope with and benefit from the changes that e-Development triggers including *gloCalization* (global interventions with local reach and local initiatives with global scope).
- e-Development dictates *increased focus on a cross-sectoral as well as a regional* approach both to be able to fully unlock and capture its value-adding potential as well as to compensate against its possible side-effects (such as domestic or regional digital and socio-economic divides that can undermine the benefits of development). Along the cross-sectoral focus theme, *a vibrant dialog and knowledge exchange among the private, educational, and R&D sectors* are crucial in achieving e-Development toward the Knowledge Economy (a propos, the Sixth Framework Programme for Research and Technological Development of the European Union has as its main focus the linkages between education and research).

- e-Development (intended as a dynamic and flexible mix of technology and development policies and interventions) is a new phenomenon: technology and development can, and should, co-exist to increase efficiency and maximize intervention impact. It leverages, catalyzes, and combines *people, culture, and technology* for optimal *availability, awareness, accessibility, and affordability* of knowledge-based goods (digital and tangible) and can serve as a powerful *communication, cooptation, and coordination* device for development.

Based on the key findings of this work in terms of what the critical success determinants for e-Development interventions are, we developed the following corollary e-Development strategy recommendations. ICT needs to be fully leveraged by e-Development, as its role is crucial in enabling, catalyzing, and accelerating e-Development interventions. e-Development interventions need to be designed with the four key dimensions (or pillars) in mind to be successful: policy making, institution building, capacity building, and investment making:

e-Development interventions also rely on and are impacted by the presence or absence of a set of key factors that serve as *enablers, catalysts, and accelerators* of e-Development and which were identified in the course of this work. There is a clear need for *an e-Development and Knowledge Economy vision and strategy* championed by the highest levels of national governments and with a gloCal element in it, namely the recognition of the challenge and the opportunity of the emergence and multiplication of global interventions.

There is also a clear need for balancing, complementing, and reinforcing *top-down public sector interventions* with *bottom-up private sector initiatives* and in particular SME support. Therefore, SME development initiatives would help unlock and capture the value-added by both e-Development and Knowledge Economy initiatives.

There is a need for *a network approach* in designing e-Development interventions, focusing on opportunities to leverage and foster connections and partnerships among knowledge-generating and sharing entities in a country's economy, such as universities, research laboratories, private sector business (large firms and SMEs), and foreign entities as well. Within this context falls the formation of real and virtual incubator networks, which is one of the pilot project recommendations in Chapter 14D of this work.

There is also a need for a *multi-layered systems approach*, where local, national, and regional challenges and opportunities are addressed in a manner that is comprehensive and systematic encouraging and leveraging gloCalization for development. In the same context, *donor coordination* leveraging ICT to minimize resource overlap and maximize intervention impact is crucial.

The role of the *diaspora* in many countries can be a very significant source of financial, intellectual, human, and social capital helping bridge the existing digital divides as well as those that may be formed or exacerbated by e-Development initiatives.

A   Improving the business environment/encouraging entrepreneurship

The business environment in most developing and transitioning countries is often severely impeded by an inefficient and bureaucratic public sector, as well as the lack of proactive business support programs. The most common problems that can be addressed with the help of e-Development applications include:

- High entry barriers due to cumbersome, costly, and lengthy start-up processes.
- High costs of doing business resulting from time- and resource-consuming administrative procedures, such as tax reporting, inspections, custom clearance, etc.
- Limited and poorly accessible information services for business development, such as on business-related laws and regulations, often overly complicated and subject to unpredictable changes.
- Corruption and red tape due to non-transparent transactions between government and private entities in areas as such privatizations and procurement.
- Lack of business development opportunities, due to limited access to finance and specialized services (especially for SMEs).

The e-Development framework allows the introduction of advanced applications that improve the traditional business and government processes, increase efficiency and transparency of interaction/transactions between the public and private sectors, and altogether strengthen the overall business environment in the country.

Start-up/investment support

Online one-stop-shop portal services can be introduced to coordinate/integrate the services of different government agencies and provide efficient customer-centered start-up support for local and foreign investment. Such systems encompass a variety of services, from information on permits and licenses, to referral to additional information sources, specialist advice, and more. The portal should be a single entry point for different start-up G2B transactions and inquiries. It would be a "one-stop-shop" window, whereas particular transactions, such as registration, tax reporting, and licensing would be performed by the relevant agencies. The portal should therefore be designed as one system/interface for all end-users.

Simplification of administrative procedures

e-Development applications can streamline the interaction between public and private sectors in many ways. Various solutions are available to improve efficiency and transparency of service provisions to entrepreneurs and facilitate business entry and operation. e-Development can be applied to improve the internal information flow among different government agencies and units providing services to the private sector. The one-stop-shop, or single-entrance point approach, is a flexible solution for most public sector structures. For example, the Center for Business Formalities in France (CFC) is a portal that collects all required information from enterprises to various government agencies, such as the local trade register, the taxation office, the administrations in charge of social security and pensions, the statistical office, etc. Once an enterprise has entered the required information in the CFC, the service transmits it to the relevant branches of the administration, simplifying all related administrative procedures.

Providing information services for business development

To improve access to vital information for businesses, a web-based information service on business-related legal and regulatory environment can be introduced. Such a web service could include sections on judicial opinions in business-related cases, draft laws and regulations, adopted laws and regulations, government directory/organization chart (with citations to laws), and Frequently Asked Questions. The site should have information in easily accessible format, with a problem-solving, "how-to" focus. For example, it could explain legal requirements on how to start a business, initiate export/import operations, etc. Ideally, the website should be part of a bigger SME-support portal. It is a relatively low-cost option that may have a very positive effect on improving the business environment. Government business-support services could also include information and training sessions on preparing business plans, new business practices, money management, foreign investment, ISO certification, tax planning, etc. One of the most creative solutions of the information services is an online benchmarking tool for quantifying performance and assessing SMEs' competitive strengths and weaknesses. Benchmarking is a systematic process for profiling and evaluating a company's effectiveness in terms of productivity, quality, innovation, and other business practices, by comparison with the "Best in Class." SMEs can be encouraged to improve their business practices by receiving objective ratings against best practice in the region.

Improving transactions between government and private entities

e-Procurement applications help streamline the way tendering is being conducted, saving time and money for both businesses and government organizations. It is a more effective way to acquire goods and services from external suppliers and provides a platform for document interchange between suppliers and buyers. Besides improving the efficiency, such a system greatly decreases the level of corruption in government procurement operations. Under a government e-Procurement system, companies need only register one single time in their area of business (e.g. office furniture, construction services, IT consulting, etc.). Whenever a public agency needs to purchase goods or contract a service, the system automatically sends an e-mail to all the private companies registered in the selected area, minimizing response time and providing an equal opportunity to all firms. The system also provides online all information related to procurement operations. At the conclusion of the bidding process, the system provides the results: the list of participants, proposals, economic and technical scores, and, lastly, the winners of the bid or contract. Privatization programs for state-owned enterprises and banks can also be enhanced with technology applications that increase transparency and reduce the lengthy process involved. A special privatization website can provide essential information about the enterprises and banks being privatized as well as procedures and requirements. The website should not be static, but allow for interaction between government authorities and potential investors.

Improving access to finance

The establishment of an online Credit Information Bureau (CIB) can facilitate openness and foster accountability within the private sector. A CIB would in fact allow entrepreneurs and banks to gather information crucial for business decision making, both in terms of partnering and lending. Information will particularly be useful for SMEs or unlisted companies where the disclosure of financial statements is not mandatory or the level of the reliability is poor. The establishment of a CIB could also facilitate integration among firms and ease the rigidities of the supply and demand sides of financing.

Online mortgage and pledge registries can assist banks in improving their provision of financial services, and to SMEs in particular, helping to register ownership and pledges, properly value the collateral, and ensure transparent and reliable flow of information. Integrated data exchange systems for financial institutions can dramatically improve the products and the dynamics of the financial system. These systems can facilitate the interconnection among different players and their relative databases and insure consistency of data according to common standards, while enhancing transparency by making information and data more easily accessible.

B   Promoting R&D networking and leveraging

Despite relatively strong education and innovation systems, many transitioning economies have a poor record of effective commercialization of their

R&D. This ineffective use of knowledge can be attributed to a weak capacity to foster R&D networking among the private sector and academia and/or poor capabilities to protect intellectual property. Thus, e-Development pilots can be used to improve the capacity of innovative enterprises, promote effective collaboration of R&D-related companies and institutions, and facilitate the effective use of the Intellectual Property (IP) system.

Promoting R&D networking and business support services

Incubators and technology parks are the main venues to create networking opportunities that foster innovation and R&D. They are designed to facilitate production and commercialization of advanced technologies by forging synergies among research centers, education institutions, and technology-based companies. Tenants of technology parks are usually small companies at an early development stage, pursuing an ambitious growth strategy based on the incubation of new ideas. To facilitate the successful adaptation and take-up of these ideas in the market place, technology parks provide financial consulting/support to seek venture capital; professional, technical, administrative, and legal assistance; information and telecommunications services; and a supportive business infrastructure.

To promote close collaboration between major R&D players, dedicated high-speed telecom networks can be created to cover public and private universities, government-supported R&D institutions, major libraries, as well as associations of private enterprises devoted to R&D promotion.

Increasing the efficiency of the Intellectual Property Rights (IPR) system

IPR management with the help of ICT applications enable entrepreneurs to use their intellectual property assets to improve competitiveness and gain strategic advantage. Effective IPR management means more than just protecting an enterprise's inventions, trademarks or copyright, but also involves a company's ability to commercialize such inventions.

National IPR Agencies can introduce online databases with functional search capabilities to allow entrepreneurs to conduct initial search on issues such as trademarks and patents quickly. The website should also provide a comprehensive IPR information service connected to a number of patent databases around the world to obtain an integrated IPR information. This can be combined with government expert services that manage and evaluate patents and trademarks to give a picture of this strategic value for companies. Virtual intellectual property markets can be designed to assist companies in commercializing the results of their R&D activities. It is a government-supported marketplace platform enabling IPR owners, potential buyers and sellers, and licensees to meet and establish contacts for commercialization of patented technologies. It provides information on what types of IPR are available for licensing, and what types of IPR customers are looking for. This service benefits SMEs that may lack the capital to take a product to market and also may be looking for licensees that may be willing to take out a license to commercialize patented technologies.

C   Facilitating SME development

Most of the applications discussed in the chapters on Improving Business Environment and R&D Promotion will have a positive impact on SME development. At the same time, e-Development allows for applications targeted specifically at SMEs. They help SMEs overcome size-related constraints that limit their capacity to access new markets, benefit from technology transfer, and tap into the global knowledge-base on the latest business practices and skills.

Strengthening networking and market access

ICT enables SMEs to strengthen linkages with large enterprises through online marketplaces. The government can provide and support a platform for such marketplaces, often as a part of a larger e-Government portal. Strong ties with large enterprises facilitate technology transfer to SMEs, and improve management and technical knowledge and skills. Finally, information and knowledge-sharing driven by ICT creates effective value-chain networks among SMEs and large enterprises, leading to sustainable industry development.

Supporting linkages between local and foreign high-tech companies

In the context of transitional and developing countries, subcontracting is one of the most efficient channels for technology transfer and skill training for domestic SMEs. Governments should support subcontracting by helping to reduce marketing barriers to foreign markets, supporting export-oriented business associations, and collecting and disseminating best practices in subcontracting in specific sectors. For these purposes, governments can create online one-stop advisory, licensing, and support portals for export-oriented ICT companies, in essence functioning as a virtual technology park/incubator.

Developing business advisory services

To address the issue of limited business and management skills among entrepreneurs, governments often encourage development of a local consulting industry. A special online portal can be created to support such efforts so that it can:

- Allow collaboration and exchange of information among the local consultants and between the local and foreign consultants;
- Interconnect advisory centers with the leading R&D and academic establishments in the country;
- Provide distance learning and re-training of the consultants;

- Provide information on the resent changes in the business regulatory environment for the consultants; and
- Help disseminate best practices and findings.

Government business support agencies can host online business advisory services provided by various private sector experts. Clients can choose an adviser from among a number of business consultants and other advisers registered with the center. Clients would be able to get a response from the selected expert within a short period of time. Further, in-depth cooperation between the adviser and the company can be conducted on an offline commercial basis.

Facilitating distance learning and training for SME

e-Learning applications can be used to allow SMEs to tap into the global knowledge-base. Enterprises in need of human development assistance should be given access to the global e-Learning networks. If infrastructure constrains prevent such an arrangement, combined methods can be utilized, where e-Learning is used to educate the trainers, which then employ traditional means of education and training for entrepreneurs.

D   Supporting rural enterprises

Rural enterprises in transitioning and developing economies, and especially in the CIS countries, have difficulties in achieving sustainable growth and development. Geographical restriction, poor technologies and business techniques, as well as lack of relevant market information deprive them of opportunities to expand sales, even if they have desirable products, good inputs, and a skilled labor force. Their major problems include:

- Lack of information on the market at both local and international levels. The issue is especially important for the countries that depend heavily on agri-business and export, such as Armenia, Moldova, Georgia, and the Kyrgyz Republic.
- Outdated technologies, know-how, and business practices. Socialist system of knowledge transfer from academia to agri-business has in many countries been practically destroyed, without effective replacement.
- Poor access to government services, such as weather forecast, business, and land registration, etc.

ICT applications, such as rural information and advisory system, e-Marketplace and e-Government, can help improve the business environment, bridging gaps between market demand and supply and enabling rural enterprises to conquer many of their inherent disadvantages. One of the most successful interventions to support rural enterprises is e-Choupal in India, designed to create a sustainable, efficient supply-chain in the agriculture sector through a vertical integration of fragmented rural farms. Even though e-Choupal is a privately owned system, it can be adopted as a government-supported solution or a public–private partnership. Another example, is Drishtee, a public–private e-Development initiative in India to create a comprehensive platform for rural networking and marketing services. It enables villagers to access both government and private sector services. The World Bank also had a successful experience in promoting rural enterprises with the use of ICT in the ECA region. The Rural Information and Knowledge System was a major part of the Agricultural Reform Implementation Support (ARIS) project implemented in the Russian Federation between 1994 and 2000. The project can serve as a base for designing rural market information systems in large countries and/or promote cross-border trade.

14
Recommendations: Potential Pilots

In this section, we propose a number of e-Development pilot projects that could be implemented as tools to innovate and learn about best ways to undertake e-Development interventions. The following criteria are recommended in the selection of pilot projects, based on best international practice. Pilot projects/interventions need to:

- Fit into the broader government policies, to gain support and become sustainable;
- Rely on permissive, if not favorable, legal and regulatory frameworks;
- Have adequate infrastructure to maintain and use the system; services should be accessible for the target audience;
- Have distinctive benefits for the owner of the project (in the most cases – a particular government agency or ministry) to be sustainable in the long run; otherwise, sabotage and bureaucratic resistance is inevitable;
- Start small and be scalable: "small" and "big" are, of course, relative terms and depend on the size of the country and other factors;
- Have a substantial and quickly achievable positive impact for private sector development and the overall business environment in the country;
- Be demand-driven: ICT should simplify services for end user; entrepreneurs will use e-Development applications only if doing so is quicker, easier, or cheaper than going through traditional channels;
- Rely on the stable institutional base, i.e. their implementation should not require major institutional reforms;
- Involve a small number of agencies since in many ECA countries interaction among ministries and agencies is notoriously poor.

Several transitioning and developing countries from the examples of pilots provided so far have already started implementing e-Development projects. The vast majority of interventions, however, deal with automation of the government back-office operations and creation of basic non-interactive websites for government agencies, with relatively rare (though successful) exceptions, such as e-Procurement in Romania and wireless business services in Estonia. While such e-Administration projects have limited direct influence on the private sector, they prepare the necessary ground for interventions related to private sector development, since practically all of them require computerization of government offices.

A   The Web-enabled pilot based on a knowledge creation, sharing, and use model (the e-Know4Dev model)

The main component of the project is the creation of *a web-based dynamic model for the creation, sharing and use of knowledge to foster economic and social development.* The model, based on a hybrid form of three leading knowledge economy architectures (Yahoo!, e-Bay, EIU), will serve as a main tool for these actors to improve their ability to communicate and share knowledge about their specific needs and services more efficiently. The model will support (see Figures 14.1 and 14.2 on p. 228):

- The creation of time, context, and user-specific content (following the Economist Intelligence Unit (EIU) model);
- The system to deliver the right content to the proper user through a user-friendly and reliable web-directory (following the Yahoo! Model);
- The establishment of a virtual market where buyers and sellers interact (following the e-Bay model).

e-Bay

e-Bay is the world's largest auction site, with 23 million registered users, operations in various countries (North America, Western Europe, and expansion in Asia). e-Bay has proven itself the most robust company of the Internet economy. It handles 79 million transactions per quarter, lists more than 5 million items for sale, and is coming ever closer to its mission of helping people trade practically anything on earth. Key to its success is the strength, scalability, and profitability of its business model: it has the largest number of sellers that attract the largest number of buyers. Likewise, the huge community of buyers keeps the sellers coming back to the site, where they are likely to get the highest bids for their items. The larger e-Bay gets, the stronger its attractiveness to both buyers and sellers alike. This is a classic network effect, where the value of a trading community or network grows by the square of each additional member. The site's attractiveness is sustained by various factors:

- Sellers can post their products, and buyers can surf the site searching for opportunities, for free (only requirement is a registration to the website);

- The bidding is conducted by the continuous exchange of e-mail between buyer and seller, supported by notifications on the development of the auctions by the e-Bay system;
- Charges apply only in case of successful transaction.

e-Bay is a very good example for the exchange mechanism between actors of the Knowledge economy: e-Bay does not create any content, it just provides a framework and structure where sellers and buyers interact. Moreover, the company's capital and investment needs are minimal (this explains the stellar returns of investment and the performance of the company). For instance, the company increased the number of auctions ten-fold while only doubling the investment (minimal fixed costs to support the framework).

Yahoo!

Yahoo! started years ago as a mere search engine. The transition to a more elaborated and complicated portal took place very quickly, when Yahoo! realized the viability of its business model based on advertising and routing users to specific websites. At the same time, Yahoo! expanded internationally its operation, creating customized portals for each country of operation. Yahoo! has had two extremely valuable competitive advantages to position itself as a market leader:

- It soon established a sound reputation as a solid player in the Internet arena (establishment of global brand name with the search engine, transition from pure search engine to portal, expansion of range of services offered, strong partnerships with content creators, etc.).
- It expanded and kept an already loyal and wide audience with its e-mail services.

Good reputation, new services and wide user base has allowed Yahoo! to sustain profitability despite the uncertainty of the Internet economy. Nowadays, Yahoo! is positioning itself as a major content aggregator and distributor, especially in Europe. To this extent, Yahoo! is focusing on designing proper strategies to face the challenges of a new market. Yahoo! is currently engaged in signing new alliances with content providers, and testing different business models to understand where the profitability of this new market relies.

EIU

The Economist Intelligence Unit (EIU) is the world leader provider of country analysis and intelligence. It started operations more than half a century ago and has immediately taken advantage of the Internet as a medium to distribute its products.

The EIU product portfolio includes reports, newsletters, alerts, and analysis on countries, regions, and industry sectors. Typical clients of the EIU are organizations that need to know about political, economic, and business developments across the world, so basically they are multinational corporations, exporters and importers, investors, financial institutions, governments, and education institutions. The business model of the www.eiu.com site is pretty straightforward: it is based on a subscription and pay-per-view basis. There are different options for customers to choose: pay a subscription for a certain period and a certain service (i.e. "business environment reports" only) or just one report.

The www.eiu.com does not include advertisement as a revenue stream and is a portal limited to the vast resources of the Economist Group (EIU, CFO, Journal of Commerce, Pyramid, The Economist, eBusiness Forum, etc.), by being a simple electronic delivery system.

B   Description of the e-Know4Dev model

e-Bay, the EIU, and Yahoo! are the most suitable examples of integrated exchange system and mechanism as facilitator for the Knowledge Economy Market. The three models present common characteristics in terms of leadership in their respective market segment, well-established reputation, and large customer base. Each one of the models offers valuable examples for the creation of a web-enabled forum.

An appropriate web-based knowledge-sharing model may take the shape of a hybrid form that leverages the success factors of each of the three models previously analyzed.

The e-Bay component may serve as channel to integrate firms and investors' efforts in the ECA region; Yahoo!'s system as a search engine and portal can serve the scope of channeling users' requests according to their needs to efficiently and easily navigate the model; the EIU model can be the basis for the creation of valuable, pertinent, and reliable content. The proposed model may serve for both for profit and not-for-profit sectors:

- For-profit model: this model may be the best solution in the case of a system established by the private sector, hence motivated and focused on revenue generation opportunities. The revenue streams of the business model for the for-profit system may hinge on e-commerce transaction revenues, subscription fees for the users, and advertisement.
- Not-for-profit model: this model may be a good fit for the creation of a knowledge creation, sharing, and use model established by NGOs, government and/or international organizations and donors. In this case, the creation, sharing, and use of content may be facilitated by public funding. Yet, the system may be gain sustainability and financial independence by auto-financing the initiative through getting revenues from advertisement.

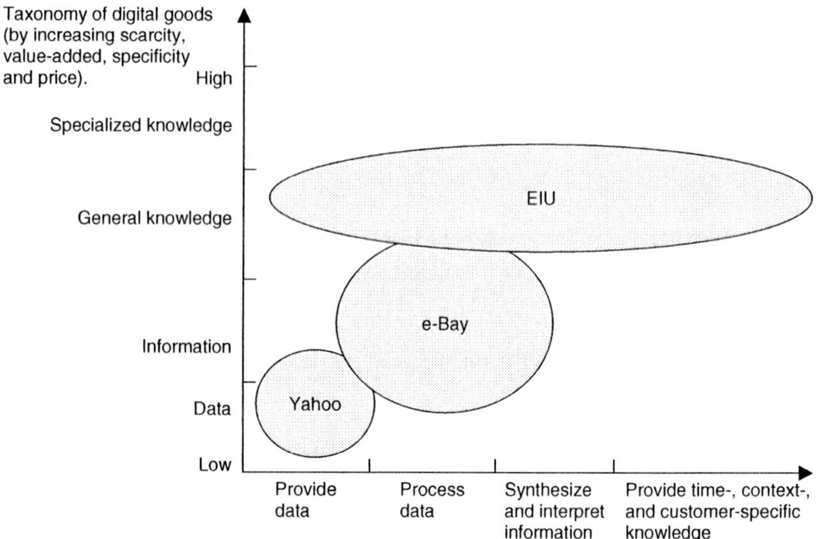

Figure 14.1   Proxies of digital goods market model

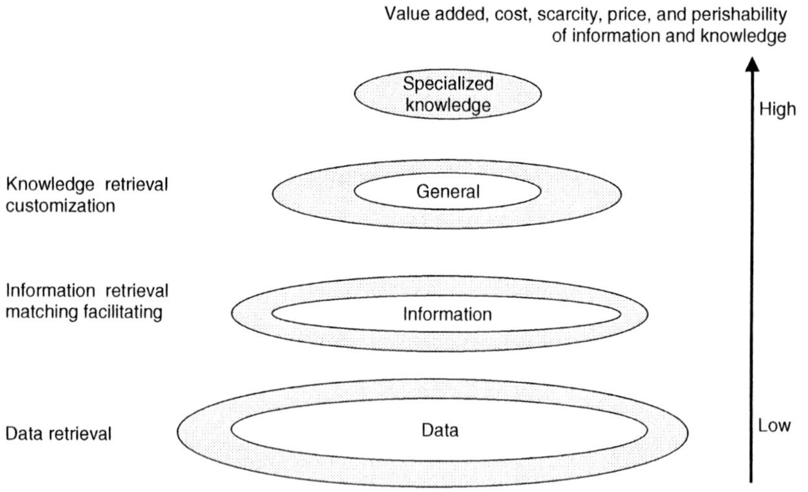

Figure 14.2   Proxies of e-Know4Dev business model

Specifically, the experience of the three models can well serve the creation of a plausible knowledge-sharing system that takes advantage of their strengths. The bidding channel created by e-Bay can serve the purpose of enabling e-Commerce transactions, where SMEs and larger firms from the ECA region interact among themselves and with international buyers and sellers. The bidding system may prove to be beneficial at different levels, since it:

- Opens up domestic and regional markets to increased competition among firms;
- Opens up international market that would otherwise be inaccessible;
- Integrates local firms into the international value-chain;
- Helps local firms to establish solid reputation both locally and internationally;
- Maximizes resources by establishing a bidding system.

The Yahoo! model serves as a good example for the structure of the knowledge-sharing system. The Yahoo! experience may be useful to design a proper application to surf, search, and use the system (so leverage the Yahoo! example focusing on its value not only as search engine, but also, and mostly, as horizontal and vertical portal). The value of a Yahoo! model as a channel to share information is crucial for various factors:

- It aggregates the content in a structured and organized way (i.e. local, regional or international). Moreover, the content is organized by field, category, temporal, and topical relevance, etc.
- It creates a flexible and dynamic system, able to be easily and constantly up-dated and integrated with new content and accessible through different devices (i.e. computers, WAP, Interactive TV (on-test), etc.).

The EIU example is relevant and valuable to stress the importance of reliable and pertinent content. The creation of specifically designed content is pivotal to the fostering of development of the private and financial sectors.

The e-Bay component of the model will create a virtual marketplace where entrepreneurs can establish direct contact with customers and consumers, and meet the increasing demand for organic products. This will further integrate micro- and SME enterprises into the international value-chain from both B2C and B2B perspectives.

The project will yield the following benefits:

- Opening up domestic and regional markets to increased competition among firms (e-Bay);
- Opening up international market that would otherwise be inaccessible (e-Bay);

- Integrates local firms into the international value-chain (e-Bay);
- Helping local firms to establish solid reputation both locally and internationally (e-Bay);
- Maximizing resources by establishing a bidding system (e-Bay);
- Aggregating the content in structured and organized way (i.e. local, regional, international). Moreover, the content is organized by field, category, temporal, and topical relevance, etc. (Yahoo!);
- Creating a flexible and dynamic system, able to be easily and constantly up-dated and integrated with new content and accessible through different devices (i.e. computers, WAP, Interactive TV (on-test), etc.) (Yahoo!);
- Stressing the importance of reliable and pertinent content. The creation of specifically designed content is pivotal to fostering development of the private and financial sectors (EIU).

C   Organic farming

Project objectives and description

The Organic Farming project aims to promote a niche and export-oriented sector of great potential for SMEs in the ECA region countries, by supporting, as its name implies, organic farming. This project also relies on the Knowledge-Sharing, Creation, and Use Model described above.

The Internet will allow farmers to access, at any time and from any location, the web-based model to improve their production capabilities (through training packages on best practices in both production and marketing; better knowledge of the demand dynamics in local, regional, and international markets, etc.). Moreover, the e-Bay component of the model will create a virtual marketplace where farmers can establish direct contact with customers and consumers, and meet the increasing demand for organic products. This will further integrate micro- and SME enterprises into the international value-chain from both a B2C and B2B perspectives.

Organic farming is a new market segment of the agri-business that offers incredible potential for developing countries:

- Increasing demand for organic food;
- Organic farming is a production process in its early stage of development, leaving vast room for new entrants;
- Organic farming is a labor-intensive industry: developing countries have large amounts of human resources available to be allocated to the agri-business, to the contrary of industrial societies.

Yet, the potential of developing countries is undermined by the complete lack of information on production techniques, marketing processes, market access, etc.

The pilot can have a positive impact on other related opportunities for private sector development: eco-tourism and software development. Several conservation areas are now in the process of being established which may further the development of organic farming and promote the eco-tourism niche market. The heavy ICT component of the pilot (the creation of a web-based knowledge facilitator mechanism) creates opportunities for a linkage between this pilot and other initiatives aimed at developing the software and IT applications sector. The need for time, context, and customer-specific knowledge can foster the whole IT sector of the region (i.e. web-development, software design, hardware procurement, IT human resources, content creation, etc.).

D The Regional Virtual Network for Enterprise Restructuring and Development (the RV-NERD pilot)

The aim of this project is the creation of a Regional Virtual Network for Enterprise Restructuring and Development (RV-NERD) to support and promote interaction among the four segments of the society and economy:

- Government (local, national and regional authorities involved in private sector development: i.e. ministries, local entities, agencies, etc.);
- Firms and companies of different sectors and dimensions (i.e. manufacturing, large-, small- and medium-, micro-sized);
- Entities of the financial sector (i.e. banks, insurance companies, venture capitalists, etc.);
- Civil society (i.e. universities, associations, trade unions and NGOs, etc.).

Each of these segments are crucial to support and sustain the goals of private sector development. The Virtual Network will be the framework to create links among these segments that would otherwise rely only on traditional means of interaction, being then heavily affected by geographic and cultural distance and barriers that hinder the development of an open market economy. The pilot is unique in its focus on creating opportunities for the four pillars of society and economy. Room for new entrants and enabling existing micro- and small-sized enterprises to improve production and penetrate international markets through an Internet-based innovative tool. They will initially be implemented in a few target countries of the ECA region. In a second phase, pilots will be implemented on a cross-regional and international scale to foster replication of successful models, thus maximizing the long-term development impact on private and financial sectors. Moreover, the knowledge-creation, sharing, and use model can be replicated globally for other sectors of interest for development strategies of the World Bank Group.

The pilot has a positive impact on the various aspects of the private and financial sectors. It includes the participations of different entities involved in the social and economic development of the ECA region. The Network is a suitable instrument to support diverse sectors of the economy, providing a reliable and replicable framework to foster development. The project will connect the various actors of the private and public sectors involved and interested in enterprise restructuring and development.

The dedicated virtual network will create opportunities for these actors to interact among each other, and ultimately create synergies. The network can later be expanded to generate greater opportunities for interaction. The link between the various actors of the private sector will be done with the support of telecenters when and where needed to insure wide participation of medium-, small-, and micro-enterprises and artisans. The essence of the project is captured in Figure 14.3 and Figure 14.4.

E Software outsourcing

The Software Outsourcing project aims to promote a niche and export-oriented sector of great potential for IT firms in the ECA region countries, by supporting software development. This project is again based on the Knowledge-Sharing, Creation, and Use model described earlier.

Experience has shown that most Western companies would be willing to outsource their software development needs if they had assurance about the quality of the work done offshore. The ECA region's countries offer a wide variety of advantages: (i) trained and available human capital; (ii) favorable environment for international investment.

There is a great potential for the ECA countries to meet the increasing demand of software outsourcing from Western markets. Global software outsourcing is a continuously growing segment of the software industry that

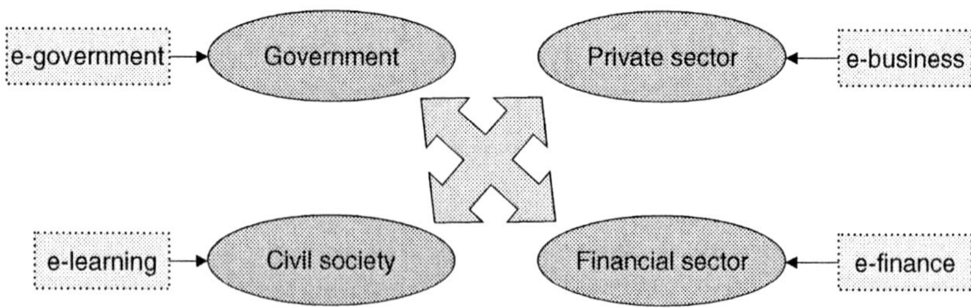

Figure 14.3 The use of ICT in the four pillars of RV-NERD

Connecting the public and private sectors to establish links for enterprise restructuring and development. In this framework each of the four components identify their capabilities to meet the others' demand and create synergies.

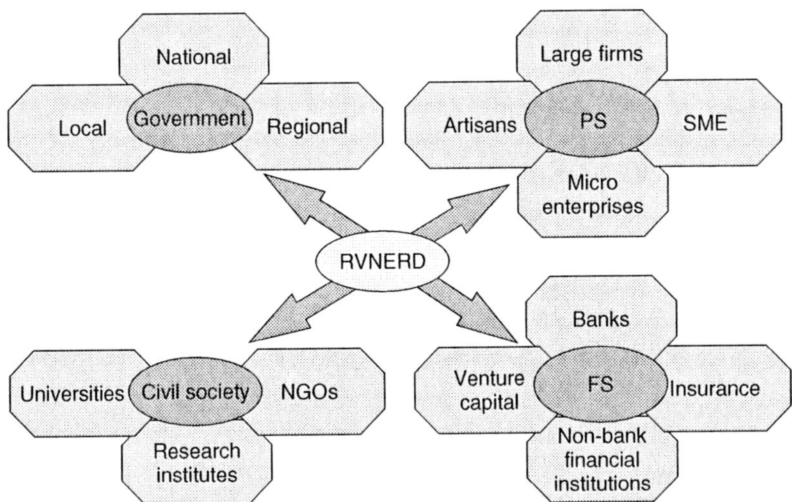

Figure 14.4   RV-NERD

Expanding the virtual network and creating opportunities for interactions

allows those transitional countries with human capital to reap the benefits of globalization. Western companies (mainly American) are willing to outsource some components of their software development due to the strategic advantages of outsourcing: cost savings, access to new labor pools, and access to new IT markets.

Software outsourcing continues to grow very rapidly and offers great potential for transitional economies. In some instances, the outsourcing industry has proven very significant for domestic economies: in 2000 software exports for India grossed USD6.2 billion. Unfortunately, the Indian example is not fully followed by transitional economies of the ECA region that have the same potential: software exports in 2000 for Russia counted for between 60 and 100 USD million. Ukraine is estimated to have had software exports of between USD20 and USD45 million.

The opportunity for transitional economies is two-fold: on the one hand they have the skills and capability to take advantage of the opportunities in international markets; on the other, they will gain competencies to sustain the growth of the local Internet economy, thus establishing their position in domestic and regional IT markets. In fact, by engaging in software outsourcing for foreign firms, software developers of transitional economies will be able to gain specific competencies to meet the demand for applications of both local and regional markets. Most of the ECA region's countries are in the process, at different degrees, of catching up with the leaders of the digital economy, and will very soon be in need of specific applications and tools (encryption, electronic signature, integrated security systems for the Internet, etc.) to sustain the development of e-Applications for both public and private sectors (e-Business and e-Government).

The transitional economies of the ECA region position themselves in an advantaged situation to engage in an industry that is labor-intensive, has relatively low barriers to entry, and few economies of scale. Local IT professionals are skilled and qualified professionals who have another "local knowledge advantage" to reap the benefit of globalization in the software industry: the localization of software packages.

In supporting the IT sector, the project aims at reducing the brain-drain, or "Diaspora", of educated and talented young professionals of the IT sector that look for professional development opportunities abroad, leaving their countries of origin and the whole local industry lagging behind market leaders.

F   Telecenters network supporting e-Content for SMEs and financial sector

The networked economy is not only widening the economic gap between developed and transitioning and developing countries, but is also creating a form of cultural differentiation between developed and developing countries. Most of the content on the Internet is from developed countries and is not specifically tailored to the needs of users of Central and Eastern Europe, both in terms of language and social relevance. The project will create a framework in which all the actors involved in e-Content will participate: academic institutions, private entities, and end-users. The structure of telecenters will allow wider participation, including the end-users (entrepreneurs) who otherwise would not have any role in the creation of content. The end-users will be able not only to access the Internet through the telecenters, but also to participate in the creation process of e-Content by providing feedback on their preferences and profiles. Moreover, the telecenters structure will function as a content clearing house allowing the many small- and medium-sized enterprises involved in the creation of traditional content to go digital.

The overall goal of the project is to help the transitioning countries of the ECA region to get adequate support for multilingual and cross-cultural content provisions and access. Low levels of adoption are also due to lack of local content. The project tries to fill this vacuum and provide connectivity at the same time, integrating the production of content and its usability at different stages of implementation. The creation of the telecenters will also support the search for new ways to bring together ideas, actions, and funds for the e-content sector in the ECA region. The telecenters will then be an integral part of the architecture to link domestic content into the international context (see Figure 14.5). The network of telecenters will link relevant

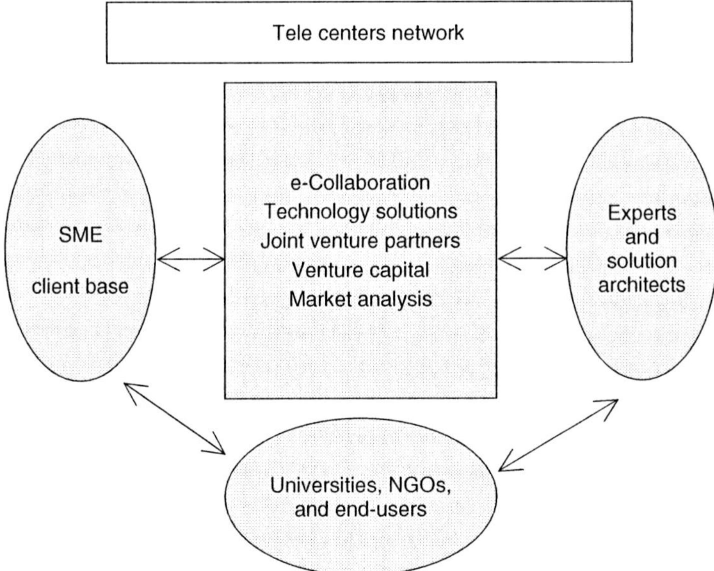

Figure 14.5   The telecenters network

players, provide guidance and advisory services to new companies, and support existing ones in finding partnership and funding opportunities. Moreover, the network will assist institutions such as schools, foundations, NGOs, and universities to play a more active role in developing the industry.

The scope of the network is to address issues related to the e-Content production industry properly:

- Skills, competencies and dynamics of the market;
- Content industry's interaction with educational institutions and end-users;
- Finding appropriate investment sources for firms involved;
- The need for promotion, marketing, and export initiatives.

The production of appropriate e-Content can overcome traditional barriers, but networks and contacts must be provided to market and finance providers. The network can serve by bridging the gap between finance and entrepreneurs.

15

Toward an Emerging Theory of Dynamic Socio-Technical Congruence in Economic Development

Comparing and contrasting our analysis of the development cases across developed, transitioning, and developing economies, we note a number of points partly corroborated by earlier conceptual and empirical research. The study and analysis of these, and similar cases, of e-Development towards the Knowledge Economy may provide a conceptual framework that could serve as an integrative bridge between macro-, meso-, and micro-economic development ideas and themes.

The overarching goal would be to attain the right *socio-technical congruence* between e-Development intervention and the type and stage of development the targeted economy is in bearing in mind the dynamic nature of both e-Development interventions and the economies they aim to advance. In other words, one could identify optimal practices and pathways in economic development in terms of *selection, sequencing, and timing decisions* undergirding e-Development interventions in order to attain a more *functional alignment* between the social, economic, and technological dimensions of the e-Development intervention and the readiness for e-Development (e-Readiness) of the targeted economy or sectors thereof (see Figure 15.1). *Functional alignment* implies that an e-Development intervention is designed in such a manner, targeted at such an entry point(s) in the economy and society, and at such a time, that the optimal configuration of critical success factors (buy-in from key stakeholders, awareness, availability, affordability and accessibility of technology, educational/health/social status of targeted social groups, and support from public and private partners in the form of public–private partnerships (PPP) among several others) will augur strongly in favor of the success of the e-Development intervention in terms of both outcomes and impacts.

The cases we use to corroborate our arguments are drawn from a number of countries and sectors in developing countries with a variety of profiles in terms of the degree, scope, and scale of the role that knowledge modalities and processes play in the development enterprise. These cases serve to illustrate vectors, actors, and crucibles of entrepreneurial development such as

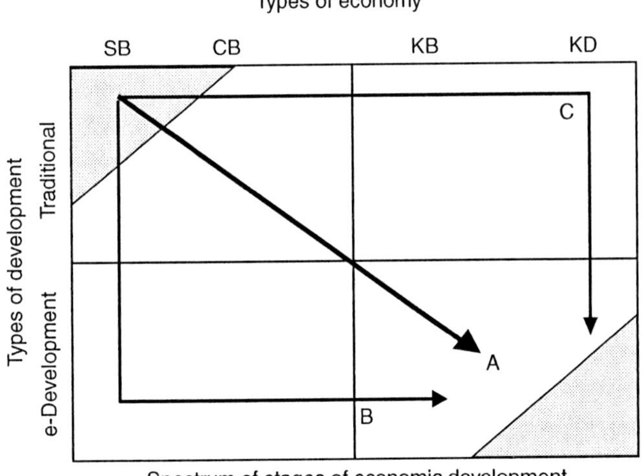

Subsistence → Emerging → Developing → Transitioning → Developed

- SF: Subsistence-focused
- CB: Commodity-based
- KB: Knowledge-based
- KD: Knowledge-driven

Attributes of pathways A, B, and C:

(A) Faster, easier and better way to move toward knowledge-based economy.

(B) Costly, slow but more common way in transitioning economies for moving towards the knowledge economy.

(C) Slowest, cost and more limited way.

Figure 15.1   e-Development pathways toward the Knowledge Economy destination

Source: adapted from Carayannis *et al.* (2005)

business incubators and networks thereof, technology and knowledge clusters, and innovation networks including agglomerations of large/small, public/private entities and partnerships focused on knowledge creation, diffusion, and use.

The central motivation for this research is our belief that the *"goodness of fit"* between the stage an economy is in and the development strategy adopted (including the use of technology and role of knowledge) determine the quality, speed, and sustainability of development" (Carayannis et al, 2005) (see Figure 15.1). In this context, our efforts focus on learning from development experiences, including among others, from SME formation and growth, to develop a methodology for establishing an optimal match typology between development stage and development strategy.

We operationalize our approach by developing and populating the following typology of *e-Development Intervention Focus*, that pivots on the level of socio-technical focus of the e-Development interventions we are reviewing (also see Table 15.1):

Table 15.1   e-Development interventions by focus

Intervention focus	Examples of projects
Macro-level	e-Sri Lanka, e-Russia
Meso-level	EU e-Signature Directive
Micro-level	HungarNet

Table 15.2   e-Development development stage and intervention focus

Development stage	Intervention focus		
	Macro	*Meso*	*Micro*
Developed	+	+	+*
Transitioning	+	−	+/−
Developing	−	−	+/−

Notes: + The countries fully satisfy the level of e-Development.
− The countries do not satisfy the level of e-Development.
+/− The countries partly satisfy the level of e-Development.
* Developed countries may encounter some hurdles at this level, but quickly find solutions to them.

- *Macro-level of e-Development* (e-Leadership and e-Strategy formulations, legal and regulatory framework interventions);
- *Meso-level of e-Development* (policies to implement the e-Leadership and e-Strategy vision such as e-Taxation, e-Government, e-Registration reforms and tax incentives to attract FDI and foster SME formation);
- *Micro-level of e-Development* (development of an educated and skilled workforce, reforms to facilitate and accelerate access to capital, formation of associations of SMEs, formation of civil society associations, and national or international networks).

To illustrate the intrinsic dimensions of the e-Development level of focus typology, we may wish to consider the following key attributes of developed, transitioning and developing economies (see Table 15.2):

- All developed economies have a strong legal and regulatory framework in place. Most, if not all of their industries are liberalized and they foster a healthy competition among market players. They all have built an adequate environment for the maturation of the ICT sector as well as for attracting FDI, which most often than not involved actions on behalf of the government, not the least being to develop a strong e-Government sector. Conversely, their main limitations reside either in the small size of their economy forcing them to become more export-oriented, or in filling the digital divide between its urban and rural areas that the country is facing.

- The transitioning economies have in common a strong basis for e-Development and a rather complete and adequate framework; the issues arise in the implementation of the strategy. Transitioning economies usually rely either on a strong, preexisting S&T heritage or on a highly educated and capable workforce. They have been working on liberalizing key industries such as telecommunications and banking. The government usually leads by example. They are more or less successful at attracting foreign capital – the more liberalized, the more foreign capital entered the country, or so it seems. In opposition, the implementation of the strategy is hampered by a lack of long-term vision and non-specific S&T and R&D policies. ICT-related costs are still relatively high, hindering a widespread ICT penetration, and access to capital is limited.
- Developing countries seem to have a relatively qualified workforce, and most often the government has a strategy, but the framework to implement it has a lot left to be desired. The government does not set an example. The legal and regulatory framework is rather unreliable and not transparent. The markets are not fully liberalized and privatization is slow. Lack of transparency and adequate protection does not attract foreign investors. Access to capital is a major hurdle for the development of the ICT sector. The population usually also lacks the basic business skills, which renders entrepreneurship a non-viable alternative.

We combine this typology with the set of tools, competencies, and applications of e-Development in the Knowledge Economy that may be grouped along four main pillars of general development to form a typology of *e-Development intervention categories* (see Table 15.3):

- **Institution building** (creation of democratic constitutional pillars, creation of central bank authorities, creation of national research and development policy-making authority, formation of tax authority, import/export finance authority, public–private partnerships for infrastructure development projects, privatization authority, etc.);
- **Capacity building** (building human capital through reforms of existing and design of new education modalities, transportation and telecommunications infrastructure building, R&D infrastructure, public–private projects for infrastructure development, training and re-skilling professionals to promote SME formation and growth, etc.);
- **Policy making** (IPR legislation, R&D tax credits, export-geared tax incentives, e-Taxation, e-Voting and e-Registration legal reforms, privatization laws and guidelines, market liberalization legal reforms, anti-corruption and pro-transparency reforms, etc.);

Table 15.3 e-Development interventions by category

Intervention categories	Examples of projects
Institution building	• Ireland: Information Society Committee • Finland: National Technology Agency • Singapore: National Computer Board
Capacity building	• HD (Human Development) Network, • The World Links for Development (WorLD), • The African Virtual University (AVU), • The Global Development Learning Network (GDLN), • The Global Knowledge Partnership (GKP) • Malaysia: Creating an infrastructure center of excellence • Australia: Empower Australia • Ireland: NetMate for Internet use in SMEs
Policy making	• Estonia: Principles of Estonian information policy • Latvia: Informatics Action Plan for years 1999–2005
Investment making	• Private Sector Development (PSD) Network, SEAF.com • Czech Republic: SME and R&D policies for innovation • Australia: Commercializing emerging technology program

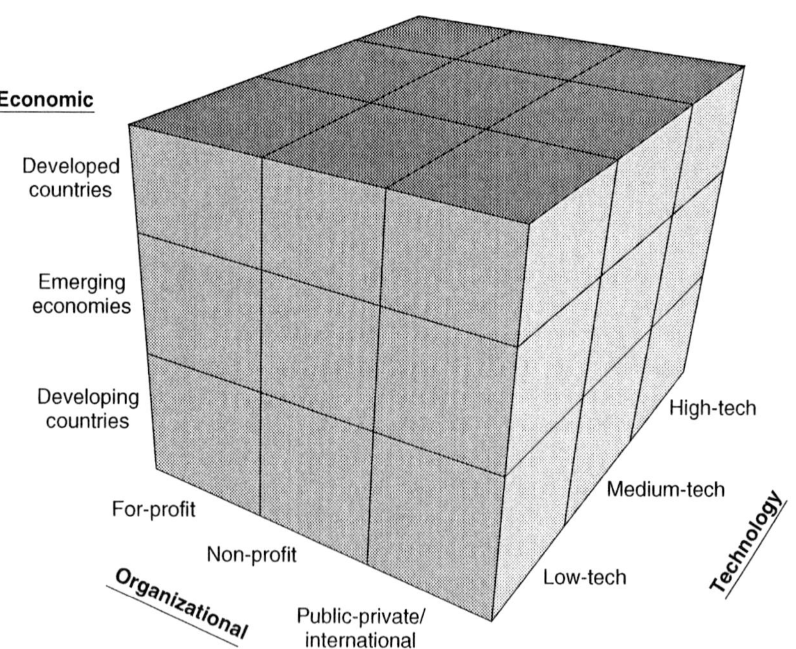

Figure 15.2 Dynamic cube of e-Development intervention strategies: three dimensions of analysis

- **Investment making** (domestic and foreign direct investments, public–private partnerships (PPP) to provide risk capital for SME formation and growth, project finance reforms to promote PPP financing, etc.).

From this new configuration of e-Development Levels and Categories we form the *Dynamic Cube of e-Development Intervention Strategies* (see Figure 15.2). In this context, the e-Readiness of an economy at a specific level and sector of e-Development intervention focus is combined with the most socio-technically congruent type of e-Development intervention over time (in a dynamic sense) to assure the best possible outcomes and impacts. The Cube in question provides a dynamic framework that could provide best practice guidance for the design and implementation of e-Development interventions on the basis of findings and critical success and failure factors identified from previous e-Development interventions on a dynamic, learning-enabled basis. Moreover, this approach will be designed to balance and leverage the natural complementarities and synergies between top-down policy-driven (mostly public-sector-derived) interventions and bottom-up practice-driven initiatives (mostly private-sector-derived and especially entrepreneur-driven).

We will summarize here the issues we attempted to address with our observations and empirical findings in the earlier parts of this book:

- How could one develop more effective and efficient mechanisms to identify, capture and disseminate critical success and failure factors and findings from ongoing e-Development interventions to enable policy-maker and practitioners to shape, evolve, and implement "smarter" e-Development strategies in real time?
- Namely, how could the most timely, appropriate and critical e-Development priorities, objectives, and goals be integrated in a strategic context of e-Development sequence, selection, and timing choices?

We could illustrate this by referring to Table 15.2, where we see that developing countries have to fulfill both the *macro- and meso-levels* of e-Development intervention focus, while transitioning countries (transitioning being the next logical step for the currently developing countries barring the *"happy accident" of country development leap-frogging* which could be enabled and triggered by "smart" e-Development strategies) already fulfill the macro-level.

Hence, developing countries find themselves at *a strategic development crossroads* where they may have to choose between following the more linear path of development passing through a transitioning stage or creating their own path on which they might achieve to catalyze and accelerate development.

There are examples of a combination or *hybrid development* enabled by e-Development interventions, such as the cases of China and possibly South

Korea as well as Russia, India, and Ukraine, where significant domestic *digital, socio-economic, and even cultural divides* formed between clusters of knowledge-based and knowledge-Driven "developed islands"[4] in a "still developing and transitioning archipelago" have been the price of development in many cases, and especially where techno-economic advances have not been met by socio-political advancements toward democratic, representative, and transparent regimes. In cases where autocracy has been empowered by economic development (and even accelerated development to boot), these divides have become a clear and present danger to the robustness and sustainability of both the economies and regimes in question as well as put the rest of the world (ROW) at risk depending on the size of the economies in question. Hence, development strategies and interventions may, especially in the long run and when leveraging technology such as e-Development, have serious implications and "fall-out" or "spill-over" effects for both the targeted economies and the ROW. On the positive side, e-Development interventions leveraging technology and knowledge stocks and flows may indeed help the world transition from a state of being confronted with natural scarcities of goods and services to one empowered by an artificial abundance of resources, ways and means for a better and more sustainable tomorrow (Figure 15.3).

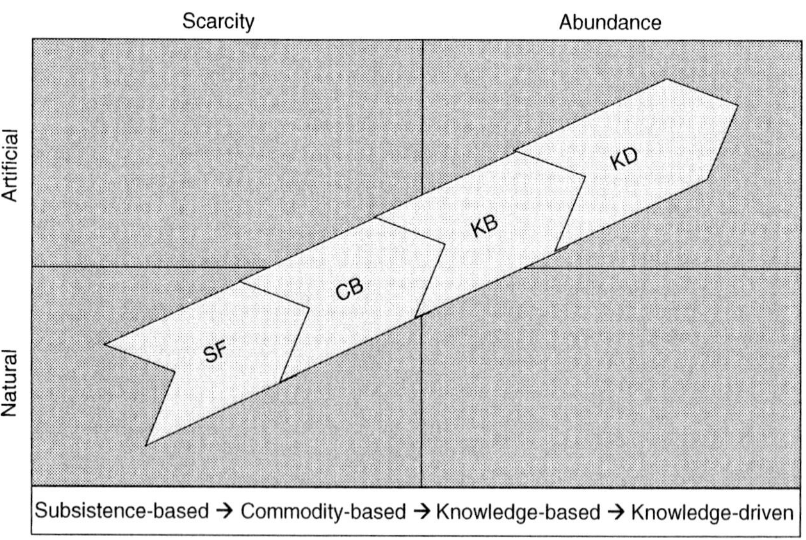

Figure 15.3 The e-Development pathway of economies in development toward the Knowledge Economy: from natural scarcity technology- and knowledge-enabled abundance

Some concluding thoughts and questions

In addition to the issues raised above, we would like to conclude this book which, like the "mission" and the "business" of development remain a work-in-progress, with the following "brain teasers" that might help engender further dialog and insights in the mutually reinforcing and complementary processes of top-down policy making and bottom-up initiatives that shape and drive development interventions and in particular, e-Development interventions toward the Knowledge Economy:

- Should a developing economy adopt a development pathway that aims at fulfilling the *macro-level* development objectives and goals (following the transitioning economies' example), or would it be "smarter" for the developing economy in question to focus on fulfilling the *meso-level* development objectives and goals?
- In the case where the *meso-level* focus is chosen, could this approach lead the developing country to "skip" the transitioning stage, "leap-frogging" toward developed economy status and what, if any, trade-offs might there be (including the *risk of technological, socio-economic, and even cultural divides* forming within a country as a result of a potentially uneven and unbalanced, accelerated development)? Moreover, what would the implications be for how the developmental stage of countries is defined and enacted?
- Could such accelerated development trajectories necessitate the redefinition of what a transitioning economy is and could such a reassessment and redefinition of objectives and goals lead to a "smarter" approach to development (by enabling more functional congruence between development conditions on the ground and development goals and objectives in the numerous reports of the MDAs and the MDGs)?

Notes

1. Networking is important for understanding the dynamics of advanced and knowledge-based societies. Networking links together different modes of knowledge production and knowledge use, and also connects (sub-nationally, nationally, trans-nationally) different sectors or systems of society. Systems theory, as presented here, is flexible enough for integrating and reconciling systems and networks, thus creating conceptual synergies.
2. We define "developing" as low and lower-middle income countries (GDP less than $2,995 in 2000), "transitioning" as higher-middle income countries (GDP between $2,995 and $9,265 in 2000), and "developed" as high-income countries (GDP $2,266 and more in 2000) (IMF, 2003).
3. The excerpts in this case study have been adapted from Nagy Hanna, 'Why ICT Matters for Growth and Poverty Revolution', *World Bank Development*, 2002; and an e-Development presentation to the World Bank by Dr. Hanna in October 2004.
4. We may also have cases of "hyper-developed" clusters, where artificial development acceleration takes place as a result of outsourcing to serve developed economies needs – this often proves unsustainable and detrimental with crowding-out effects and large fluctuations of capital flows. Along with developing or transitioning countries there may also be developed countries' examples that border on this category – see the case of Ireland (Carayannis, Hagedoorn and Alexander, 2001).

References

American Chamber of Commerce (2001) *Offshore Software Development in Russia.*

Asian Development Bank (ADB) (2001) *Toward e-Development in Asia and the Pacific: A Strategic Approach for Information and Communication Technology.*

Barab, S. A. and T. M. Duffy (2000) "From Practice Fields to Communities of Practice," in D. H. Jonassen and S. M. Land (eds), *Theoretical Foundations of Learning* (Mahwah, NJ: Lawrence Erlbaum).

Belcastro, H. (2002) *Internet as a Tool for Communication, Information and Participation among Tertiary Students in Namibia.* The Communication Initiative.

Bose, K. (2003) "An E-Learning Experience: A Written Analysis Based on my Experience with Primary School Teachers in an E-Learning Pilot Project," *International Review of Research in Open and Distance Learning.* University of Botswana.

Braga, C.A. *et al.* (2002) *Globalization and Technology: You Can't Put the Genie Back in the Bottle Again.*

Braun, P. (2002) "Regional Tourism Networks: The Nexus between ICT Diffusion and Change in Australia," *Information Technology and Tourism*, 6(4), pp. 231–43.

British Broadcasting Corporation (BBC) (2003) *South Africa School goes Hi-Tech.* BBC Website.

Brookes, M. and Zaki Wahhaj (2000) "The 'New' Global Economy—Part II: B2B and the Internet," *Global Economic Commentary*, Goldman Sachs, February 9, 2000.

Carayannis, E.G. (1992) "An Integrative Framework of Strategic Decision Making Paradigms and their Empirical Validity: The Case for Strategic or Active Incrementalism and the Import of Tacit Technological Learning," *RPI School of Management Working Paper Series*, 131.

Carayannis, E.G. (1993) "Incrémentalisme Stratégique," in *Le Progrès Technique* (Paris, France).

Carayannis, E.G. (1994a) "Gestion Stratégique de l'Acquisition de Savoir-Faire," in *Le Progrès Technique* (Paris, France).

Carayannis, E.G. (1994b) The Strategic Management of Technological Learning: Transnational Decision Making Frameworks and their Empirical Effectiveness, Published PhD dissertation (Troy, NY: School of Management, Rensselaer Polytechnic Institute).

Carayannis, E.G. (1998) "Higher Order Technological Learning as Determinant of Market Success in the Multimedia Arena; A Success Story, a Failure, and a Question Mark: Agfa/Bayer AG, Enable Software, and Sun Microsystems," *International Journal of Technovation*, 18(10), pp. 639–53.

Carayannis, E.G. (1999) "Fostering Synergies between Information Technology and Managerial and Organizational Cognition: The Role of Knowledge Management," *International Journal of Technovation*, 19(10), pp. 219–31.

Carayannis, E.G. (2000) *The Strategic Management of Technological Learning: Case Studies from Power Generation, Transportation, Pharmaceuticals, and Software US and European Firms* (CRC Press).

Carayannis, E.G. (2001a) *The Strategic Management of Technological Learning* (Boca Raton, FL: CRC Press).

Carayannis, E.G. (2001b) "Learning More, Better, and Faster: A Multi-Industry, Longitudinal, Empirical Validation of Technological Learning as the Key Source of Sustainable Competitive Advantage in High-Technology Firms," *International Journal of Technovation*.

Carayannis, E.G. (2002) "Is Higher Order Technological Learning a Firm Core Competence, How, Why, and When: A Longitudinal, Multi-Industry Study of Firm Technological Learning and Market Performance," *International Journal of Technovation*, 22, pp. 625–43.

Carayannis, E.G. (2004) "Measuring Intangibles: Managing Intangibles for Tangible Outcomes in Research and Innovation," *International Journal of Nuclear Knowledge Management*, 1(1).

Carayannis, E.G. and J. Alexander (1999) "Winning by Co-opeting in Strategic Government-University-Industry (GUI) Partnerships: The Power of Complex, Dynamic Knowledge Networks," *Journal of Technology Transfer*, 24(2/3), pp. 197–210.

Carayannis, E.G. and J. Alexander (2004) "Strategy, Structure and Performance Issues of Pre-competitive R&D Consortia: Insights and Lessons Learned," *IEEE Transactions of Engineering Management*, 52(2).

Carayannis, E.G. and D. Popescu (2005) "Profiling a Methodology for Economic Growth and Convergence: Learning from the EU e-Procurement Experience for Central and Southern Eastern European (CSEE) Countries," *International Journal of Technovation*, 25(1), pp. 1–14.

Carayannis, E.G. and M. von Zedwitz (2005) "Architecting GloCal (Global-Local), Real-Virtual Incubator Networks (G-RVINs) as Catalysts and Accelerators of Entrepreneurship in Transitioning and Developing Economies: Lessons Learned and Best Practices from Current Development and Business Incubation Practices," *International Journal of Technovation*, 25(2), pp. 95–110.

Carayannis, E.G. and D. Campbell (eds) (Forthcoming, Summer 2005) *"Mode 3" Knowledge Creation, Diffusion and Use in Innovation Networks and Knowledge Clusters: A Comparative Systems Approach Across the United States, Europe and Asia* (Praeger Books/GreenWood Press).

Carayannis, E.G. *et al.* (1994a) "A Multi-National, Resource-Based View of Training and Development and the Strategic Management of Technological Learning: Keys for Social and Corporate Survival and Success," *39th International Council of Small Business Annual World Conference*, Strasbourg, France.

Carayannis, E.G. *et al.* (1994b) "The Strategic Management of Technological Learning from a Dynamically Adaptive, High-Tech Marketing Perspective: Sustainable Competitive Advantage through Effective Supplier-Customer Interfacing," *University of Illinois at Chicago/American Management Association Research Symposium on Marketing and Entrepreneurship*, Paris, France.

Carayannis, E.G. *et al.* (2005) "Technological Learning for Entrepreneurial Development (TL4ED)," *International Journal of Technovation*, forthcoming.

Carayannis, E.G., J. Hagedoorn and J. Alexander (2001) "Strange Bedfellows in the Personal Computer Industry: Technology Alliances between IBM and Apple," *Research Policy*, 30(5).

Chilean Economic Development Agency (CORFO) (2003a) *Invest@Chile, High Technology Investment Program*.

Chilean Economic Development Agency (CORFO) (2003b) *Invest@Chile, High Technology Investment Program. IT Penetration*.

Chomsky, N. (1993) *Language and Thought* (Rhode Island: Moyer Bell).

Chomsky, N. *et al.* (1971) *Chomsky: Selected Readings* (NY: Oxford University Press).

Cohen, W.M. and D.A. Levinthal (1990) "Absorptive Capacity: A New Perspective on Learning and Innovation," *Administrative Science Quarterly*, 35(1), pp.128–52.

Commission of the European Communities (1997) *Commission Recommendation on Improving and Simplifying the Business Environment for Business Start-Ups.*

Connectivity for Educator Development (Connect-ED) (2003) *Connect-ED Homepage.*

Cooksey, B. (2001) *Higher Education in Tanzania: A Case Study* (New York: Carnegie Corporation of New York).

Dahlman, C. and J.E. Aubert (2001) *China and the Knowledge Economy: Seizing the 21st Century* (World Bank Institute).

Darch, C. and P.G. Underwood (1999) "Dirt Road or Yellow Brick Superhighway? Information and Communication Technology in Academic Libraries of South Africa," *Library Hi Tech*, 17(3), pp. 28–9.

Development Gateway (July 2003) *E-Learning. Government ICT Policy and Plans – A Catalyst for e-Learning.*

Digital Opportunity Initiative (DOI) (2001) *Creating a Development Dynamic: Final Report of the Digital Opportunity Initiative, July 2001.*

Digital Partnership (DP) (2003) *Demonstration Partnerships.* Digital Patnership Online. International Business Leaders Associations.

Dodgson, M. (1991) *The Management of Technological Learning: Lessons from a Biotechnology Company*, De Gruyter Studies in Organization, 29 (Walter de Gruyter Inc).

Dodgson, M. (1993) *Technological Collaboration in Industry: Strategy, Policy, and Internationalization in Innovation* (Routledge).

Dyker, D. and S. Radosevic (2000) *Building the Knowledge-based Economy in Countries in Transition – From Concepts to Policies*, Working Paper (World Bank & EU DGXII TSER).

Easterly, W. (2002) *The Elusive Quest for Growth: Economists' Adventures and Misadventures in the Tropics* (Cambridge, Mass: The MIT Press).

Ernst, M. (2003) *Chile toward the Information Society.* Government of Jamaica, Cabinet Office.

Federal Computer Week (2004) *Study: U.S. not Sole e-Government Superpower.*

FID (1998) "New Information and Communication Technologies: Social Development and Cultural Change," *FID Bulletin.*

Garud, R. and M. Rappa (1994) "A Socio-cognitive Model of Technology Evolution: The Case of Cochlear Implants," *Organization Science*, 5, pp. 344–62.

Garud, R. and P. Nayyar (1994) "Transformative Capacity: Continual Structuring by Inter-Temporal Technology Transfer," *Strategic Management Journal*, 15, pp. 365–85.

Goldstein, A. and D. O'Connor (2000) *e-Commerce for Development: Prospects and Policy Issues* (Paris: OECD).

Guanhua, X. (2000) Speech at the International Seminar on Technological Innovation, Beijing, September 5–7.

Guisheng, W. Regional (2000) "Distribution of China's Science and Technology and Economic Development," presentation to the International Seminar on Technological Innovation, Beijing, September 5–7.

Halpern, D. (1989) *Thought and Knowledge: An Introduction to Critical Thinking* (Lawrence Erlbaum).

Hanna, N. (2003) *Why ICT Matters for Growth and Poverty Reduction*, Development Gateway website.

Hansen, M. T. (1999) "The Search-transfer Problem: The Role of Weak Ties in Sharing Knowledge across Organization Subunits," *Administrative Science Quarterly*, 44(1), pp. 82–111.

Iansiti, M. and K.B. Clark (1994) "Integration and Dynamic Capability: Evidence from Product Development in Automobiles and Mainframe Computers," *Industrial and Corporate Change*, 3(3), pp. 557–605.

International Monetary Fund (IMF) (2003) *External Debt Statistics: Guide for Compilers and Users – Appendix III, Glossary* (Washington DC: IMF).

International Telecommunication Union (ITU) (2001) *ITU ICT Statistics Online.*

Jelinek, M. (1979) *Institutionalizing Innovation: A Study of Organizational Learning Systems* (New York: Free Press).

LearnLink: Digital Tools for Development (LearnLink) (2003) *Digital Opportunities for Development: A Sourcebook for Access and Applications.*

Marshall, A. (1965) *Principles of Economics* (London: Macmillan).

Matthew J. (1996) *Organizational Foundations of the Knowledge-Based Economy* (Paris: OECD).

Mintzberg, H. (1989) *Mintzberg on Management* (New York: The Free Press).

Mutula, S. (2002) "E-Learning Initiative at the University of Botswana: Challenges and Opportunities," *Campus-Wide Information Systems*, 19(3), pp. 99–109.

Nonaka, I. (1988) "Creating Organizational Order out of Chaos: Self-Renewal in Japanese Firms," *California Management Review.*

Nonaka, I. (1994) "A Dynamic Theory of Organizational Knowledge Creation," *Organization Science*, pp. 14–37.

Nonaka, I. and H. Takeuchi (1995) *The Knowledge-Creating Company: How Japanese Companies Create the Dynamic of Innovation* (New York: Oxford University Press).

ONETOUCH-SYSTEMS (2003) *E-Learning for Millions: OneTouch Helps Launch North America's Largest Unified Educational Network.*

Orbicom (2003) *Internet site.* http://www.orbicom.uqam.ca/

Organisation for Economic Co-operation and Development (OECD) (1996) *The Knowledge-Based Economy* (Paris: OECD).

Organisation for Economic Co-operation and Development (OECD) (2000) *Measuring the ICT Sector* (Paris: OECD).

Organisation for Economic Co-operation and Development (OECD) (2001a) *Innovative Clusters: Drivers of National Innovation Systems* (Paris: OECD).

Organisation for Economic Co-operation and Development (OECD) (2001b) *e-Learning: The Partnership Challenge* (Paris: Centre for Educational Research and Innovation).

Polanyi, M. (1958) *Personal Knowledge* (Chicago: The University of Chicago Press).

Polanyi, M. (1966) *The Tacit Dimension* (Routledge).

Prime Minister of Japan and His Cabinet (2001) *Reform Schedule-Main Points.*

Prime Minister of Japan and His Cabinet (2003a) *e-Japan Strategy II.*

Prime Minister of Japan and His Cabinet (2003b) *e-Japan Priority Policy Program.*

Reisman, A. (1989) "A Systems Approach to Identifying Knowledge Voids in Problem Solving Disciplines and Professions: A Focus on the Management Sciences" *Knowledge in Society: The International Journal of Knowledge Transfer*, 1(4), pp. 67–86.

Reisman, A. and L. Zhao (1991) "A Taxonomy of Technology Transfer Transaction Types" *Journal of Technology Transfer*, 16(2), pp. 38–42.

Richardson, M. (2001) *The Knowledge Economy…No more Business as Usual* (University of Auckland).

Routti, J. (2003) "Research and Innovation in Finland – Transformation into a Knowledge Economy," in *Competitiveness and the Knowledge Economy Research and Innovation Strategies: Cases of Chile and Finland*, presented June 2, at the Inter-American Development Bank, Washington, DC.

Schmitz, H. and K. Nadvi (1999) "Clustering and Industrialization: Introduction," *World Development*, 27(9), pp. 1503–14.

Schon, D. (1983) *The Reflective Practitioner: How Professionals Think in Action* (New York: Basic Books).

Schumpeter, J. (1942) *Capitalist, Socialism and Democracy* (New York: Harper Press).

Sciadas, G. (2003) "Monitoring the Digital Divide . . . And BEYOND". Orbicom.

Shannon, C.E. and W. Weaver (1949) *The Mathematical Theory of Communication* (Urbana: University of Illinois Press).

Simon, H. (1969) *Sciences of the Artificial* (Cambridge, MA: MIT Press).

Sternberg, R. and P. Frensch (1991) *Complex Problem Solving: Principles and Mechanisms* (Hillsdale, NJ: Lawrence Erlbaum Associates).

Teece, D., G. Pisano, and A. Schuen (1990) *Firm Capabilities, Resources, and the Concept of Strategy*, CCC Working Paper, 90–8 (Berkeley, Illinois: University of Berkeley).

United Kingdom Department of Trade and Industry (UK DTI) (1998) *Our Competitive Future: Building the Knowledge Driven Economy* (London: UK DTI).

United States Agency for International Development (USAID) (2003) "Teachers get Connected in Uganda," *USAID*, Bureau for Africa, Newsletter.

USBE&IT News Services (2004) *Pushing IT Skills in Africa with HBCU Help.*

von Hippel, E. (1988) *The Sources of Innovation* (Cambridge, MA: The MIT Press).

Wender, E.C. and W.M. Snyder (2000) "Communities of Practice: The Organizational Frontier," *Harvard Business Review*, 78(1), 139–45.

Wenger, E. (1998) *Communities of Practice: Learning, Meaning, and Identity* (New York: Cambridge University Press).

Wenger, E. (2004) "Knowledge Management is a Donut: Shaping your Knowledge Strategy with Communities of Practice," *Ivey Business Journal*, 68(3).

World Bank (1998) *World Development Report 1998/1999: Knowledge for Development.*

World Bank (2000) *Vietnam's Tale of Two Cities.*

World Bank (2000) *World Development Report 1999/2000: Entering the 21st Century.*

World Bank (2005) *World Development Indicators Online.*

World Bank Institute (2001a) *China and the Knowledge Economy.*

World Bank Institute (2001b) *Republic of Korea: Transition to a Knowledge-Based Economy.*

World Economic Forum (2002) *The Global Competitiveness Report 2001–2002* (New York: WEF & Harvard CID/Oxford: OUP).

World Tourism Organization (WTO) (1999) *Marketing Tourism Destinations Online* (Madrid).

Bibliography

Australian Bureau of Statistics (ABS) (2001) *Australian Economic Indicators.*

Australian Government (2001) *Backing Australia's Ability: An Innovation Action Plan for the Future.*

Australian Government (2005) *Internet Site* http://www.fed.gov.au/KSP/

Central Statistics Office Ireland (CSO) (2002) *Information Technology Principal Statistics.*

Centre of Information Technologies of Education. *Internet Site* http://www.ipc.lt

Chaumeil, T. (1999) *The Internet in Argentina: Study and Analysis of Government Policy,* e-OTI.

Costarricense.com. *Internet Site* http://www.costarricense.com/

Department of Communications, Information Technology and the Arts (DCITA) Australian Government (2001) *Information Technology Online (ITOL) Program.*

Department of the Taoiseach of the Reopublic of Ireland (1999) *Implementing the Information Society In Ireland: An Action Plan.*

Economic Development Board of Singapore, Representative Office, Washington, DC.

Economist Intelligence Unit (EIU) (2001) *Country Data.*

Economist Intelligence Unit (EIU) (2001) *Country Profiles.*

Economist Intelligence Unit (EIU) (2001) *Country Reports.*

Economist Intelligence Unit (EIU) (2001) *Economic Survey.*

Economist Intelligence Unit (EIU) (2001) *Pyramid Research e-Readiness Ranking.*

e-Government in New Zealand. *Internet Site* http://www.e-government.govt.nz/

Ennis Information Age Services (2002) *Ennis Information Age Town Project.*

Financial Times Online. *Country Survey Finland 2001.*

Financial Times Online. *Country Survey Singapore 2001.*

Finnfacts (2002) "V. Finland in a Changing World Economy" in *The Story of Finland.*

Finnish Information Society Development Centre (TIEKE) *Internet Site* http://www.tieke.fi/

Finnish National Fund for Research and Development (SITRA) (1998) *Quality of Life, Knowledge and Competitiveness.*

Government of Singapore. *Internet Site* http://www.gov.sg

Grant Thornton International (1999 and 2000) *European Business Survey.*

Harris, R. (1998) *Malaysia's Multimedia Super Corridor* (University Malaysia Sarawak).

infocom. *Internet Site* http://www.infocom.lt/

Infocomm Development Authority of Singapore (IDA) *Internet Site* http://www.ida.gov.sg

Information Society Commission (1998) *First Information Society Commission Report.*

Information Society Commission (2000) *Benchmarking Ireland in the Information Society.*

Information Society Research Centre. *Internet Site* http://www.info.uta.fi/winsoc/

Information Society Steering Committee (1996) *Information Society Ireland: Strategy for Action* (Dublin: Forfas).

Information Technology Association (ITA) South Africa. *Internet Site* http://www.ita.org.za/

International Institute for Management Development (IMD) (2001) *World Competitiveness Yearbook 2001.*

International Monetary Fund (IMF) *International Financial Statistics (IFS).*

International Telecommunications Union (2001) *The e-City: Singapore Internet Case Study*.

Joyce, A. (2000) *Education and Training For All* (European Schoolnet).

Kable. *Internet Site* http://www.kablenet.com/

Kogod School of Business at American University (2001) *IT Landscape in Argentina*.

Ministry of Economy of the Republic of Lithuania. *Internet Site* http://www.ukmin.lt

Ministry of the Interior of the Republic of Lithuania. *Internet Site* http://www.vrm.lt/

Ministry of Trade and Industry (MTI) of Singapore (2001) *Economic Survey*.

Ministry of Transport and Communications Finland. *Internet Site* http://www.mintc.fi

National Information Technology Council of Malaysia. *Internet Site* http://www.nitc. org.my/nita/index.shtml

Organisation for Economic Co-operation and Development (OECD) (2001) *Telecommunications Outlook 2001, New Zealand*.

ReSET. *Argentina Profile*.

RIPE Network Coordination Centre. *Internet Site* http://www.ripe.net/

SEE Online. *Internet Site* http://www.southeasteurope.org/

Seismas (Parliament) of the Republic of Lithuania. *Internet Site* http://www.lrs.lt/

Singaporean Embassy to the USA, Washington, DC, USA.

Statistics Finland (1999) *On the Road to the Finnish Information Society II*.

UK Department of Trade and Industry (DTI) (2000) *Business in the Information Age: International Benchmarking Study 2000*.

Index

Printed in the United States
65664LVS00001B/127-129